W9-AHO-019

My People the Sioux
New Edition

BY
Luther Standing Bear

Edited by E. A. Brininstool

Introduction by Richard N. Ellis

Introduction to the New Bison Books Edition by
Virginia Driving Hawk Sneve

UNIVERSITY OF NEBRASKA PRESS
LINCOLN AND LONDON

IN LOVING MEMORY OF
MY FATHER
CHIEF STANDING BEAR THE FIRST
A WARRIOR OF DISTINCTION
A GREAT LEADER AND COUNSELOR AMONG HIS PEOPLE
IN LATER LIFE AN EARNEST CHRISTIAN
WHO WALKED THE TRAILS OF PEACE AND HARMONY
CONSTANTLY STRIVING FOR
THE BETTERMENT OF HIS RACE

Introduction © 1975 by the University of Nebraska Press
Introduction to the new Bison Books edition © 2006 by the Board
of Regents of the University of Nebraska
All rights reserved
Manufactured in the United States of America

First Bison Books printing: 1975

Bison Books edition reproduced from the 1928 edition published
by Houghton Mifflin Company. Introduction by William S. Hart
and photographs omitted.

Library of Congress Cataloging-in-Publication Data
Standing Bear, Luther, 1868?–1939.
My people the Sioux / Luther Standing Bear; edited by E. A. Bri-
ninstool; introduction by Richard N. Ellis; introduction to the new
Bison Books edition by Virginia Driving Hawk Sneve.—New ed.
p. cm.
ISBN-13: 978-0-8032-9332-8 (pbk.: alk. paper)
ISBN-10: 0-8032-9332-1 (pbk.: alk. paper)
1. Standing Bear, Luther, 1868?–1939. 2. Teton Indians—Kings
and rulers—Biography. 3. Teton Indians—History. I. Brinin-
stool, E. A. (Earl Alonzo), 1870–1957. II. Title.
E99.D1S73 2006
978.004′9752440092—dc22   2006016620
[B]

INTRODUCTION TO THE NEW BISON BOOKS EDITION

Virginia Driving Hawk Sneve

My People the Sioux is Luther Standing Bear's autobiography, written when he was fifty years old. Born in the 1860s, Luther was one of the first Sioux children to attend school, where he learned to speak, read, and write English and mastered a trade at Carlisle Indian School in Pennsylvania. Without this education, he could not have written *My People the Sioux* or the three other books he published.

Carlisle Indian School was opened in 1879 by Richard H. Pratt, an army man. The school was run like a military institution with an aim to civilize the Indian students by "killing the Indian, to save the man."[1] The students were immersed in the dominant white culture. After their long hair was cut and they answered to their white names, they were required to speak only English and to learn a trade. Students also had music and art classes and attended Sunday school and services in the town of Carlisle.[2]

The school gave its students opportunities to interact and live in the white world, which reservation boarding schools established later could never do. In addition to regular school concerts, to which the public was invited, the school band performed at football games, expositions, and even in presidential inaugural parades.[3] During the summer months, students were enrolled in the "outing program," which placed them in jobs with non-Indian families, for which they earned their first wages.[4]

In his recollections, Luther remembers how he gave up his Indian name, Ota Kte, in a classroom at Carlisle. He was handed a long stick and told to point it at one of many words written on the blackboard. He could not read the words—names found among the white people. After the stick landed on "Luther," he was instructed to memorize the name because he could no longer be Ota Kte. Luther felt sad at the loss but was pleased that he learned his new name more quickly than the other Indian students. Once he had a white man's name, he had to have his hair cut. His head felt bare and cold, and Luther wondered if he had become an imitation white man. Still, he was proud of his new jacket, shirt, pants, and shoes, none of which he had ever worn in his young life. This mixture of feelings was a perplexing dilemma for Luther and other educated Indians who wanted to retain Indian ways but who also liked the new life. A few individuals acculturated and adjusted to the pull of both worlds, but most chose one over the other—either staying Indian or assimilating into the white world.

The greatest change experienced by Luther's generation was in education. Before reservation life, there were no formal classrooms in a band's camp, but the children were surrounded by caring adults whom they watched and emulated. There was no written language, so important values and family and tribal histories were told by elders to a younger generation within a close *tiyospeye* (extended family). When that free way of life ended, the children were taken from their homes. They, along with hundreds of other children, lived and studied within the confines of brick walls under the stern instruction of one teacher.

Luther's compositional style reflects what he studied in school. His white teachers must have influenced his use of the word "Sioux," rather than "Lakota" or "Dakota." "Sioux" is from the Ojibwa word *Nadewesou*; it has been translated to mean "treacherous snake," the name of the Ojibwa's enemy. In one sentimental passage, Luther recalls, "Nature seemed to hold us in her arms. And there we were contented to live in our humble tipis." The word "humble" is used after Luther's exposure to white culture and views.

Often, Luther also uses analogies from the white world: "Our women wore dresses with open sleeves, and, when a person stood behind them as they were pulling on the skin [to be tanned], they resembled angels flying, as the big sleeves flapped back and forth." During his first buffalo hunt, he fired three arrows into a buffalo, and the beast did not die: "I began to think that buffalo had all the nine lives of a cat." Cats were not part of Indian life until reservation settlement. He uses scientific theory when describing the first white men his people saw: "They had hair all over their faces, heads, arms, and hands. . . . None of us had ever seen a gorilla, else we might have thought that Darwin was right concerning these people."

The first part of *My People the Sioux* recalls Indian life, when "we had everything provided for us by the Great Spirit above. Is it any wonder that we grew fat with contentment and happiness?" Luther fondly writes of how children played. Boys used small bows and blunted arrows, which required hand-eye coordination, learning skills needed to be hunters and warriors. Girls played with dolls in small tipis and mimicked their mothers in keeping house and tending to family. Young boys and girls played together, but as they grew, they separated into gendered games. Boys spent more time with men, and girls with women.

When the "Iron Snake," or railroad, started to run through native land, curious Indians quietly studied it. But when a thirsty party of warriors stopped at a depot, the station master refused them water. This angered the Indians, but rather than kill the white man, they tore up the railroad track and wrecked the train. Although Luther had been named Ota Kte (Plenty Kill) because his father, Standing Bear, had been a warrior who had killed many enemies, Luther learned as a young boy that killing white men was not an honorable deed because they were the weaker race. As more whites came to Sioux land, though, Luther recalls, "This was the beginning of our hatred for the white people." Confrontations between whites and Indians became violent, culminating in the Battle of the Little Big Horn, the pacifying of Sioux chiefs, and the death of Crazy Horse.

The federal government provided annuities to the Indians in exchange for the land occupied by whites. Ration day was attended by women, who were allotted food depending on the size of their families. Flour, unknown to the Indians, was considered useless and was dumped into ravines, but the sacks were saved and made into boys' shirts. Indians had to be taught how to make fry bread and how to roast and grind coffee, but they immediately took to syrup and sugar. Their high protein diet of lean buffalo changed when they could no longer hunt, and they became dependent on the annuity issue of fat pork and beef on the hoof. Eventually, bootleggers came with alcohol. When Luther recalls, "None of this was really good for us," he unknowingly foretells of diabetes and alcoholism, which would have devastating effects on Indian health, family, and society.

Standing Bear, Luther's father, greatly influenced the young boy. Luther notes how his father was among a delegation of Sioux leaders who went to Washington DC to see the "Great Father," Rutherford Hayes. The representatives presented their grievances to the president, who assured them that the wrongs would be corrected, but the delegation went home with only presents and empty promises. Standing Bear returned dressed in white men's clothing and with an awareness of the whites' great numbers and power. He realized that the Indians would lose in a fight and that the better course was to live like the whites.

Luther greatly admired his father, who taught his son to be brave and unafraid to die. Doing a brave deed brought honor to one's family, and Luther longed to accomplish such a deed. Knowing that his father believed that education was the path the Indians must follow in order to survive in a white world, Luther volunteered to go to Carlisle Indian School. He thought that he would leave the reservation and "stay away long enough to do some brave deed, and then come home again alive." At that time, Luther did not understand what education was or how long he would be away from home.

Luther decided to learn white ways and language so that he could serve his father as an interpreter and keep books for his father's store, which was one of the first Indian-run enterprises on the reservation. Luther also recruited for Carlisle, visiting the reservation periodically to show off his new clothes, language, and skills, which persuaded parents to send their children to the school.

Luther eventually left Carlisle permanently "with a better understanding of life. There would be no more hunting— we would have to work now for our food and clothing. It was like the Garden of Eden after the fall of man." His words showed the white influence on his education, and he had a mixed reception at home. Some were proud of his achievement, while others did not like that Luther had become a white man.

Luther became a teacher and was a lay reader in the Episcopal Church, and soon he became a family man as well. He and Nellie DeCory, a half-blood, were married and had children. His mother-in-law, a full-blood who had completely adapted to her white husband's way of life, did not like that Luther was also a full-blood. But his father-in-law approved of the marriage and helped the young couple by providing household goods and cattle.

Luther was now an adult with family responsibilities, and he was concerned about reservation affairs. He actively intervened to settle a dispute over distribution of goods. He helped the reservation agent calm a disgruntled band and prevented a violent confrontation. Later, Luther tried to dissuade his father's band from joining the Ghost Dance movement. His father and stepmothers lived at Pine Ridge Agency, but one of Luther's brothers was a scout who witnessed the massacre of Big Foot's band, including women and children. Luther was extremely upset: "There I was, doing my best to teach my people to follow in the white men's road—even trying to get them to believe in their religion—and this was my reward for it all! The very people I was following—and getting my people to follow—had no respect for motherhood, old age, or babyhood. Where was all their civilized training?" Despite these feelings, Luther still tried to emulate the whites. After he became a teacher on Pine Ridge, he organized adult Indians into a club with the purpose of getting information to the uneducated parents of his students. These gatherings were the forerunners of tribal councils, which were later established to govern the reservations.

Unlike other Indians of his time, Luther was able to buy ranch land on which to raise cattle and horses, although he still had to collect rations and annuity goods from the government, as he had no cash to buy food for his family or feed for his horses. When rations were no longer given, Luther was able to find three jobs because of his education, which also gave him opportunities to help his people. "When they came to the agent's office for their money, I gave them the book in which they were to sign their names. In the evening I was at the store to wait on them, talking to them in the Sioux tongue. When they went to church, I stood before them and preached to them in their own language." Luther used his education in another way when he joined Buffalo Bill's Wild West show. On the show's European tour, he served as interpreter and mentor for seventy-five Indians. The most difficult part of the job was to keep the Indians sober.

Luther began writing his memoirs after he was fifty, and perhaps this distance of years caused a stoic tone to his recollections. After returning home from Europe, Luther's matter-of-fact prose tells of how he was in a train wreck and badly injured. He seems to write without feeling about the deaths of two of his children. Regarding an event that would have struck gratitude in an Indian man's heart, Luther only musingly recalls: "It is a great honor to receive the title of 'Chief,' but there is much hard work about it also."

It was with regret that Luther decided to leave the reservation: "I discovered that as long as I was on the reservation I was only a helpless Indian, and was not considered any better than any of the uneducated Indians." He moved to Iowa, then to Oklahoma, and finally to California. There he acted in films, but he did not approve of the inaccuracies of how Indians were portrayed. Then he began to write. Luther was one of the first published Native authors to present Native American views—specifically, those of the Sioux, which differed from the military, government, and missionary accounts. After his experiences on the reservation, he became an advocate of bilingual education: "The Indian children should have been taught how to translate the Sioux tongue into English properly; but the English teachers only taught them the English language, like a bunch of parrots." He felt that, even though the Indians became book-educated, they knew very little else of the white world.

Luther's written works gave a Native perspective, which

led to sympathy for the plight of the Indians from his white readers. Years later, Indians criticized him for becoming a white man. It was a difficult decision for Luther, as he loved the Indian ways, but his choice was determined by his education at Carlisle. There he learned to live in the white world and use English, which allowed him to write a firsthand account of his people's transition from freedom to reservation life.

NOTES

1. Barbara Landis, "Carlisle Indian Industrial School Research Pages," http://www.carlisleindianschool.org.
2. Landis, "Carlisle Indian Industrial School."
3. Landis, "Carlisle Indian Industrial School."
4. Landis, "Carlisle Indian Industrial School."

PREFACE

THE preparation of this book has not been with any idea of self-glory. It is just a message to the white race; to bring my people before their eyes in a true and authentic manner. The American Indian has been written about by hundreds of authors of white blood or possibly by an Indian of mixed blood who has spent the greater part of his life away from a reservation. These are not in a position to write accurately about the struggles and disappointments of the Indian.

White men who have tried to write stories about the Indian have either foisted on the public some blood-curdling, impossible 'thriller'; or, if they have been in sympathy with the Indian, have written from knowledge which was not accurate and reliable. No one is able to understand the Indian race like an Indian.

Therefore, I trust that in reading the contents of this book the public will come to a better understanding of us. I hope they will become better informed as to our principles, our knowledge, and our ability. It is my desire that all people know the truth about the first Americans and their relations with the United States Government.

I hereby express my appreciation for assistance in the preparation of the manuscript of this book and the photographs used, to my good friends Mr. E. A. Brininstool, of Los Angeles, and Mr. Clyde Champion, of Alhambra, California; also to my niece Was-te-win and her husband William Dittmar, whose aid and encouragement have been of the utmost value to me.

CHIEF STANDING BEAR

CONTENTS

INTRODUCTION

We did not think of the great open plains, the beautiful rolling hills, and winding streams with tangled growth, as
"wild." Only to the white man was nature a "wilderness" and
only to him was the land "infested" with "wild" animals and
"savage" people. To us it was tame. Earth was bountiful and
we were surrounded with the blessings of the Great Mystery.
Not until the hairy man from the east came and with brutal
frenzy heaped injustices upon us and the families we loved
was it "wild" for us. When the very animals of the forest
began fleeing from his approach, then it was that for us the
"Wild West" began.

> Luther Standing Bear, *Land of the
> Spotted Eagle*, p. 38.

As a Lakota, a member of the Teton or Western
Sioux, born in the decade of the 1860s, Luther Standing Bear grew to young manhood during years of crisis
for the Sioux and other tribes of the Great Plains. He
was raised in the traditional manner to be a successful
hunter and warrior and a respectful and productive
member of Sioux society. But while he was still a boy
the traditional life of the Sioux was undergoing
dramatic change. The great Sioux Reservation, established by the controversial Fort Laramie Treaty of
1868, came into being about the time of his birth. Although some Tetons, notably Red Cloud and American
Horse of the Oglalas and Spotted Tail and Two Strikes
of the Brules, began to live near agencies established
for them, many of the Tetons continued to live the old
way of life until military campaigns following the Custer battle on the Little Big Horn in 1876 forced the
Sioux people to conform to a reservation life.

Change accelerated after the military defeat of the Sioux, and in the years that followed, virtually every important institution in Sioux life was subject to change. The disappearance of the buffalo and confinement to the reservation caused the erosion of old traditions and forced the Sioux to depend upon the government for food and other necessities of life. Warrior societies were weakened, and normal avenues of social and political advancement were closed. Opposition to government programs by traditional chiefs such as Red Cloud and Spotted Tail caused dramatic confrontations at the agencies and led to efforts to weaken positions of leadership and to create rival leaders who were more sympathetic to the will of agents and Washington officials. The establishment of agency police responsible to the Bureau of Indian Affairs provided another attack upon Sioux institutions and traditions and further strengthened the position of the Indian agent. Government support of missionaries helped to undermine Sioux religion, as did the prohibition against the Sun Dance, the most important religious and social event in the yearly cycle of Sioux life. Efforts to convert Sioux warriors into sedentary agriculturalists were at odds with Sioux traditions and desires, and finally government education programs were developed in an effort to speed acculturation and prepare the Sioux and other Indians for assimilation into white society.

Government officials were opposed to all manifestations of Indianness and were devoted to the goal of stripping away the traditional way of life and replacing it with that of white America. Young Standing Bear, or Plenty Kill as he was named, was subjected to the buffeting caused by reservation life and by changing federal policies and was himself a product of those policies. *My People the Sioux* is his autobiographical account of his traditional Sioux boyhood and subsequent changes in his life and the life of his people.

The lack of first-hand Lakota accounts of these turbulent and transitional years makes Standing Bear's autobiography especially valuable. He effectively portrays the change from the old way of life. Trained to be an effective hunter, he participated in his first buffalo hunt and graphically describes the excitement, confusion, and fear, and the pride in his first kill. The disappearance of the buffalo, however, forced the Sioux to rely on cattle, the evil-smelling spotted buffalo, and other goods supplied by the government. The Sioux were issued flour, but as they did not make bread and were not instructed in the use of flour, they usually threw it away and used the sacks for shirts and other items. They were issued green coffee beans and eventually learned that it had to be roasted, but when that was accomplished, they lacked coffee mills. As the drink was black and bitter, some thought it was medicine, and his mother added plenty of pepper to it on the assumption that the stronger and more bitter it was, the better it would be as medicine.

Other adjustments also had to be made, and Plenty Kill personally made the choice to attend the new government school at Carlisle, Pennsylvania. He had been raised to be brave and had been instructed to die on the battlefield while young rather than die of old age. Therefore, he chose to go with the whites because it would demonstrate his bravery. He did not know whether he would survive or not, and as the group of Sioux children traveled eastward to Carlisle they expected to be killed and feared that they would fall off the end of the flat earth.

The journey and the first weeks at Carlisle were a new and trying experience for the Sioux. The trip by train, little houses all in a line, drew crowds of loud and curious whites, and life at Carlisle with new clothing, food, rules, and restrictions required a tremendous adjustment. The "civilizing" process began at Carlisle, he wrote, and it began with clothes. Whites believed the Indian children could not be civilized while wearing moccasins and blankets. Their hair was cut because "in some mysterious way long hair stood in the path of our development." They were issued the clothes of white men. "High collars, stiff-bosomed shirts, and suspenders fully three inches in width were uncomfortable, while leather boots caused actual suffering," Standing Bear later wrote. Red flannel underwear, which caused "actual torture," he remembered as the worst thing about life at Carlisle.[1]

The Indian school at Carlisle was the creation of Richard Henry Pratt, an army officer who had been placed in charge of Indian prisoners in Florida and who became convinced that the government should intensify efforts to educate American Indians. Pratt, although a military man, became the superintendent of Carlisle and had a major influence on Indian education during his twenty-four years in that office. He agreed with the growing sentiment that acculturation was necessary and believed that all evidence of Indian culture should be eliminated and replaced with the culture of the white man. In Indian affairs, he once said, "I am a Baptist, because I believe in immersing the Indians in our civilization and when we get them under holding them there until they are thoroughly soaked."[2]

Pratt used the Carlisle school to implement this philosophy. The use of native languages was forbidden, and the children actually had to obtain permission to speak in their own language when their non-English-speaking relatives visited them. They were also given English names, and Standing Bear describes how they were asked to pick a name from a list on a blackboard. He happened to choose Luther and thus became Luther Standing Bear in the government records.

Standing Bear's account gives some idea of the tremendous adjustments that had to be made by Indian children who had been transported from the warmth and security of family and culture to the alien world of the whites where even communication was difficult, if not impossible, because teachers did not speak any Indian languages. However, Standing Bear made the necessary adjustments and even was selected to work in the great Wanamaker department store in Philadelphia.

Eventually he returned to his own people where he learned how difficult it was for a young Indian, the proud possessor of an education, knowledge of the English language and white culture, and the strange clothes of the whites, to readjust to reservation life and find a satisfactory application of the trade that he had learned at Carlisle. The difficulties of "returning students," as they became known, were serious and continued to disturb white educators. Returning students, for their part, often found that they were between the two cultures and were not fully accepted by either. Many discovered that employment was not available and ultimately rejected their entire educational experience and "returned to the blanket" by casting off all white ways and embracing their own culture. Others found it more convenient and satisfying to remain in urban centers as members of the larger white society.

Standing Bear was more fortunate than most. Armed with a recommendation from Richard Pratt, he secured employment as an assistant teacher in a government school on the Rosebud Reservation at a salary of three hundred dollars a year. Bureau employees were enthusiastic in their praise of him and described him as "diligent and faithful, persevering and trustworthy," and as a "very competent mixed blood." When he moved to Pine Ridge in the 1890s with the approval of the Secretary of the Interior, he received a better position with the government.[3]

As the years passed, Standing Bear found other employment. He was an agency clerk, opened a small store, became an assistant minister, owned a ranch, and eventually joined Buffalo Bill's troupe and went to Europe with the Wild West Show. Ultimately he went to California, where he appeared in many movies and lectured widely. It was during his California years that Standing Bear wrote four books, *My People the Sioux* (1928), *My Indian Boyhood* (1931), *Land of the Spotted Eagle* (1933), and *Stories of the Sioux* (1934). A leading member of the Los Angeles area Indian community, Standing Bear had many friends, both Indian and white. Those who studied with him remember him fondly and mourned his passing in 1939 while he was working on the film *Union Pacific*.[4]

My People the Sioux was published when the author was some fifty years of age. As it is based upon his memory, it is not surprising that there are factual errors. Although Standing Bear states that he is an Oglala, it appears that he actually was a Brule. George Hyde, whose extensive research on the history of the Sioux included work in written records and oral traditions of the Sioux people, believed that the elder Standing Bear, father of Luther, was a Brule. His band, the Wears Salt band, was Brule, and he was listed on the agency rolls as a mixed-blood, Hyde found. Hyde believes that his conduct verifies that he was a mixed-blood because he was the only Brule who ran a store in the old days.[5] Other government records support Hyde, and the record of the agreement for land allotment in 1889 lists the elder Standing Bear as a member of the Brules. Nor is there any question that the Standing Bear family lived at the Spotted Tail Agency and Rosebud Reservation, the home of the Brules.[6]

Some of the confusion undoubtedly comes from the fact that when the government allotted land at Rosebud and Pine Ridge, Luther Standing Bear and his brother Henry both moved to the Pine Ridge Reservation and received their allotments there. Government records list Luther Standing Bear as Pine Ridge allottee No. 4644 and indicate that he was three-quarters Indian and one-quarter white. The allotment schedule at Pine Ridge also listed his date of birth as 1863, as did the census of 1932; so there is some question whether government records are accurate or whether Standing Bear was correct in stating that he was born in 1868.[7]

There is also the possibility that Standing Bear overemphasized the importance of his father, who is described as a major political figure among the Sioux. According to this account, the father was one of those who helped persuade Crazy Horse to surrender in 1877. He is also credited with preventing Spotted Tail and Red Cloud from shooting Crazy Horse as he lay dying from a stab wound, and with carrying the pipe to the Ghost Dancers in the stronghold and persuading them to surrender after the massacre at Wounded Knee. Published histories do not indicate the involvement of the elder Standing Bear in these events, nor do they mention him as a significant Sioux leader. The letters received by the Indian Office also fail to verify these claims, although the absence of such information is not conclusive.

Another point of controversy is the author's description of Spotted Tail, the best-known Brule leader, who was killed by Crow Dog, a member of the same tribe, in 1881. There is no evidence to support the charge that Spotted Tail had secretly sold Sioux land or that he had stolen another man's wife and that tribal chiefs had agreed in council that he must be killed for his transgressions.

Whatever the inaccuracies in *My People the Sioux*, it remains an important book and serves as something of a milestone in the development of American Indian literature. Standing Bear was one of the first well-known Indian authors and his books were reviewed by the *New York Times* and other newspapers. They undoubtedly broadened the public's knowledge of American Indians and the Sioux in particular. Coming as it did in 1928, during a period of intense criticism of federal Indian policy and the year that the critical Meriam Report was also published,[8] *My People the Sioux* deepened public sympathy for the Indian people.

By 1933, when *Land of the Spotted Eagle* was published, John Collier had become Commissioner of Indian Affairs, and the movement to reform Indian policy was well underway. The changing climate of public opinion permitted Standing Bear to become more openly critical of government treatment of Indians. In language similar to that used by Vine Deloria, Jr., and other modern Indian spokesmen, he said that there was no Indian problem created by Indians, but that it was due to whites and their inability to seek understanding and achieve adjustment. "Who can say that the white man's way is better for the Indian?" he wrote. "Where resides the human judgment with the competence to weigh and value Indian ideals and spiritual concepts or substitute for them other values?"[9]

Standing Bear had few kind words for the Bureau of Indian Affairs, its treatment of the Sioux, and its administration of "the government prison" known as the reservation. The government goal of acculturation, he felt, was ill conceived:

> The attempted transformation of the Indian by the white man and the chaos that has resulted are but the fruits of the white man's disobedience of a fundamental and spiritual law. The pressure that has been brought to bear upon the native people, since the cessation of armed conflict, in the attempt to force conformity of custom and habit has caused a reaction more destructive than war, and the injury has not only affected the Indian, but has extended to the white population as well. Tyranny, stupidity, and the lack of vision have brought about the situation now alluded to as the "Indian Problem."[10]

Like many other Carlisle students, Standing Bear had a high personal regard for Richard Pratt but criticized government policies. He believed that white people had much to teach Indians, but that Indian people also had much to teach whites. He had seen at first hand the operation of government schools on reservations and found little good to say about them. One of the first day school teachers did not even know how to drive a team and wagon when he arrived at the reservation. When out for a drive one day, he neglected to put the brake on and his horse ran downhill. The terrified teacher then thrust his leg between the spokes, thinking it would stop the wagon, and suffered a broken leg for his efforts. Other teachers were afraid of the Indians and had no preparation for teaching children who did not speak English. Standing Bear urged that teachers in Indian schools be bilingual and that they use bilingual instruction.[11]

He believed that Indians should teach Indians and that Indians should serve Indians, especially on reservations. He complained, as many Indian leaders do today, that on reservations the positions of importance were held by white employees instead of trained Indians. "Every reservation could be well supplied with Indian doctors, nurses, engineers, road- and bridge-builders, draughtsmen, architects, dentists, lawyers, teachers, and instructors in tribal lore, legends, orations, song, dance, and ceremonial ritual," he wrote. "The Indian, by the very sense of duty, should become his own historian, giving his account of the race —fairer and fewer accounts of the wars and more of statecraft, legends, languages, oratory, and philosophical conceptions," he continued. "No longer should the Indian be dehumanized in order to make material for lurid and cheap fiction to embellish street-stands. Rather, a fair and correct history of the native American should be incorporated in the curriculum of the public school."[12] Indians should be taught their own history, he suggested, and he recommended the creation of schools where tribal art and Indian thought would be taught on the Indian pattern by Indian instructors. All Americans, he believed, would benefit, for "in denying the Indian his ancestral rights and heritages the white race is but robbing itself."[13]

In the expression of these beliefs Standing Bear was ahead of his time. Although reformers like John Collier also favored a revival of native arts and crafts, wanted to reform Indian education, and favored the employment of Indians by the Bureau of Indian Affairs, and many Indian leaders held similar views, Luther Standing Bear was unique in that he stated these views through the medium of books at a time when an Indian author was a rarity. His criticism of Indian education, his call for employment of Indians in positions of authority in the Bureau of Indian Affairs, his recommendation for the adoption of bilingual education and the teaching of American Indian history and culture, his belief in the preservation of Indian culture, and his criticism of discrimination against Indians in the motion picture industry are all timely today, and others still echo his statements. Standing Bear would be pleased with the existence of college courses in American Indian history, although he undoubtedly would be unhappy that more institutions of higher education have not begun similar programs, and he would support the Native American Studies programs run by Indian instructors that exist today. He would be overjoyed with the existence of new developments such as the American Indian Law Program directed by Philip "Sam" Deloria at the University of New Mexico and efforts to attract Indian students into graduate programs by that and other institutions; he would speak alongside Louis Ballard, noted Indian composer, when he criticizes the motion picture industry and the entertainment industry in general for continued discrimination against Indian performers and for continued distortion of the image of Indian people.

My People the Sioux and Standing Bear's other books are not superb examples of literary art, and Standing Bear lacked the sophistication and skill of modern Indian authors like Vine Deloria, Jr., or M. Scott Momaday; but despite inaccuracies and a certain naiveté, his books are still worth reading. They are important in the development of American Indian literature and provide useful information on the Sioux and their relations with the government.[14]

INTRODUCTION

NOTES

1. Luther Standing Bear, *Land of the Spotted Eagle* (Boston: Houghton Mifflin, 1933), pp. 232–33.

2. Richard H. Pratt, *Battlefield and Classroom: Four Decades with the American Indian, 1867–1904*, ed. Robert M. Utley (New Haven: Yale University Press, 1964), p. 335.

3. Daniel Dorchester, Superintendent of Schools, to Commissioner of Indian Affairs, August 3, 1891, Letters Received, 1881–1907, Records of the Bureau of Indian Affairs, RG 75, National Archives, Washington, D.C.

4. Letters in the files of the Bureau of Indian Affairs that praise Standing Bear can be found in 63456-1934-Pine Ridge-034, Central Correspondence Files, 1907–1939, Records of the Bureau of Indian Affairs, RG 75, National Archives; Shiyowin Miller to Richard Ellis, July 10, 1973, in possession of author.

5. George E. Hyde, *Spotted Tail's Folk: A History of the Brulé Sioux* (Norman: University of Oklahoma Press, 1961), p. 288 n.

6. *Senate Exec. Doc. No. 51*, 51 Cong. 1 sess., pp. 51, 242.

7. James McGregor to John Collier, January 16, 1935, 63456-1934-Pine Ridge-034, Central Correspondence Files, 1907–1939, Records of the Bureau of Indian Affairs, RG 75, National Archives.

8. Lewis Meriam et al., *The Problem of Indian Administration* (Baltimore: Johns Hopkins Press, 1928), commonly known as the Meriam Report, presented the results of a survey, conducted by a private foundation, of economic and social conditions among American Indians. The grim picture it painted of the Indians' situation, along with recommendations for reform, made a strong impact on government policy.

9. *Land of the Spotted Eagle*, pp. 248–49, 251.

10. Ibid., p. 248, and Luther Standing Bear, "The Tragedy of the Sioux," *American Mercury* 24, no. 95 (November 1931): 273–78.

11. *Land of the Spotted Eagle*, pp. 18, 241–42.

12. Ibid., p. 254.

13. Ibid., pp. 254–55. In 1933 Standing Bear wrote President Franklin D. Roosevelt proposing a bill that would require public schools to teach a course on Indian history, religion, philosophy, art, and culture (Standing Bear to Roosevelt, May 2, 1933, 22628-1933-013, Central Correspondence Files, 1907–1939, Records of the Bureau of Indian Affairs, RG 75, National Archives).

14. Shiyowin Miller and Warcaziwin deserve a special note of thanks for sharing their memories of Luther Standing Bear.

MY PEOPLE THE SIOUX

MY PEOPLE, THE SIOUX

.·.

CHAPTER I

PLENTY KILL

THE Sioux tribe, to which I belong, has always been a very powerful nation. Many years ago they traveled all over the Western country, hunting, camping, and enjoying life to its utmost, in the many beautiful spots where they found the best wood and water.

It was in a cold winter, in the month when the bark of the trees cracked, in the year of 'breaking up of camp,' that I was born. I was the first son of Chief Standing Bear the First. In those days we had no calendars, no manner of keeping count of the days; only the month and the year were observed. Something of importance would, naturally, happen every year, and we kept trace of the years in that manner. After I went to school and learned how to 'count back,' I learned that that year of 'breaking camp' was A.D. 1868; the month when the bark of the trees cracked was December. Consequently I was born in December, 1868.

My mother was considered the most beautiful young woman among the Sioux at the time she married my father. Her name was 'Pretty Face.' My grandfather — my father's father — was a chief, and accounted a very brave man. He had captured many spotted horses from other tribes in their wars with one another. Therefore, when my father was born, he was given the name of 'Spotted Horse.' This he kept until he was old enough to go on the war-path and earn his own name. He once told me how he received the name of 'Standing Bear.' His story, as near as I can remember it, was as follows:

'One of our hunting scouts returned with the news that the Pawnees were on our hunting-grounds and were killing our game; so all the braves prepared themselves for war. We knew we had a hard enemy to face, as the Pawnees were very expert with the bow and arrow. If one of these Pawnees was knocked down, he was just as liable to arise with his bow in hand, or even if lying flat on his back, he would have an arrow in his bow all ready to let drive.

'We started and traveled quite a long way. When we came up over a hill, we could see the Pawnees down in the valley. They had just finished killing a lot of buffalo, and the game lay scattered here and there. Each man was busy skinning the animal he had killed. Our men rode into them as fast as they were able. I was riding a sorrel horse at this time, and he was a good runner.

'When the Pawnees saw us coming, they scattered to get their horses and leave. We gave chase after them. I took after some men who went over a hill, but they had too good a start, and I knew there was no use tiring my horse out chasing them, so I turned back. As I was nearing my own people, I observed several of them in a bunch, and I rode in close to see what was the matter.

'When I got there, the Sioux were all in a circle around one Pawnee. His horse had got away from him in the excitement and he was left on foot. But he had a bow and arrow in his hand and was defying any of the Sioux to come near. He was a big man and very brave. When our men would shoot an arrow at him and it struck, he would break the arrow off and throw it away. If they shot at him and missed, he would pick up the arrows and defy the Sioux to come on.

'Then I asked the men if any one had yet touched this enemy. They said no; that the man appeared to have such strength and power that they were afraid of him. I then said that I was going to touch this enemy. So I fixed my shield in front of me, carrying only my lance.

'The Pawnee stood all ready for me with his arrow fixed in his bow, but I rode right up to him and touched him with my lance. The man did not appear excited as I rode up, but he shot an arrow at me, which struck my shield and glanced off into the muscles of my left arm.

'Behind me rode Black Crow. The third man was Crow Dog, and the fourth man was One Ear Horse. We four men touched this enemy with our lances, but I was the first. After the Pawnee had wounded me, the other men expected to see him get excited, but he did not lose his nerve. As soon as I had passed him with an arrow through my arm, the Pawnee had a second arrow all ready for the next man.

'The second man was shot in the shoulder, and the third man in the hip. As the last man touched the enemy, he received an arrow in the back. In this manner the Pawnee shot all the four men who had touched him with their lances. We had all gained an honor, but we were all wounded. Now that four of our men had touched the enemy, he was so brave that we withdrew from the field, sparing his life.

'We were some distance away when I began to feel very sleepy. Old Chief Two Strikes and Broken Arm, my uncle, got hold of me to keep me from falling off my horse. This was a very peculiar sensation to me, and something I had never experienced before. The last I remembered was as if falling asleep, but in reality I had only fainted.

'While I was sleeping peacefully (as it appeared to me) I heard an eagle away up in the sky. He seemed to be whistling, and coming nearer and nearer, descending in a circle. Just as the eagle came very close to me, I awoke, and there I saw the medicine man running around me in a circle with one of the whistles made from the bone of an eagle's wing. It was the medicine man who had awakened me from my seeming sleep. Then Chief Two Strikes (who was a very old man) and Broken Arm helped me home.

'These men all sang my praises as we entered the village. Then a big victory dance was given, and great honor was bestowed upon me. At the next council Chief Two Strikes proposed me as a chief, because I was brave enough to face the enemy, even if that enemy was ready to shoot me. So I was accepted and elected as a chief under the name of "Standing Bear."'

That is how my father's name was changed from 'Spotted Horse' ('Sunkele Ska') to 'Standing Bear' ('Mato Najin'). In those days every warrior had to earn the name he carried.

Before my birth, my father had led his men many times in battle against opposing tribes. He was always in front; he was never known to run away from an enemy, but to face him. Therefore, when I was born, he gave me the name of 'Ota Kte,' or 'Plenty Kill,' because he had killed many enemies.

I would like to state that in those days it was considered a disgrace, not an honor, for a Sioux to kill a white man. Killing a pale-face was not looked upon as a brave act. We were taught that the white man was much weaker than ourselves.

Soon after I was born, one of our scouts came into camp one day, and very excitedly stated that a big snake was crawling across the prairie. This caused much excitement. Close observation revealed the fact that a stream of smoke was following the supposed snake. It was the first railroad train of the Union Pacific Railroad. To the Indians this was a great curiosity, and they would climb high in the hills to watch the train run along and listen to the funny noises it made. When they saw that the 'snake' ran on an iron track and did not leave it, they began to be a little braver, and came in closer to better examine the strange affair.

One day some of a war-party of our tribe were returning home. They were very thirsty, and stopped at the railroad station to get some water. The white man in charge of the station compelled them to leave without giving them any water. He was perhaps afraid of Indians, or possibly had done something to them and thought they had come to punish him. His actions made the Indians very angry. They thought it was strange that the white people would run a railroad train across their land, and now would not even let them have a drink of water.

So the war-party came home and reported the treatment they had received from the white man. A council was called, and it was decided to do something. My mother heard the men talking, and, after leaving me in the care of my grandmother, she took a short-handled axe and followed the men. When they came to the railroad track, it was decided to tear up some of the rails and the pieces of wood to which they were fastened. My mother cut the ties and the men hauled them away, after which the whole band went back a mile or so and waited to see what would happen when the train came along.

When the train crew sighted the Indians in the distance, they began to shoot at them. The Indians then whipped up their ponies and gave chase. The men on the train were so busy jeering at the Indians and making fun of their attempt to catch up with them that they failed to watch the track ahead, not suspecting that the Indians would be smart and cunning enough to lay a trap for them. When the train reached the broken spot, it ran off the track and was badly wrecked.

My mother had hidden near by, and after the train smash-up she ran to it. It happened to be a freight, carrying supplies of all sorts to the distant West, and among the cargo was quite a quantity of maple sugar, gingham, and beads. My mother obtained from this train wreck the first beads ever seen by the Sioux Nation. Prior to that time, all the fancy work on moccasins or clothing was made with porcupine quills, which were dyed. In using these quills, the women would hold them in their mouths until soft, then, when they were used, the quill was flattened with the finger nail.

Being a very smart woman, my mother conceived the idea of using some of these beads in place of the quills, to see what they would look like. She beaded a strip of buffalo skin, using yellow beads for the background, instead of the white ones which are now used so much. This beaded strip she sewed on a buffalo calf skin, which I wore as a blanket. So I was the first Sioux Indian to wear beads around my body on a blanket.

The summer following my birth, the northern Sioux came to visit us. This must have been about the time of the sun dance, a religious ceremony which brought the entire tribe together. There was a creek running near our camp in the Black Hills which was swollen from the heavy rains. My mother had pitched our tipi near a spot where the water was shallow, and, as it was the best crossing, the visitors splashed through the water on their ponies and came up the hill past our tipi, where my mother had placed me, wrapped in my buffalo skin blanket carrying the beaded strip. She had placed a large basin of 'wasna,' or Indian hash, beside me, as a welcome to our guests, and I was the 'reception committee.' All the Indians, as they passed, stopped to pet me and get some hash. My mother did this in honor of my father.

Sometimes the little incidents of our lives stand out more prominently than the more important ones. One of my earliest recollections is of a time when we were moving camp at night. I was asleep in a 'hunpa wanjila,'or travois, as it is called to-day. One of the horses turned, causing the poles to cross and pinch me quite severely on the hip. I awoke, crying, and my mother had to come and quiet me. After I had grown up, I mentioned this little incident to my mother, and she said I was about two years of age when it happened.

In those days we knew nothing of Christmas, with its giving and receiving of gifts, as do the children of all nations to-day, but, when boys or girls were old enough to walk alone, they received useful articles. Many games were made for us by our parents. About the first gift I received from my father was a bow and arrows. He made them himself, painting the bow red, which signified that he had been wounded in battle. The arrows were likewise painted red. As I was very young at the time, the arrows were fashioned with knobs on the end, instead of the sharp points, and the bow was not a strong one to pull. That bow and arrows was the beginning of my Indian training. It was to be my weapon in war, and was to get my food for me; so I must always keep it near me. My father taught me how to hold the bow correctly in my left hand, and pull the string back to my body with the right. The arrow was to be placed on the left side of the bow, over my thumb. My father cautioned me always to take good aim, and to be very careful of this bow and arrows. Some day, he said, he would like to see me go on the war-path and earn my own credits. So I kept my bow and arrows near me all the time, as it told of my father's bravery, of which I was very proud, as every one in camp knew my father had been wounded in battle.

We boys would play around camp and shoot, but we had to find our lost arrows, and sometimes this was not an easy task, but my father taught me how. As soon as I was able to sit on a pony, he gave me one for my own. It was an important event in my young life when I was given my own pony. The Indian ponies were gentle little animals. When they were feeding on the plains, we boys could walk right up to them and they did not seem scared — in fact, they were so gentle that we caught them by hand. The blackbirds always stayed around the pony herd when it was feeding, as they got their own meal through them without any trouble, because the ponies, in walking about through the grass, would scare up myriads of grasshoppers, which the blackbirds eagerly snapped up. So the blackbirds and the Indian ponies always were friends. It was a common sight to see several of the birds perched on a pony's back at the same time.

One day my father took me out to shoot a bird. He instructed me how to crawl along the ground to get near my quarry. We went out to the field where the ponies were grazing. Father and I crawled real near them, but they were not in the least frightened. I used the knob arrows, but, try as I might, I could not shoot a bird, so we went back to camp. This made me feel rather sheepish, as I wanted to please my father.

The following day my cousins and uncles were going out bird-hunting, and I trailed along with them. This day I killed my first bird. The event brought a thrill to me! When we arrived back to camp, my father was so happy that his son had killed a bird! He notified the camp crier to announce that his son 'Ota Kte,' or 'Plenty Kill,' had killed his first bird, and that Standing Bear, his father, was giving away a horse in consequence. In all Indian camps there is an old man who acts as a herald to make announcement of importance. On this occasion the horse was given to an old man who was very poor.

This was the beginning of my religious training. When I was born, my father prayed to the Great Spirit to make a warrior of me, and to do this I was compelled to shoot straight. So when I killed my first bird, we believed this was an answer to my father's prayer, and, when a prayer was answered, we always sacrificed something. Thus, this sacrifice was given to an old man who was too poor ever to return the kindness.

Now I began to feel that I was a very big boy, and the whole camp took notice of me. Soon came the fall of the

year and the time to move camp. While the older people
were discussing moving, my cousins and uncles were busy
planning a deer hunt. I listened to all they had to say. It
was planned to start out when the camp broke up and hunt
a little to one side. My relatives never dreamed of my following them, and were too busy looking for game to pay
any attention to me.

When we started out, my cousins really meant to keep
in sight of the moving camp, but we kept drifting away a
little farther all the time. As the sun arose high in the
heavens, it grew very hot. We had now lost sight of the
camp altogether, and could find no water to quench our
thirst. I was suffering very much and began to cry. The
big boys now took notice of me and began to worry. We
were in an unpleasant predicament. Fortunately one of
the boys soon killed a deer. One of my uncles caught some
of the warm blood in his hands and gave me a drink of it.
The blood was far from cooling, but it quenched my thirst.
The boy who had killed the deer cut it up, giving each of
us a share, as we had all been hunters together that day.
Being the smallest boy in the party, I was given the smallest piece of meat.

The older boys tied up my share of the deer meat and
hung it on my back. It was now getting well along toward
evening, and we were on foot, walking back to try to
locate the camp. I was very tired, but did my best to be
brave and keep up with the other boys. Suddenly we saw
a solitary horseman ride up against the skyline on a distant
hill and come toward us. He was leading an extra pony.
We did not know whether he were friend or foe, and the
big boys got ready to fight, if necessary.

When the man on the pony saw us, he signaled. It was
my father, out searching for us. I was so glad to see him.
The extra pony was my own little animal. Father lifted
me to its back and placed one of the smaller boys on behind me, taking another little fellow up behind on his own

mount. In this way we returned to camp, very tired, and so happy to be home again.

Then father called the old camp crier to announce that his son 'Ota Kte,' or 'Plenty Kill,' had brought home his first meat, and that Standing Bear was giving away another pony in consequence. This pony was given to another old man. My father felt so proud of me that he was happy to do this.

CHAPTER II

THE TIPI

Our home life began in the tipi. It was there we were born, and we loved our home. A tipi would probably seem queer to a white child, but if you ever have a chance to live in one you will find it very comfortable — that is, if you get a *real* tipi; not the kind used by the moving-picture companies.

When I was a boy all my tribe used tipis made of buffalo skins. Some were large; others were quite small; depending upon the wealth of the owner. In my boyhood days a man counted his wealth by the number of horses he owned. If a tipi was large it took a great many poles to set it up; and that called for a great many horses to move it about when camp was broken.

A small tipi required about twelve poles to set up, and they were not very long, so that only about two horses were required when on the move. But a large tipi required from twenty-five to twenty-seven poles, and it was necessary that they be quite a bit longer. It required about six horses to transport properly a large tipi when camp was broken. We were at liberty to move any time we chose. So, if a man wanted a large tipi, he must first be sure he had horses enough to move it.

My father's tipi was the largest in our tribe. When we made camp, all the rest of the tribe would camp at a distance, as they were afraid the wind might get too strong in the night and knock our tipi over on them.

At the top of the tipi were two flaps which served as wind-breaks. If the wind blew too hard from the north, then the flap on the north side was raised; if it came from the south, the south flap was raised. Our tipis were always set up facing the east, so we always had the west at our backs.

In case of rain, both flaps were closed down and tied to a stake driven in the ground. If a tipi was set up right, there never was any smoke inside, as the flue was open at the top. If snow fell heavily, it banked up all around the outside of the tipi, which helped keep us warm. On nights when there was a cold, sleeting rain, it was very pleasant to lie in bed and listen to the storm beating on the sides of the tipi. It even put us to sleep.

To erect a tipi properly, three poles were first laid on the ground, one longer than the others. The long one was to serve as the front-door space. These three poles were tied together with a rawhide rope and then were raised up. The tipi covering was then laid on the ground and doubled over. One pole was then laid on the center of the back and tied at the top.

All the other poles were placed around the three poles which were now standing, except two, and they were left for the flaps. After all the poles were in place, the one that supported the tipi was placed. One end of the tipi was now pulled around to the front-door space, and the other end was pulled around to meet it.

A boy would then climb to the top of the tipi and put the pins in the front to hold the tipi together. The women then staked the tipi down with larger pins made of cherry wood. These stakes were about fifteen inches long, and the bark was left on them for about two inches. This kept the tipi from slipping up on them.

In the center of the tipi a large fire was built, and it was nice and warm, regardless of the weather outside.

Doubtless you are wondering what sort of furniture we had in our homes at that time. We did not have very much, but there was sufficient to keep us happy.

We used no high bedsteads. We had a tripod tied to-

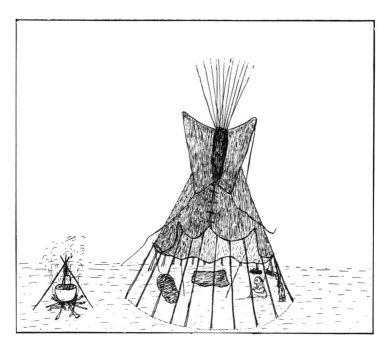

THE TIPI IN SUMMER AND IN WINTER
From drawings by the author

gether with a buckskin string. Straight branches were also strung to a buckskin thong, and these hung down in front of the tripod. These branches varied in size, and were narrow at the top and wider at the bottom. They were attached to the buckskin thong in such a manner that they could be rolled up when it came time to move camp. On top of these small branches was hung a buffalo skin. This was fastened on top of the tripod by the nose. The branches kept the buffalo skin from sinking in between the two sticks of the tripod and served as a back-rest. These tripods stood about five feet high. The skins were quite long, so that a portion of them trailed on the ground. In the center, another skin was laid. This made a very pretty bed and was fine to sleep in. The beds were made all around the sides of the tipi.

At the rear of the bed, against the tipi wall, a tanned hide was tied to the poles, on which was painted the history of the family. These were to the Indian what pictures were to the white man's home. This painted robe could be worn as a blanket when attending a dance.

At the back of the bed, and in front of this painted skin, the woman of the house kept all the rawhide bags. These bags were very fancy affairs. They were made by the women. When a buffalo skin was brought in for this purpose, it was first staked to the ground and the women scraped all the meat off. The skin was then washed with water to make sure it was clean. While the skin was yet damp, it was painted. Our paints in those days were made from baked earth and berries. The paint-pots were turtle-backs. The brush used by the artist was not really a brush, but a small bone, rather ragged on the edge, so it would hold the paint. The straight-edge or ruler was a very straight stick.

Then the woman who was to act as the artist got everything ready to decorate the hide. The paints were mixed with water. The woman kneeled on the skin and designed her patterns, putting in all the colors which she thought. pretty and suited her fancy.

The bag had to be painted in such a manner that the two sides, when folded over, met in the center. Holes were made along the edges of these two ends, and a buckskin string was run through to serve as a tie-string. The decorated side of the bag was tied together. The other side also had a buckskin string, which was fastened to the saddle when on the move.

After the big bag was made, the scraps from the hide were used up. Some pieces were cut for moccasin soles. These were not painted; but the pieces which the women expected to make bags from were all painted at the same time as the big bag. The women made one little bag which served as a sort of workbox. In this the woman kept all the tools she needed in her sewing — the awl and sinews. She also made another to hold her comb. In those days a comb was made from the tail of the porcupine. Another bag held paints and brushes; sometimes knife-cases were made from any of the left-over pieces of hide. All these were painted in pretty designs, and this work was always done by the women. The bag that held the war-bonnet was also painted and decorated, but all war articles were painted by men.

Some of these bags held the dried meat for the winter's supply. Others held sinew and scraps of skin and moccasin soles. In fact, these bags served the Indian just as the white man's trunk is used by him. The bag that held the war-bonnet always hung on the tripod of the bed. It never was laid on the ground.

Other bags which held the clothing of the family were made and decorated with dyed porcupine quills. These were made round, from tanned buffalo skins. The woman cut out the size she desired, then sewed it with sinew, with buckskin tie-strings attached.

In those days we used to eat the porcupine. Every

portion of the body was utilized. The hair was used in the manufacture of the dancing-headdress; the tail was made into a comb; the quills were dyed by the women and used for a variety of purposes in their fancy work.

This porcupine-quill work was quite an art. The pulling of the quills required some time, and one had to be careful that the quills did not get into one's fingers. The dyeing of these quills was also quite a scientific art.

In decorating a bag, the woman would place several of the dyed quills in her mouth. This dampened them, and she would then flatten them with her finger nails and run them through little holes made with an awl. Several colors would be used in the work, and, when it was finished, the woman had a very pretty design. Several rows of quills were put around the bag. If a fancy bag was desired, a few tassels were added to the sides.

When these round bags were in place on top of the rawhide bags, and the painted skin was hung up behind them, and the beds all made and a fire burning, the tipi looked just as neat as any white man's house.

When we were all settled for winter, our women fixed up the tipi as comfortably and inviting as possible. Not for Thanksgiving Day, for we were taught to give thanks every day. Not for Christmas or New Year's, because we knew nothing of these holidays of the white man. It was solely for our own pleasure, and the assurance that we were safe for the long winter months.

The entrance to the Black Hills was through a narrow passage known as 'Buffalo Gap.' The wild animals came in through this gap for protection from the icy blasts of winter; and the Sioux likewise went there. There were springs of clear water and plenty of wood. Nature seemed to hold us in her arms. And there we were contented to live in our humble tipis all through the rough weather.

After a time, of course, our tipis would begin to get old and worn. The poles would commence to break off. Then was the time to think of getting new ones. The entire tribe was in the Black Hills, where they could get all the poles they wanted. They used fir pines, as they were the straightest, and could be found in all sizes. The men would chop down as many trees as they needed and haul them to camp one at a time. First, the bark was peeled off, with all the small limbs. When all the trees had been brought to camp, one would be leaned against a standing tree for a brace. A block of wood was fastened to the butcher knife to be used as a draw-shave. Before the Indian had steel knives he used a sharp stone to do this work. As most of the poles were cut to about the required size, it was not very hard work to finish them. The Indian had no boss standing over him, and he took his own time.

After the poles were all finished, they were arranged in conical form to dry out. If one began to get crooked during this drying-out process, it was turned around with the crook on the outside. This served to straighten the pole. It required about three days for the poles to dry and 'season.'

While the stronger of the men were preparing the poles, the old men also found plenty of work to do. They made the stakes which were to hold the tipi down, and prepared the pins that were to hold the tipi together in front. After they had those finished, they made some other sticks about two feet long, with a hole in one end through which was passed a rawhide thong. These were used in moving camp. All tipi poles had a hole in one end. When it came time to break camp, these small sticks were tied to as many of the tipi poles as a pony could comfortably carry on one side. The rawhide string from the small stick was slipped through the holes in the tipi poles, which kept them from slipping and being lost.

Now that all the poles, sticks, pins, and stakes were prepared for the new tipi, the next and hardest job was to get the skins with which to cover the tipi poles. The entire tribe started to move to northern Nebraska, as they knew this to be a good hunting-ground. Scouts were sent out ahead to locate the buffalo herds. When they returned with the location of a herd, the hunters would prepare to start out on the hunt.

All the relatives now assembled and entered into an agreement that all the skins from the first hunt were to go to the head of the band. If they did not secure enough hides from the first hunt, then the next one was also to go to him. The hunters would kill as many buffalo as possible, and the skins were removed very carefully. As they were to be used for tipi coverings, there must be no holes in them.

As soon as the hides were brought in, the women spread them on the ground and pegged them out while they were yet fresh, with the flesh side up. Three or four women would then commence to remove all superfluous bits of meat from the hide. In this work they used a piece of flint or a sharp stone before steel and iron came into use among them. These 'fleshers' were shaped like a crowbar with teeth in the end. The handle was covered with buckskin, with a buckskin string attached to tie up around the wrist, which helped to hold the instrument.

After all the meat was removed from the skin, and it had dried out, it was turned over with the hair on top. Then, with a tool made of elk-horn, they scraped off all the hair. This instrument, clasped in both hands, was used by the women, who worked it toward them. They were very expert in this work.

When the hair had all been scraped off, it showed a layer of skin which was dark. This was also removed, showing another layer of white. This the women took off carefully in little flakes, and it was used in making a very fine soup. The brains and liver of the buffalo were cooked together, after which this mixture was rubbed all over the skin. It was then folded into a square bundle for four or five days. Several of these bundles of skins would be piled on top of each other.

A frame was now built on which to stretch the skin after it was opened. This frame was made of round poles tied together at the four corners with rawhide thongs. When the skin was opened, it was damp. It was fastened to the frame with rawhide rope run through the peg-holes around the edge of the hide. The mixture of brain and liver was now all scraped off, and the skin washed with water until perfectly clean. The women then went all over the skin with a sandstone, which made the hide very soft.

A braided sinew was then tied to a naturally bent tree, and the other end fastened to a stake driven in the ground. This made the sinew taut, like a bowstring. The skin was then taken off the frame and pulled back and forth on this sinew, by the women, until it was very soft. The effect of this was to produce a beautiful white tan.

At that time our women wore dresses with open sleeves, and, when a person stood behind them as they were pulling on the skin, they resembled angels flying, as the big sleeves flapped back and forth.

These skins were now ready to be put away until enough more were finished to make the tipi. While some of the women were busy tanning the skins, others were engaged in cooking, making dried meats, and getting all the sinew on the poles to dry. The sinews were the cords in the animals, and were used by the women in lieu of thread. There was no waste, I can assure you. When a sufficient number of skins for one tipi were finished, that part of the skin which had the holes in was trimmed off and the hides were patched together.

To begin to measure a tipi, two poles were laid on the ground and were squared off. All tipis were made to look as if they were sitting down. When the skins were being sewed together, the women put them down on these poles and made a circular bottom, much the same as the white women make a circular bottom skirt. When enough skins were sewed together to fit in between these two poles, then it was put around the back pole. More skins were then sewed on until it came back to the front pole again. A small extra piece of skin was allowed in the center, at the top of the back. It was to this piece that the rawhide rope was tied to fasten the tipi to the pole. This was the last pole to be lifted in erecting the tipi.

In those days our women did not have any 'sewing circles,' but, when a tipi was to be made, they all got together with their sinews and awls — the latter made from the wing-bone of an eagle. They would all sit down and laugh and joke as they punched the holes with the awl and threaded the sinews which had been saved from the remains of the buffalo. This did not seem like work to our women.

When the new tipi was all ready to be put up, the old one was taken down, but the skin covering was not thrown away. Every bit of it was utilized to some good purpose. It was well smoked, and that made it waterproof. All the long winter, leggins and moccasins were made from the smoked skin. Sometimes a quiver was made to hold the bow and arrows. Later, when the Indians began to get guns, they also made cases for them out of the old hide, so that it was all utilized.

We did not have many cooking-utensils. When a buffalo was killed, the men were very careful in removing the stomach so as not to puncture it. The inside lining (or tripe) was washed and hung up on four sticks. This made a sort of bag suspended from the center of the sticks. All the meat was then washed and placed in the stomach-bag. Water and salt were added. Stones were then heated in a fire near by and put into this bag. The hot stones soon made the water boil, the meat was cooked, and presently we had soup all ready. We then sat down to a feast.

For plates we used the backs of turtles, while some were

made from sections cut from trunks of trees and hollowed out. Spoons were made from the horn of the buffalo and the mountain goat. These horns were boiled until soft and then cut down the center. While they were yet hot, the men fashioned them into spoons. Some of these horns were larger than others, and from those was made a sort of dipper.

After all the soup and meat was cleaned out of the bag, it was then cut up and eaten. This was a great saving in dishwashing, as there were no pots to wash and our dishes were very few. At that time we knew nothing of coffee or bread. Our entire bill of fare consisted of meat and soup.

If the tripe was to be eaten without being made into a soup-bag, the outside skin was taken off very carefully. This skin was very strong. It was cleaned and tanned and hung inside the tipi to hold water. We did not need a cup with this sort of water-bucket. All that was necessary, when one wanted a drink of water, was to press the bottom up and the water came to the mouth of the bag. Occasionally our mothers would put wild mint leaves in the bag, and when we drank the water through these leaves, it tasted very good. In the summer time this water-bag was suspended under a tree, and we children did not have to go inside the tipi for a drink.

Our Indian women also made a delicacy called 'wasna,' or Indian hash. It was prepared by chopping up the bones and boiling them until soft and the grease came to the top. This was skimmed off and laid aside. Some dried meat was roasted and pounded fine with a stone hammer. Sometimes choke-cherries were added. Grease was then melted and mixed with the pounded choke-cherries and meat. This hash would keep for some time if rightly prepared. The women usually kept a skin from the tripe in which to wrap this hash, and it would harden somewhat after the manner of the white man's head-cheese.

When a big feast was to be held, the woman who could

bring out one of these skins full of hash felt very proud. When a man started on a long journey he usually carried some of this hash with him, as did the men who were going out on the war-path, as it was then not necessary to light a fire, which might betray the Indians to their enemies.

If a change in the bill of fare was desired, the women pounded some dried roasted meat until it was soft and tender. It was then served with the grease from the cooked bones — the same as the white man uses butter to add to the taste of his steak.

In the early spring, when we moved away from our winter quarters, our band of Indians looked better than any circus parade. Each family had its place in line. Nobody was ever in a hurry to get ahead of those in advance — as the white man in his automobile tries to do in this day and age.

In traveling, the ponies carrying the tipi poles of one family, went along together. Then came the pony that carried the tipi covering. This was folded in such a way that there was equal weight on each side. Next came the ponies with the bags. The rawhide bags hung on the saddle, one on each side of the pony. On top of these were the round bags, and in the center of these was that portion of the bed made from the branches strung on buckskin. As this was usually decorated, when rolled up it showed a great variety of colors.

The very young babies rode in a travois drawn by a very gentle pony, which the mother of the baby led, riding on her own pony. We bigger boys and girls always rode our own ponies, and we had plenty of fun chasing birds and hunting, until we came to the new camping-ground.

In all this hustle and bustle of moving, getting the children ready, and starting on the road, in spite of the fact that there were several hundred people, there was no confusion, no rushing hither and thither, no swearing and no 'bossing.' Every one knew we were moving camp, and each did his or her duty without orders. The entire camp would be on the road without any noise.

The old men of the tribe would start out first on foot. They were always in front, and we depended on them. They were experienced and knew the lay of the land perfectly. If the start was made before sunrise, it was beautiful to see the golden glow of the coming day. Then the old men sat down to wait for the sunrise, while the rest of us stood about, holding our horses. One of the men would light the pipe, and, as the sun came over the horizon, the entire tribe stood still, as the ceremony to the Great Spirit began. It was a solemn occasion, as the old man held the bowl of the pipe in both hands, and pointed the stem toward the sky, then toward the east, south, west, and north, and lastly, to Mother Earth. An appeal was made during this ceremony; the men smoked, after which the pipe was put away. Sometimes there would be something to eat on these occasions. After this ceremony was over, somehow we felt safer to go on.

The old men took the lead again, and when they reached a nice grassy place, with plenty of wood and water, they sat down. We then knew they had found a camping-place for the night, and everybody was happy. Every one then got busy locating a place to pitch his tipi. But there was no mad rushing around; we all took our time. Each woman put up her own tipi. Soon the whole camp showed a great circle of tipis, the fires were started, and we were shortly ready to eat. Meantime, the men turned the horses loose and attended to their wants.

Sometimes we would start off again the next morning. Sometimes we remained in one place several days. But as we were on our way to our summer home, in the northern part of Nebraska, and the distance was considerable, we children were anxious to be on the go again.

If there was any dispute about starting, the old men

went to their tipi and counseled together. If it was decided to make a long journey the next day, one of the men would go around and warn every one to get to bed early, so as to be all prepared to start early in the morning. The women would make preparations to carry water along, in case we did not find any on the day's march.

Very early the following morning, we could hear the call of the old man as he passed along by the tipis. He would call out 'Co-oco-o!' This meant, 'Get up' — and we did. There was no asking of questions, such as, 'What time is it?' 'Can I lie a little while longer?' We boys always arose at once, to show that we were young men.

Our journey consumed quite a while. But we stopped when we wanted to and stayed as long as we pleased. There was no great rush. But finally we reached our destination, and our camp was soon settled. Then a scout was picked to go out for buffalo. When the scout returned, the hunters started out, camp was moved near to the place where the buffalo had been located, so the work would not be so hard on the women by being a great distance from camp. When the fresh meat was brought in, we all had a big feast, and were well pleased and satisfied to go to sleep at the end of another day.

Soon the hot summer days arrived. Perhaps the reader may think we had an awful time in a closed tipi, but not so. Forked branches were cut from the box-elder tree. While this is a very soft wood, at the fork of a branch it is tough. The branches were cut four or five feet long. Sometimes ash was used, but box elder was better.

The tipi, all around, was staked down with pins. The women would pull all these pins out on hot summer days, which left the tipi loose around the bottom. The forked ends of the box-elder branches were then placed through the holes around the edge of the tipi, which elevated the edge some little distance, quite like an open umbrella. This not only increased the size of the tipi, but made the amount of shade greater. When the tipis were kept nice and clean, it was very pleasant to stroll through a great camp when all the tipi bottoms were raised.

During the heated portion of the day, our parents all sat around in the shade, the women making moccasins, leggins, and other wearing apparel, while the men were engaged in making rawhide ropes for their horses and saddles. Some made hunting arrows, while others made shields and war-bonnets. All this sort of work was done while the inmates of the camp were resting.

We children ran around and played, having all the fun we could. In the cool of the evening, after the meal was over, all the big people sat outside, leaning against the tipis. Sometimes there would be foot races or pony races, or a ball game. There was plenty we could do for entertainment. Perhaps two or three of the young men who had been on the war-path would dress up in their best clothes, fixing up their best horses with Indian perfume, tie eagle feathers to the animals' tails and on their own foreheads. When they were 'all set' to 'show off,' they would parade around the camp in front of each tipi — especially where there were pretty girls.

We smaller children sat around and watched them. I recall how I wished that I was big enough so I could ride a perfumed horse, all fixed up, and go to see a pretty girl. But I knew that was impossible until I had been on the war-path, and I was too young for that. Before we could turn our thoughts toward such things, we must first know how to fish, kill game and skin it; how to butcher and bring the meat home; how to handle our horses properly, and be able to go on the war-path.

When the shades of night fell, we went to sleep, unless our parents decided to have a game of night ball. If they did, then we little folks tried to remain awake to watch the fun. We were never told that we must 'go to bed,' because we never objected or cried about getting up in the morning. When we grew tired of playing, we went to our nearest relatives and stayed at their tipi for the night, and next morning went home.

When a thunderstorm threatened, every one ran to his tipi. All the forked branches were pulled out, and the sides of the tipi were lowered. If a high wind accompanied the storm, the women, boys, and girls were all hustling, pounding the stakes into place with stone hammers. Then the long branches from the box-elder tree were carried inside the tipi to be used as braces for the poles, which kept them from breaking in. After the storm had passed, how fresh and cool all the earth seemed!

Such was the life I lived. We had everything provided for us by the Great Spirit above. Is it any wonder that we grew fat with contentment and happiness?

CHAPTER III

GAMES

Now I was beginning to consider myself as a big boy, and naturally did not run to my mother with every little thing. When we children were not playing together, I spent my time looking for game or fishing. One day my mother went to see her mother, who lived some little distance from us. My mother belonged to the Swift Bear band. When night came and she did not return for supper, I did not cry. Some other women came to our tipi, and they were very good to me. My father thought Mother would soon return.

Some days afterward, one of my uncles of the Swift Bear band saw me playing, and beckoned me to come to him. He took me to my mother. What a wonderful feeling it was again to be with my own mother. She combed my hair, gave moccasins to me, and also some nice things to eat. And I was really happy to be petted. She never mentioned to me about going back to my father, and, in fact, never thought of returning.

One day, when I was playing outside, my father called for me. I went home with him, and he gave me a horse and all the things necessary to make a man of me. When I went inside the tipi, the two women were still there, and they both called me 'son.'

These two women were the two wives of my father. They were sisters. We all lived in the same tipi, and they were both very good to me. But when their own children came, there was a difference.

In this day, such an arrangement would make it very hard for the children, but in my time it made life better for me. There were more relations to look after me. My father's parents had both passed to the Great Beyond.

But my own mother yet had both her parents, and so did my stepmothers. So I had four grandparents, and they were all good to me. It was the duty of the grandmothers of the tribe to look after the children. When my brothers and sisters went over to see their grandmother and I went along, she did not have things as nice for me as for her own daughter's children.

When I visited my mother's mother, she made nice things for me, and that made up for what I lost from the others. My own mother had two sisters, and they each had two children. My mother had one daughter before she married my father, and the girl lived with her. I now had two homes — one at my father's and one with Mother. When I would go to visit Mother, her sister's children, and my own sister and I would call on my grandmother. We called all 'brothers and sisters.' The term 'cousin' was not used.

Grandmother had as many bladder skins tanned as there were children. These skins were used in the place of paper bags, and she always kept them clean and put away until we visited her. On such occasions Grandmother would make some 'wasna' for us. There was not as much grease added as in that made for the older people. Grandmother would add a little sugar and choke-cherries for us children.

When it was all made, she would fill the little bladder bags and give one to each of us. We ran and played and ate our hash from these bags, as white children of to-day eat candy. After we had emptied the bags, we returned them. We enjoyed our stay, as we had plenty to eat. Grandfather had a big place, and it made him very happy to have all the children with him. He was a very industrious old man. His name was 'Wo-wa-se,' or 'Labor.' This name really suited him, as he was always busy. Grandfather was a very good man, and he liked my father. So as there was no trouble between my parents, I went back and forth at will.

We were now safely settled for the winter in the Black Hills, and we began to prepare things for our winter games.

When our people killed a buffalo, all of the animal was utilized in some manner; nothing was wasted. The skins were used as covers for our beds; the horns for cups and spoons, and, if any of the horns were left, they were used in our games.

The whole side of the buffalo was roasted. After all the meat had been cleaned from the bones, my father took six of the ribs and placed them together. He then split a piece of cherry wood and put the ends of the bones between the pieces of wood. The whole affair was then laced together with rawhide rope on both ends of the bones. On top of these bones, Father fastened a buffalo head, with rawhide ropes. Then he made a string of rawhide which was fastened to the front of the contrivance to pull it with. This was my rib sleigh or 'can-wo-slo-han.' After sliding down in the snow a few times, these bones would become smoother than most of the steel runners on the sleds of to-day. We could use them in winter on the snow, and in the summer for sliding down the grassy slopes. The ribs, or runners, never became rusty, and if we moved camp we did not have to pack our sleds along. Where there were more buffalo, there were plenty more ribs to make other sleds with.

One of the games we played was called 'hu-ta-na-cu-te.' There is no word or name in English for this game, but it was played somewhat on the order of the white man's game of 'hockey' on the ice, only instead of hitting, we threw. Our game was made from the end of a buffalo rib. This bone was about six inches long. One end was shaved down to a round point, somewhat resembling the letter 'U.' The other end was squared off, and the marrow cleaned out. Two small round sticks were inserted at an angle, and a wedge put between them. Then two feathers

Ta-hu-ka-can-kle-ska, a Summer Game for Boys

Winter Game of Hu-ta-na-cu-te on Ice

Winter Game of Pte-hes-te on Ice or Frozen Ground

Pa-slo-han-pi, a Winter Game for Women on Ice or Frozen Ground

SIOUX GAMES
From drawings by the author

were put on the ends of these two sticks, and we were all ready for our fun.

Sometimes the snow would be falling fast when we were getting ready to play this game. I was one of the lucky boys to own a knife of my own. This acted as a sort of magnet to draw the other boys to me. They would all sit around in our tipi waiting for a chance to use my knife to whittle at a bone. The boys were all good to me.

In our country it grew very cold. The snow would freeze very hard after it fell, making the surface as smooth as glass. After the snow had frozen hard, we would start to play the 'hu-ta-na-cu-te' game. We would take opposing sides, and each side tried in every way to get the advantage over the other. Sometimes the game would be played against a bank to see if the boys could go over the top.

The 'hu-ta-na-cu-te' would be held in the right hand, between the thumb and second finger. The first finger would be placed between the two feathers over the plug. Standing in a row, we boys would throw this on the ice or snow full force. If thrown right, and if it landed on the flat side of the point, it would go a long distance. Some of the more expert players could even make it go away up in the air.

Occasionally the feathers would not get placed just right on the 'hu-ta-na-cu-te,' and it would not fly straight. Then the feathers must be adjusted until it would. Some of us became very expert in this game, and could throw it a great distance. The one who could throw farthest was the winner. On clear days we played this game dressed in breech-cloth and moccasins only. In those days we did not have the white man's shirt and stockings; but we did not feel the cold, as the game was very exciting and the exercise kept us warm.

We had another game called 'pte-hes-te.' This was made from the tip end of a buffalo horn. We would shine the horn nicely and cut off about three or four inches. A long stick was placed in the open end and wedged in all around to hold the stick as near the center as possible. Only one stick was used in this game. Feathers were split and wrapped on the stick with sinew, much the same as we made our arrows, only we used two bunches. When the feathers were dyed bright colors, they looked very pretty, and helped guide the instrument. The 'pte-hes-te' was held in the right hand by the stick, and swung back and forth over the shoulder and then thrown down along the icy ground. It would go fast and much farther than an arrow. We had to be very careful to have these made straight, as they were much heavier than the 'hu-ta-na-cu-te,' and if they hit you, they might kill.

We also had another game called 'can-wa-ki-ya-pi,' a sort of top game. It was made from the limb of a tree, tapered to a point. We had little whips made from a stick, with a strip of buckskin for a lash. We spun the top between the fingers and whipped it to keep it in motion. In all natural wood you will find a heart right in the center. My father drove a piece of bone that was very sharp into the heart of my top for a peg. When all the boys were playing 'can-wa-ki-ya-pi,' or top game, it was interesting to hear the tops spin and sing.

Perhaps you will wonder what the girls did. Among Indians, girls and boys play different games, and are always separated from each other. I think that is one reason why our girls grew up to be very nice young women.

The first girls' game I shall mention was called 'pa-slo-han-pi.' This was made from the end of a buffalo or elk horn, much the same as the 'pte-hes-ta,' which the boys played.

The handle of the 'pa-slo-han-pi' was quite long, and there were no feathers attached. With the first finger of the right hand on the tip end of the stick, the girl threw the 'pa-slo-han-pi' from over the shoulder, much the same

way a girl throws a stone, only it would glide when it
struck the ice. The one who threw farthest was declared
the winner. Some of the girls were very skillful at the
game.

Another game was 'i-ca-slo-he,' a sort of game of marbles, but it was played in the winter on the ice. The girls
would offer a prize for the winner. Probably you will
wonder where we got our marbles. In this world of ours
the One above, who has always provided for His children,
helped us, in our amusements as well as in our daily work.
On our reservation we found very nice round stones. If
any of the boys found round stones, they would give them
to their mother, to be presented to some girl.

The girls would first put some brush on the ice to be
used as a seat. Then they would choose sides. The good
players always tried to remain together, so they could win
the prize. The girls sat opposite each other, choosing the
distance before the game started. Each side had a small
piece of wood in front of them, which they called 'un-
pa-pi.' The first side to play took all the marbles on their
side. Then the leader threw them all, one at a time. If
she knocked the block of wood away from in front of the
others, they threw over their prize. If the prize happened
to be a string of beads, and it caught the block of wood,
then they won it back. But the other side had to try to
win it by hitting their block of wood. Sometimes a string
of beads would go back and forth several times. When one
side lost their prize, then they started with the marbles
again. Occasionally the small boys, bent on mischief,
would slide over the ice and catch the beads and run away
with them, whereupon the girls would chase us to recover
the beads.

The 'ta-si-ha' is a game played by the young ladies,
although occasionally the young men tried their hand at it.
This was for those who were in what the whites would
call the 'junior age,' and it was played on winter evenings.

This game was made from the ankle bones of the deer. After the bones had all been cleaned, they were strung on a buckskin string, with the narrow end down. At the narrow end a tassel of little stones, tied together, was hung. After the Indians began to get beads they made this tassel from them. There were about eight of these bones used in the game, each of which fitted into the wide end of the other. At the other end of the buckskin string was fastened the long bone of an eagle's wing. Nowadays they use a piece of steel wire.

If the young women were playing among themselves, they would choose sides; but if the young men were to take part, they would take the opposing side. They held the eagle wing-bone in the right hand and the tassel in the left. Then they would swing the string of bones out in front of them. If they succeeded in catching the first bone, they played again. If a miss was made, they passed the 'ta-si-ha' to the next one in line. If the player caught the bone ten times in succession, it counted for one win. After catching the first bone ten times, they would start on the second, third, fourth, etc., until they caught the entire ten. Then they would catch the tassel, which would be called one game.

The players would always try to get the best of the opposing side. Sometimes they would play with one hand held behind them. At other times they would hold the 'ta-si-ha' in the left hand. It was great fun to watch this game. Some of the young men were so bashful they would cover their faces, not caring if they won or lost. All they desired was to be near the girl they loved. Some of these young men would have their fingers covered with German silver rings which they wanted the girls to see — much the same as the white youth who wears a diamond wants to 'show it off.'

Our people believed that all work and no play was not good for any one. So the older people had a game called 'hanpa-pe-cunpi.' It was also known as the 'moccasin' or 'hand game.' It was played somewhat after the manner of 'button, button, who's got the button?' But our play was more dignified. It required two men who were very skillful in concealing a small stick in the hand. There were two small sticks used, each about two inches long, and tied in the center with a string of dyed buckskin, some colored red and others blue, to represent the different sides playing against each other. In the center, between the players, were ten long sticks. These were used to 'keep tally' on. One man took charge of the score.

One whole band would play against another. When we would hear the men of our band talk about going over to another band to play the 'hand game,' we would get quite excited, and long for the day when we were grown up so we could play this game. Every one in camp would then get busy, looking around for something to be put up as a prize. There were blankets, otter skins, buffalo robes, moccasins — in fact, anything they could afford to donate.

After the sun had set and the shadows began to fall, our band would be ready to start. The men would go first, then the women, while we children stayed in the rear. Everybody would start to sing about the hand game, to let the other band know our band was coming, and it also served as a sort of challenge. The largest tipi was quickly cleared, all the beds being taken to another tipi. Indian perfume was then put all around, which filled the tipi with a delightful odor.

The players also were perfumed. They would enter first and take their places in the center of the tipi on one side. The women arranged themselves behind, and we children hung back in the rear of the women.

After our players were all seated, the other band would come in and seat themselves. They took the same formation on the other side of the tipi. One of the old warriors held the two sticks, and when every one was seated, and all was quiet, he recounted his deeds in war. After he had finished, he would hand the sticks to two men of one side who he judged were able to uphold the honor of their band. The opposing side selected one man to act as 'guesser' for their band. He would take his seat directly in front of the two players.

The game would begin with singing, the players slapping their hands together and hitting the ground, then putting their hands behind their backs and going through all sorts of motions to deceive the guesser. These motions were kept up all through the singing. As the song came near to the end, the guesser had to tell in which hand both players held the little piece of wood. If he pointed to the left hand, it meant that he had concluded the wood was in their left hands; and the same for the right hands. If the guesser put his hand right in front of him, with the thumb pointing one way and the finger the other, it meant that the players held the wood in the two outside hands. If he pointed straight out, it meant they held the wood in the center hands.

If the guesser made a mistake, the players received two of the long sticks for their side. If he guessed right on one of the players, it gave the players' side only one stick, while the player who fooled the guesser played alone. He had to be very careful after that, because it was much easier where the guesser had only one man to watch.

Sometimes a young woman or a young man would get up and commence to dance for the purpose of distracting attention of the guesser. It was very hard to keep the mind on both players when the dancers' bells were ringing. If the guesser missed on the man who was playing alone, it gave the players' side another stick, and both men played together again.

As soon as the guesser had caught both men correctly, they handed over their little sticks to the other band, and the same tactics were repeated. The important thing was to keep the long sticks away from the opposing band, and, if the guesser did not prove to be very skillful, he was replaced by some one else.

When one side had won about eight of the ten long sticks and were playing again, the excitement would be great. But if the guesser could beat the two men on the first call, they had to hand over the small sticks to the other party. The two long sticks remained in the center, and were yet to be won.

It might happen that the opposite side might begin to have better luck, and might win the two sticks in the center. Then, if they won again, they would begin to take the sticks from the other band.

When one side had won the ten sticks, it counted as one game. The best two out of three games was the way it was usually played. After the game was over, the losing side would set up a big feast for the victors, besides giving all the prizes.

The band which won would then go home, singing and rejoicing on the way. Then they waited for the losers to 'stage a come-back.' If they did not do this, then the winning band would go to another tipi to play the game, and try to win once more. My father was chosen many times to act as guesser for his band, and he was very skillful at it.

In those days it was great fun to attend a game of 'han-pa-pe-cunpi' with the whole family. The men would play it away into the night, with every one watching very intently. When we children grew sleepy, we lay down and went to sleep.

If the men wanted to smoke, but one pipe was used, and this was passed between the men. No drinks were served which took away the senses of our men and women, so no one grew boisterous. We had no bad words in our language, so none were used. Truly, our sleep was a healthful one.

I have spoken of the 'i-ca-slo-he' or marble game for the

young women, but there was a marble game for the small boys also. It was an indoor game, to be played on cold winter nights when a fire was built. We would find some round stones and get the bark of a tree, or a smooth, flat piece of stone. If we could find neither bark nor flat stone, we would use our hand or forearm. This we held at an angle. We would pull some ashes out of the fire and mark trenches through the piles. Then we would start our marbles down grade, and the marble which went over the greatest number of trenches won the game. While we all worked very hard to make our marbles go farthest, there was no cheating, but the game was played fairly.

Another winter game, to be played out of doors, was the 'i-pa-ho-tun-pi,' or popgun game. In the olden times the popgun was made quite short, from ash or any wood that had a big heart. A hole was drilled through the heart of the wood. Perhaps you will wonder how this was done, inasmuch as we had no drills or wire at that time. It certainly did require some patience. The worker would take a thin stick and burn it on the end until it was red, when he would press it into the heart of the ash stick. This was repeated over and over again, and required considerable time before the hole was drilled through.

When the gun was finished, we had to get the ammunition. Sometimes we used the root of the fox medicine plant. We would peel off the outside bark and chew the inside until the sap was all gone, when it became quite a hard ball. A small ball was first inserted in the barrel of the gun, and allowed to roll down to the end until we could feel it. Then we put in a larger one. This left a small air space between the two balls. With a stick which would just fit into the gun barrel, we would push. This would shoot the 'bullet' out with some force, and it made quite a noise.

All through the winter we enjoyed ourselves, but soon the melting of the snow would warn us that spring was coming, and that it was time for new games. The big boys would be overhauling their bows and arrows, and then we knew it was time for the ' bow game.' They gathered a big pile of brush and stacked it hard against a bank. Then the boys would line up for the play. One arrow was shot into the brush-pile, leaving the feathers sticking out. This was the goal. The player stood his bow on the ground, with his hand resting on the top. The bowstring faced the brush-pile. The side of an arrow was hit against the bow-string, and the string, being taut, caused the arrow to spring back, and it would stick in the bush. The arrow that had its feathers nearest the original arrow in the brush won the game. This game was for the big boys only, and, as each contestant had his arrows painted so he would know them, it was not hard to locate them.

The singing of the meadowlarks would presently draw our attention away from the bow game, and we would start off to hunt these birds. The larks in our State, at that time, talked the Sioux language — at least, we inferred that they did; but in California, where I now live, it is impossible to understand them. Perhaps they are getting too civilized. In our country, we little fellows thought these birds were our enemies, because they would say things to us that we did not care to hear. They would call out a boy's name, and say that 'his mamma wanted him,' or some other objectionable expression in bird talk. So we did not like to have these birds come near us. Those early songsters were wise birds, and sometimes we would hunt all day and get nothing. We used blunt arrows in hunting birds, but when out after rabbits, we took our wooden-pointed arrows. These were not given to us until we were considered able to handle them right. Off we would start, and presently strike the fresh trail of a rabbit. As soon as we killed one, we would have a feast. We carried no matches, but we knew how to make a fire by rubbing two sticks together. We would roast the rabbit and have a fine time. After we had enough of it, we would go home, tired but happy.

Perhaps some of the boys would suggest that we go fishing, and off we would start — minus pole, line, sinker, or hook. All we carried was our bows and arrows. Do you wonder how we got any fish with bows and arrows? The first thing we did was to catch our ponies. We would pull a few black hairs from the tail. These we tied about two lengths long and wound a few of them together. This was our fish-line. We carried along a bit of buffalo meat if there was any. When we came to the river or brook, we got a long branch of the willow tree and tied the hair-line to it. The piece of meat we would tie to the end of the line with sinew. This combination made a very good pole, line, and bait. The bait was thrown into the stream, and soon the fish would be attracted by the meat. Soon a big fish would come along and swallow the bait, and he was quickly jerked out of the water.

The boys who did not own a pony from which to get hair for a line had another method of fishing. They took the branch of a willow switch and made a loop on one end with sinew or braiding. They would lower this into the water, and, when a big fish tried to pass through it, he was soon landed on the bank. Occasionally the boys would shoot the fish with the bow and arrow, using an arrow with extra long shanks. In those days it did not take long to get enough fish for a feast, and we roasted or boiled them — that is, if we could find a can. If we caught more than we could eat, we carried the fish home on a 'stringer' made of a small branch. In those days the fish were good to eat. Nowadays I cannot eat fish at all.

One of the games we played was called 'pa-slo-han-pi.' It had the same name as a girls' game, but was played differently. The 'pa-slo-han-pi' was a long stick, six or seven feet in length, made from a willow tree. In the early spring, the thin bark of the willow peels very easily. A straight thin piece of the bark was cut off. This was repeated until the stick was clear of the bark. Then we took these thin pieces and wound them about the stick in various designs. We next made a fire and piled brush on. When this began to smoke, we held these long sticks in until all the raw part of the branch had a yellow tinge, caused by the smoke. Then we unwrapped the bark, and the stick was marked very prettily, with yellow and white. Occasionally some of the boys would make their designs black by burning the stick with a different wood. We would make six or eight of these sticks before we started to play the game.

It was played somewhat on the order of the white boy's 'follow your leader.' The 'pa-slo-han-pi' was held in the right hand, between the thumb and second finger, the tip of the first finger being on the top of the stick. When all was ready, we all stood in a line.

In the girls' game they threw the 'pa-slo-han-pi' over the right shoulder, but the boys glided the stick over the moccasin, a log, or a stone. The foot was held up, and the stick shot over the moccasin by a swift throw of the hand. This made it travel a long distance, and the player who could send his stick farthest won all the other sticks. The contestants would all throw one stick apiece, then we would all run to see whose stick traveled farthest. Each player knew his own stick by the design on it.

Our women had a summer game called 'tan-pa.' On our reservation we had wild plum trees. The women took about seven of the seeds of the plum, and on each side burned different marks. Each mark counted for a certain amount. Then a basket was made of the flat grass that grew in the swamps near the cat-tails. These baskets were about five inches across and an inch and a half deep, and were made heavy on the bottom.

Thirty long sticks were used for chips or tally-cards. When everything was ready to start the game, the women got together and put up their prizes, as the white women do to-day when they play euchre or 'five hundred.'

There was no limit to the amount of players in this women's game of 'tan-pa.' Sometimes they chose partners, sometimes three would play together; again, each would play for herself. The prizes consisted of sinew, porcupine quills, beads, rawhide, or buckskin. Sometimes one of the women would put up a pair of moccasins. Nowadays they can go out and buy a prize for very little money; but when an Indian woman put up a prize, it meant something because of the hard work it had cost her.

When they grew tired of playing for points, they would change the game and play for pairs. The leader took the basket, with the three middle fingers on the inside, and the thumb and small finger outside. She shook the basket around to mix up the seeds, and then thumped the bottom on the ground. This would cause the seeds to jump into the air and fall. If she landed a pair of one marking, that gave her side one stick, and she played again. If the second play showed no pairs, she handed the basket over to the other side.

The grown men had a game called 'pa-in-yan-ka-pi.' This was a large hoop made from the wood of the ash tree, to about the size of a wagon wheel. On four points of the hoop the men cut a spot about two inches long and made designs. They covered these marks with red and yellow paint, and each of the marks counted for a certain number of points. Four sticks were used, each about four feet long, made of ash. Two of the sticks would be tied together with buckskin, about six inches from the bottom, and again about ten inches from the bottom. The upper string was shorter than the lower one, making a sort of fork, with two prongs. Two men were selected who were good runners, and each carried one of these pronged sticks. The players wore only a breech-cloth, as they wanted nothing to hamper their movements. The main object was to knock one of the hoops down with one of the sticks, on a mark corresponding with the color of the buckskin their stick was tied with.

One of the men rolled the hoop as fast as he could. Then the two runners started after it with their sticks, ready to knock it down if they got close to it. When the hoop went down, every one rushed forward to see what the mark was and to note the score. It quite resembled a football game, because the winners yelled just as the white folks do at a ball game.

Sometimes the old men who were watching the game would begin to boast about how they played the game when they were young, and how fast they could run. Then the young men would commence to tease their elders to give them an exhibition of their ability. It was an exciting moment when the old men would drop off their blankets and start. Of course they could not give very much of an exhibition, but it pleased them immensely when the younger men applauded them, and the winner felt very proud.

We had foot races for all ages of the tribe. Sometimes one whole band would race against the other for prizes. Pony races were very common, and the exercise kept us all in fine trim physically.

Now for American baseball. Remember, I say AMERI-CAN baseball — not English. WE were the only real Americans. This game makes me laugh, as so few white people had any idea we ever had such a game. First, let me relate a little incident: One time I made a bow and arrow for a little white boy. His aunt grew quite indignant that her nephew wanted to play Indian. He came to me and said his aunt did not want him to play with a bow and arrow. She wanted him to play a real American game, like baseball.

Poor little fellow! How hard it would have been for him to play the REAL AMERICAN baseball, because it was so different from the English (or white man's) way of playing the game.

At the time of year when the bark of the trees was easy to peel off, a crowd of us would start out to get the second growth of the ash. Second-growth branches were always straight. It was real fun, as all ages of the tribe gathered these sticks. After getting back home, the men would build a fire and hold a stick over it until the bark started to burn. Then the bark was peeled off, which left a nice white wood. Next, the end was bent in the shape of a shepherd's crook, and tied with a rawhide string in that position to dry and set. After the stick was dried out in this shape, the rawhide string was removed, and a piece cut off the end of the stick so that it somewhat resembled the golf sticks of the white man. The handle was just long enough for a man to be able to reach the ground and hit a ball while running. These were the bats used in the game. Each man had his own, and it was decorated to suit himself.

The ball was made from scraps of buckskin, wound together, and then covered with a piece of buckskin and sewed with sinew. These balls were very hard, and about the size of an ordinary baseball.

When the ball and bats were all ready for use, a collector went through the camp and gathered all the articles which were to be used as prizes. It was really funny to see the way in which this man laid out his prizes so they would show off to the best advantage. When he reached our side of the camp, he compared the prizes we were to give with those he already had. If an otter skin had been put up by the opposite side, then some one on our side had to be just as liberal and also donate an otter skin. When calico was donated, they measured off the amount in yards. You could not give three yards and expect nor hope to win six. Both sides had to make donations of about equal value. After the prizes were all collected, they were carried to the middle of the camp or field. The collector remained with them to watch them.

The young men who were to play were now busy painting their bodies and fixing their hair. Then they would run up and down, warming up for the game. Every one was anxious to have the game start. The children got their ponies and rode them to a place where they could watch the game. Every one but the players was on horseback, in a big circle. The camp was about a mile or so across, and one tipi at each end was chosen as goals. Any number of players could participate in this game. Sometimes there were as many as fifty men on a side, each one having a bat.

There were no foul lines. The main object was to get to the goals first; the ball was not to be touched with the hand, but must be hit with the bat or kicked.

When the players were ready, a man threw the ball up in the air, and as it came down the men on both sides tried their best to drive it toward their finishing-line. If the ball was driven to the side of the camp, it caused a scramble for all the people near by to get out of the way. We little fellows on horseback would whip up our ponies and run as fast as we could to watch the ball. The men who played this game were all fast runners, very strong and fine-looking. They wore only the breech-cloth and plain moccasins; sometimes they ran in their bare feet.

I remember one time when they were playing this game, and we were all watching them, the ball came to our side. We got out of the way as fast as our ponies could carry us, and then watched to see what would happen. Two of the best runners were after the ball, and as they came together one young man was lifted off his feet and thrown. He struck a small tipi and knocked it down, but that did not seem to worry him in the least; he got after the ball and drove it back. Such playing required all a man's strength.

Two out of three games had to be won by one side, and

then they carried all the prizes home to their camp. The greatest excitement was caused when each side had won once, and it came time for the last play. The ball would be down near the goal, with every one on that side shouting for victory. Suddenly one hit would drive the ball into the field again. There it would perhaps be met by one of the out-fielders (as you would call them). If he was an exceptionally good player, he would knock the ball over the heads of the players and into the tipi.

What shouting and singing there would be as the victors went home! When this game was played at night, it was for every one. The ball used in the night game was about three times larger than the one used in the day game. It was made of buckskin stuffed with deer hair. This made it very soft, and it would not go very far, and if one happened to get struck by it, it did not hurt very much. When we little fellows knew the night game was going to be played, we got our bats and started with all good intentions to get into the game. We would expect to hit the ball at least once; but when we would see the men coming our way, we would change our minds and run away from the ball as fast as we could.

Sometimes the women played the game alone. One of my cousins was such a fast runner that when she got after the ball the others usually gave up the chase. She was a very tall young woman. She is now an old woman. Her name is Mrs. Black Horn, and she still resides at Pine Ridge Agency, in South Dakota.

When we were quite small, we all sat around in the evening to hear our older people talk of hunts, battles, fishing, and moving. Like the children of to-day, we tried to imitate. The old men would relate how they had sent out a certain scout and what news he brought back, and about how the hunt started. So we children wanted a buffalo hunt all our own. We had no toys, of course, but we did not complain, but started to make some ourselves. We would get some adobe mud, work it until it was easy to model, and very soon we had a great array of horses. We used slough grass for the legs of these horses.

Sometimes we made our horses from the branches of the red willow tree. We could make four different colors. If we used the willow as it was on the tree, the horse was plain red; if we took off the first bark from the legs, it resembled stocking-legs. Peeling off the bark produced a yellow horse; or we could make spotted horses by picking at the bark here and there.

Then we would make little men from these branches also — that is, if our horses were made from the willow. If we made adobe horses, then we modeled adobe men. After the horses were all made, we would go out where the real horses were grazing and pick up dried manure chips and call these the buffalo, because they were brown.

We made little bows and arrows, and then divided into bands, like the grown folks. If we let the girls come into this game, it was more fun, as they would make little tipis from the leaves of the cottonwood tree, and fasten them together with a small twig. When the girls had plenty of these made and they were scattered around, it quite resembled a big camp.

Then we boys would make-believe send out a scout, and after he returned we would all start with our imitation horses to get the buffalo. We would play by the hour at this game of chasing the buffalo.

While we were getting the cottonwood leaves for the girls, we would sometimes break off a forked stick, and they would use this to make a doll. These dolls were not very handsome affairs, as they had no arms; but when they were wrapped in a piece of buckskin, they looked good to us Indian children.

The women could make very nice dolls from the scraps of buckskin, which they stuffed with deer hair. These were unbreakable, and when dressed looked very pretty. The girls would keep these dolls for a long time.

As the girls grew toward young womanhood, they were taught to imitate their mothers in everything. They were taught to tan buckskin and sew it together to make a tipi. They used poles from the willow tree seven or eight feet long, and these made fine tipis. However, but few of the girls could afford such a luxury, and the girls who could were very proud to show them off.

In our play the girls would usually decide where the village was to be pitched. Some of us boys had our own ponies and we would suggest having a battle and attacking the camp. This was lots of fun. Some of the girls had their dolls in little carriers, and they would run, and the boys on their side would fight us. If a boy fell off his pony while in the camp of the enemy, one of us would be brave and try to rescue him.

After the battle was over and peace reigned, if the opposite side had lost all their horses, then the boys would drag the tipi poles over to another place, and the camp would be set up again.

While this was all in play, it was just like the stories which were told to us at home. There was no roughness shown among the children, nor was any advantage taken of any one. We always 'played fair,' as we were taught to be fair in all things.

If any of the older people were passing, they would stop and watch us at our play. If they happened to be passing through the spot where our miniature camp of adobe horses and men was set up, they were always very careful not to break any of our playthings and spoil our fun.

Our playthings were all outside, so we did not need to put them away; in that way they did not muss up the tipi. But if a heavy rain came up in the night, our adobe toys looked very miserable the next morning. But there was plenty more adobe and lots of trees from which to manufacture more toys, and we did not cry or worry about the loss.

CHAPTER IV

A BUFFALO–HUNT AND A BATTLE

ABOUT 1875 we were camped near the big White River, some forty miles east of the Black Hills. The Sioux tribe then numbered about twenty thousand souls, as the Pine Ridge and Rosebud Reservation Indians were together.

My father came home from council one day, and told my mother to get ready to move, as the tribe was going to the northern part of Nebraska, where the indications of buffalo were then very plentiful.

Early the following morning I was called to climb to the top of the tipi and remove the pins, or little sticks, that held the tipi together. In a few minutes it was down, and we were moving toward the south. We boys climbed on our ponies and rode alongside the moving caravan, chasing everything in sight. We made three camps before we arrived at the point where it was thought likely the buffalo would be.

At sundown we all gathered together about a big fire made of buffalo chips, which burned like coal. It was a calm, clear night, and the smoke from the camp-fire went straight up into the air. All the older men got together and were talking about something in a very quiet way. Finally two of them arose and looked all over the assemblage, apparently searching for some one. Finally they picked a young man, not very large or stout, but withal a very reliable man in every way. He knew every foot of the country and where to locate the water-holes. He was brave, and perfectly able to travel alone at night in all sorts of weather, and was also able to protect himself if he encountered enemies.

This man was chosen as a scout. After being notified, he went to his tipi to get what he intended to carry with him.

When he returned, all I saw him have was his quiver full of arrows and a very strong bow. He wore nothing but a breech-cloth and plain moccasins. Around his neck was a twisted buckskin string which held his bag of medicine. When he returned to the gathering, about twenty men and women were singing for him. He ran around the fire three times, and the fourth time he sped off into the darkness. The fire was then extinguished.

The old man who always acted as herald then came around to every tipi, warning the inmates to be very quiet. The moon was shining, although it was yet very early. But we were warned that if we played, we must be careful not to make any noise. It seemed as if even the babies, dogs, and ponies minded the order.

Our scout remained absent all night. Early in the morning the same old man passed by every tipi before sunrise. He called out 'Co-o-co-o!' which meant, 'Get ready!' In a short time every tipi was down. As soon as the old man had passed, fires were made, breakfast cooked, and the camp was moving before sunrise.

Twelve old men were the leaders of this camp. One of them carried a burning buffalo chip on the end of his lance. They went away up on a hill, where they could be seen for a long distance. Here they built a big fire. They did not attempt to avoid being seen, as there were no enemies around.

While these men were watching for the return of the scout, the others dismounted and took off their saddles to give the horses a rest, and to dry the backs of the animals if they had become sweaty. The women were busy repacking their bundles. Even we boys found many things to keep us busy.

Presently one of the old men arose and exclaimed, 'Hi-ye-he!' which meant that our scout was returning. Then we were very happy. The fire was rebuilt by adding more chips, and the men gathered halfway around the flames, all sitting down, with the women and children behind them. The dogs and ponies also instinctively drew closer, as if they, too, wanted to hear the report.

One old man near the fire held the pipe of peace, which he pointed in the direction from which the scout was approaching. We could see him at a great distance on top of a hill. Here he stood for quite a while. Finally he ran to the east about a half-mile, then about the same distance toward the west; then he ran straight toward where we were gathered around the fire.

We all understood, when he ran to the east and then to the west, that he had seen many herds of buffalo. He approached the fire on the opposite side from us. Then he sat down, and the old man offered him the peace pipe. He stretched out both arms, passing the pipe three times, but the fourth time he accepted the pipe. After drawing a few whiffs he handed it back. Everybody exclaimed, 'Ha-ho!' meaning 'Thank you.' His reason for smoking the peace pipe was that he would tell nothing but the truth.

After this ceremony, the scout started in to tell where he had seen the buffalo, how many there appeared to be, and how quietly they were resting and not being disturbed by any enemy. This was all good news, because the buffalo would have acted as if restless if enemies were near. When the scout pointed he used his thumb instead of the first finger. His work was now finished, and he returned to his tipi.

The old man who carried the pipe now gave the order to move ahead. The buffalo were not far distant, so the hunters began to get ready for the attack. They went ahead of our camp, riding their ponies and leading the best horses. As no extra weight was ever put on these fast horses, they were always fresh and ready for a long run as soon as the buffalo were sighted.

Yet, even though the hunters knew where the buffalo were, they were not allowed to get ahead of each other.

If one buffalo was shot, it would stampede the entire herd; so the men were to keep together, because this hunt was for the winter's supply of meat. To make sure that none of these hunters tried to be tricky and get ahead of some other hunter, three men rode with them with war-clubs in their hands, which they were to use on any hunter who tried to 'get funny,' as the white man calls it. It was very seldom that a hunter was foolish enough to do anything which called for such punishment.

The three men with the clubs ran to the top of a hill. They figured out the best place to go in order to get as close to the herd as possible without being detected. Soon they told the hunters to get on their best horses. The men rode without saddles, the reins being held on their bridle-arm. As the horses were trained hunting animals, they knew just what was expected of them.

As soon as the hunters appeared at the top of the hill, the buffalo sighted them. Some of the animals were lying down quietly. Now they began to rise and huddle together, viewing the approaching horsemen with symptoms of alarm. The three men with the clubs were still riding back and forth, watching the hunters, as it was not yet just time for the slaughter to begin. As they drew closer to the herd, the command was given to them to commence the attack.

The men were all ready and impatient. They rode as fast as possible, and when they sent an arrow into an animal, it was shot so as to penetrate the heart if possible. Soon a great cloud of dust arose, as the buffalo stampeded, and the hunters had to be very watchful that they were not surrounded and trampled beneath the hoofs of the ponderous beasts. The dust was so dense that it was impossible to see very far in any direction. Hunting buffalo under these conditions was a very dangerous proposition.

The men killed only what they thought was enough for the camp. They did not pursue the animals all day, nor did they kill for sport. When they returned home with the meat, we were all very happy. The women cooked, and then began to prepare dried meat for the cold days that were to come. Quite often the snow lay very deep in the winter, and our hunters could not get out for many days; but if there was plenty of dried meat we did not worry.

Soon after this hunt, we moved our camp up on the 'Minia-tanka-wakpala,' or 'big water creek,' which, interpreted into English, means the Niobrara River. We still numbered about twenty thousand. We had plenty of dried buffalo meat, but, as the weather was pleasant, one of the men went out deer-hunting. We all liked a change of meat.

This hunter soon returned, and reported that he had seen smoke in the distance, and that the deer were moving away from that direction very rapidly. That night all the chiefs and warriors held council. They selected three men to go out and scout around to determine the cause of the smoke. Then an order was issued that nobody in camp was to light a big fire. Every one must remain quiet, and the ponies kept close at hand.

There was not very much sleeping done in camp that night. Some of the men remained with their horses, and the young men kept watch around the camp all night. We had to be very careful, not knowing but that enemies had scouts out watching our camp.

The next day about noon the scouts returned. They reported seeing some Pawnee Indians on our hunting-grounds. These Indians were our enemies. Instantly all the warriors began to get ready to go on the war-path, and great excitement prevailed.

My father brought his own horse in, as well as an extra one for me. He was ready, and wanted me to go with him. All the chiefs had gathered in a large tipi to a council, and one of the men came out and turned my father's horses loose. This meant that they did not want him to go. But he was a very brave man; so he got his own best horse and started off alone toward the enemy. As soon as the braves saw him leave, they did not wait, but got on their ponies and started after him, leaving our village without any men to defend it, save the old men.

My grandfather told me he was not going to fight, but was going after buffalo, as we were out of fresh meat. So he saddled a horse for me to accompany him. We did not go very far until we heard a thundering of hoofs. Looking over the hill we observed about a hundred buffalo coming toward us. Grandfather got me safely behind the hill and told me to be careful, as our enemies, the Pawnees, had doubtless frightened these buffalo. The noise made by the approach of the animals sounded like an earthquake, and the thought that perhaps the Pawnees were right behind them was not a very comforting one for a little fellow like myself. Grandfather told me to remain where I was, while he gave chase after the animals.

The buffalo came running along and Grandfather started after them just as they turned off at the hill. He wore only a breech-cloth and moccasins. After the buffalo had all passed, I looked over the hill. There was my grandfather, with his two braids of hair tied together, skinning a buffalo, which he had killed without any noise.

Leading my horse, I walked over where he was and sat down to watch him skin the buffalo. Every once in a while I would glance uneasily about, as we knew our enemies were very near. Soon the skin was off, and then the butchering began. My grandfather carried very sharp knives, also a few small sticks, which the old men called 'pipe trimmers.'

He cut out a fine piece of tripe, or lining of the stomach of the buffalo, washed it in the blood and gave it to me to eat raw, with some of the marrow from one of the front leg bones. I obtained this marrow with one of the small sticks which he gave me. The Sioux in those days learned to eat raw meat, so when we were in the enemy's country and did not dare light a fire, we could still get along. To the white boys or girls of to-day, this would not appear very appetizing; but we were taught to eat what was considered good for us, and not to ask questions about it. We did not know what it meant, in those days, to be anæmic.

My grandfather was very busy while I was eating. He put the skin of the buffalo over my horse, with the hair side down, after tying all the meat together with rawhide ropes which he cut from the raw skin. He then hung the meat over my horse's back against the flesh side of the buffalo skin. After it was all ready, he pulled the skin over to cover the fresh meat, and I climbed on top to ride. There was such a big load that my two legs stuck out very straight.

We reached the village safely, and everybody was so glad we had some fresh meat. A big fire was then built, and the whole sides of the buffalo tied to sticks and swung back and forth over the fire. While the meat was roasting, the women pulled weeds and strewed them on the ground to sit on. A shade was also erected. After the meat was done to a turn, we had a real barbecue, which was heartily enjoyed, in spite of the fact that we had no coffee, bread, or cake; but we were very thankful for the fresh buffalo meat.

In a few days we saw some of our war-party returning. One of the men in advance was waving a scalp. This caused great excitement. The men paraded around the village; but my father came home between two young men, being badly wounded. He went right to our tipi. Everybody appeared to be happy and rejoicing. I went in to see my father.

He was sitting on a buffalo robe, with his back against a tripod of wood. He was very quiet, so I did not go near him, as I knew he was wounded and would soon have the medicine man. So we boys decided to go bird-hunting. When we returned I went to our tipi. My father was telling some of the old men about the fight. It seems that the Pawnees had moved north, as the game was more abundant there. They knew this was the hunting-ground of the Sioux, so the warriors had secreted their women, children, and horses in a dry creek bed. As our tribe came over, the Pawnees expected they would run into them, and were on the lookout. My father rode his horse in quite near to them, and then turned away, confident that some of the enemy would follow him. He had a very swift horse, which made it difficult for the Pawnees to overtake him. But they rode after him, which gave some of our men a chance to surround and kill several of them. My father then tried the same tactics a second time; but not many of the Pawnees pursued him, as several of the first band of the tribe had not returned.

But the Sioux were spoiling for a fight, and they charged right at the Pawnees. Several hundred of them were killed in the battle which followed, and many of their women, children, and horses were captured.

When my grandfather asked my father if he had killed any of the enemy, he replied, very calmly, 'Oh, I only killed seven of them.' My father never got excited over anything. Finally he remarked that they had several of the Pawnees as prisoners, and that they were being held in one of the tipis.

The next day several of the boys, myself among the number, wanted to see these prisoners. The village was about one mile in width, and we walked across to the place where they were being held. Among the prisoners was a tall, slim youth, and we wanted to play with him very much — just so we could touch him. This was the first opportunity we boys had had to touch an enemy. So we coaxed him to come out of the tipi and show us how fast he could run. As he had been wounded, he could not make very fast speed; but we were satisfied with having had the chance to touch him.

Soon the chiefs held a council, and it was decided to send the prisoners home. Each man who had captured a prisoner was to give that person clothing and a horse. It cost something to capture a man or a woman in those days. All the Pawnees were dressed in Sioux clothing and started up the hill in company with some of our own braves. They were escorted quite a distance from our camp and turned loose.

We watched the prisoners leave with some of our own warriors, and never expected to see the strangers again. But when I was in Carlisle Indian School, in Pennsylvania, some Pawnee Indians were brought in, and among them was the tall, slim boy. We recognized each other immediately.

Now that the prisoners had left, every one in our camp got ready for the big victory dance. All the men who had been in the battle took part, each man dressed in the clothing he had worn in the fight. Those who had been wounded painted the spot a bright red, to represent blood. If a horse had been wounded, the animal was brought into the dance and painted where it had been struck by a bullet. Even the horses received praise for the part they had taken in the battle.

The scouts who had gone out first wore eagle feathers which had been trimmed down. Those who had killed an enemy wore an eagle feather straight up at the back of the head. If he had been wounded while killing an enemy, the feather was painted red. Those who had worn war-bonnets in the fight also wore them in the dance. Some carried scalps. There were no false credits given at this dance, but every warrior received his just merits. One could easily tell just what the standing was of those who participated in the dance. Several days were consumed before the victory dance was finished. Then we all settled down again in peace and quiet.

CHAPTER V

MY FIRST BUFFALO

ONCE we were camped between the White River and a place known as Crow Butte. As usual, every one in camp seemed to be having a good time. One day I observed a great many horses near our camp. They were such beautiful animals, sleek and fat. I asked my stepmother where the horses came from. She told me the Great Father at Washington had sent them to be given to us. I was very happy, thinking I should get one, as I was now regarded as a young man.

A chief from each band was chosen to distribute the horses to his own people. As the name of each chief was called, he was given as many small sticks as there were horses allotted to his band. My father was called, and he received his bunch of sticks. Then he told all the young men who wanted horses to come to his tipi. As each man came in, he was given a stick, which signified that he was to receive a horse from my father when the animals had been turned over to the camp.

After he had given out all the sticks, there were still two young men without horses. But Father did not let them go away disappointed. He picked up two sticks and gave one to each man. He then said he would give them each a horse from his own herd, as he had already allotted all the animals which the Government was to present them.

Although we had nice ponies in our band, they were nothing as compared to the horses the Government sent. My father would have liked one of them himself, but he was a chief, and was obliged to look out for his people first. How different from the methods of the 'big man' among the whites of this day and age! Before he gets in office he is ready to promise anything and everything to those who can put him there by their votes. But do they keep their promises? Well, I should say not! After they are elected, the first thing they do is to feather their own nests and that of their own families.

But the Indian chief, without any education, was at least honest. When anything was sent to his band, they got it. His family did not come first. He received no salary. In case of war he was always found at the front, but when it came to receiving gifts, his place was in the rear. There was no hand-shaking, smiling, and 'glad-handing' which meant nothing. The chief was dignified and sincere.

One day we boys heard some of the men talking about going to the agency. They said the Government had sent some spotted buffalo for the Indians. This was the name the Indians gave to the cows, there being no word in the Sioux tongue for the white man's cattle. Our own wild buffalo had been disappearing very rapidly, as the white people had been killing them as fast as possible. We were very happy to learn that we were to receive more meat, this being our main diet. We had heard about these spotted buffalo, but had never seen them.

So we got on our ponies and rode over to the agency with some of the men. What a terrible odor met us! It was awful! We had to hold our noses. Then I asked my father what was the matter around there, as the stench was more than I could stand. He told me it was the odor of the spotted buffalo. Then I asked him if we were going to be obliged to eat those terrible animals. 'The white people eat them,' was his reply.

Now we had several white people around us, but they were all bald-headed. I began to wonder if they got that way from eating those vile-smelling cattle. I then recalled that buzzards were bald-headed, and they lived on carrion, and I began to feel sorry for the white people who had to live on such stuff.

Each man was called to receive his cattle, and as they were driven out of the corral they were shot down. Here and there, all about, one could see cows lying where they had been shot down, as they did not care to drive them near their homes. They skinned the cow, cutting out the tenderest parts, and roasted it right there. This roasting killed most of the odor. Then they took the skin and traded it off for calicoes and paints. If they happened to cut the tail off while skinning the animal, and brought it to the trader later, he exchanged some candy for it, to give to the children. The Indians soon 'wised up' to this, and thereafter demanded something for the tail, whether it was on the hide or off it.

Did you ever stop to think of the difference there is in meat that is killed while in a contented state, and meat that is carried in trains day after day on the hoof? Some of these poor animals stand so closely together in box cars that they have no room even to lie down and get rested, and if they do, they are poked in the ribs by men on the cars just for the purpose of keeping the animals on their feet. We knew the difference — which was the reason we could not eat this sort of meat when we first began to receive it.

In spite of the fact that we received plenty of beef and rations from the Government, we were hungry for buffalo meat, and we wanted the skins. So one day we left the agency without a permit. We were very independent in those days. We started for the northern part of Nebraska, as we knew that section to be good hunting-grounds.

I had been out with my father and grandfather many times on buffalo-hunts, but they had always attended to the killing, and I had only assisted in the eating afterward. But this time I was going as a hunter. I was determined to try to kill a buffalo all by myself if possible. My father had made me a special bow and some steel-pointed arrows with which to kill big game, and this was to be my first chance to see what sort of hunter I was.

A scout had been sent out, and one morning, very early, he reported that there were some buffalo near. Everybody, including myself, began to get ready. While one of my stepmothers was helping me, she said, 'Son, when you kill a buffalo, save me the kidney and the skin.' I didn't know whether she was trying to poke fun at me or to give me encouragement. But it made me feel proud to have her talk like that to me.

But my father always talked to me as if I were a man. Of course I now felt that I was big enough to do a man's work. The night before the hunt, my father instructed me as follows:

'My son, the land on which these buffalo have been found is reported not to be rough, and you will not have to chase the buffalo into dangerous places, as the land is very level. Whatever you do, watch the buffalo closely. If the one you are after is running straight ahead and not turning, then you can get in very close, and you will stand a good chance to shoot it in the heart. But if you observe the buffalo to be looking at you from the corner of its eye, then look out! They are very quick and powerful. They can get their horns under your horse and toss him high in the air, and you might get killed.

'If you hit in the right spot, you may kill the buffalo with only one arrow, but if not, you will have to use more. If your pony is not fast enough to catch up with the buffalo, the best thing you can do is to shoot an arrow right behind the small ribs. Perhaps it will reach the heart. If the buffalo runs down a hill or into a bank, then you have another chance. Shoot at the joint of the hips, then your buffalo will sit down and you can take your time to kill it.

'Keep your eyes open! In the beginning there will be lots of dust, but after you pass through that, it will be clear, and you will be able to see where you are going.'

This was the first time I was to go on a hunt after such large animals. I had killed several small animals, but a buffalo is far from being a small creature, and you can imagine that I was greatly excited.

Early the next morning every one was ready for the start. I carried my bow in my hand, as there was not room for it in my quiver where I kept my arrows. I rode a little black mare, a very fine runner that could cover the ground like a deer.

Two men on beautiful horses rode in front of us. This was for the purpose of keeping order in the party. There was no chance of one man getting ahead of the others and scaring the game. We all had to keep together and stay behind these men.

They rode to the top of a hill where they could get a good look at the herd and figure if there was any better place from which to approach it. We always got as close to the buffalo as possible, because it makes the meat tough to run an animal any farther than necessary.

After looking at the herd from various positions, they chose what was considered the most advantageous spot. Here they cautioned the hunters to change to their running-horses and be all ready. I did not have to make any change, as the little black mare was all the animal I had. I saw some of the men tying their two braids of hair back, and others, who wore shirts, began rolling up their sleeves. They wanted their arms free once they began shooting. They fixed their quivers on the side instead of carrying them on the back. Nobody wore any feathers or carried any spears or lances.

The extra horses were hobbled and left in the charge of an old man. When the two riders gave the command, everybody started right up. Of course I was right at the front with them. I wanted to do something brave. I depended a great deal on my pony, as I knew she was sure-footed and could run as I wanted her to.

At the top of the hill, all the hunters turned their horses loose, and the animals started in running like the wind! I whipped up my little black mare and nearly got ahead of the others. Soon I was mixed up in the dust and could see nothing ahead of me. All I could hear was the roar and rattle of the hoofs of the buffalo as they thundered along. My pony shied this way and that, and I had to hold on for dear life.

For a time I did not even try to pull an arrow from my quiver, as I had all I could do to take care of myself. I knew if my pony went down and one of those big animals stepped on me, it would be my last day on earth. I then realized how helpless I was there in all that dust and con-fusion, with those ponderous buffalo all around me. The sound of their hoofs was frightening. My pony ran like the wind, while I just clung to her mane; but presently we came out of the dust.

Then I observed what my father had told me previously. I was quite a bit ahead of the buffalo now, and when they caught sight of me, they started running in two different directions. When I looked at those big animals and thought of trying to kill one of them, I realized how small I was. I was really afraid of them. Then I thought about what my stepmother had said to me about bringing her a kidney and a skin, and the feeling that I was a man, after all, came back to me; so I turned my pony toward the bunch which was running north. There was no dust now, and I knew where I was going.

I was all alone, and I was determined to chase them, whether I killed one or not. By this time I could hear shots fired by some of the hunters who carried guns, and I knew they were killing some. So I rode on after this small bunch, and when I dashed behind them, I pulled out one of my arrows and shot into the middle of them. I did not even know where my arrow went, and was just thinking of quitting when I observed a young heifer running slower than the others.

This encouraged me, so I whipped up my pony again and took after her. As I came close, she stopped and turned. Then she started running in another direction, but I saw she was losing fast. She was not as big as the others, so I was not afraid. I made up my mind I was going to kill that buffalo if it took all the arrows in my quiver.

I rode right up alongside the buffalo, just as my father had instructed me. Drawing an arrow from my quiver, and holding to my pony with all the strength of my legs, I fitted the arrow and let drive with all my strength. I had expected to kill the buffalo right quick, but the arrow went into the neck — and I thought I had taken such good aim! But the buffalo only shook her head and kept on running. I again caught up with her, and let another arrow loose, which struck near the heart. Although it was not fired with sufficient strength to kill at once, I saw that she was fast weakening and running much slower. Then I pulled my third arrow and fired again. This went into the heart. I began to think that buffalo had all the nine lives of a cat, and was going to prove about as hard as a cat to kill, when I saw blood running from her nose. Then I knew she would have to drop pretty soon. I shot my fourth arrow into her, and she staggered and dropped over on her side, and was soon dead. So I had killed my first buffalo.

When I examined the fallen animal and noted that I had shot five arrows into her, I felt that this was too many arrows for just one buffalo. Then I recalled that my father had once killed two buffalo with only a single arrow. He knew he had hit the first one in the right spot, as the arrow penetrated very deeply and he simply rode up alongside, drew the arrow through, pulled it out again and used it to kill the second one.

As I stood there thinking of this, it made me feel ashamed of my marksmanship. I began to think of pulling all the arrows out but one. In fact, I had started to do this, when a remark that my father had once made to me came into my head. It was, 'Son, always remember that a man who tells lies is never liked by anybody.' So, instead of trying to cheat, I told the truth; and it made me feel happier.

I took all the arrows out and started in to skin the buffalo. I was doing splendidly until I tried to turn the animal over. Then I discovered that it was too heavy a task for me. As I had but one side skinned I began to think of removing the kidney and cutting out a nice piece of meat for my stepmother. Just then I heard some one call me. I got on my pony and rode to the top of the hill. There I saw my father, who had been looking for me. He called to me, but I just rode back to my buffalo. He knew something had happened, so came over, and then I pointed to the dead buffalo, lying there half-skinned.

He was so pleased that I had tried to do my best. Then I told him about the number of arrows I had had to use, and where each one had struck. I even told him how I had shot my first arrow into the whole bunch, not knowing where it had landed. He laughed, but he was proud of me. I guess it was because I had told the truth, and not tried to cheat or lie, even though I was just a youngster.

Then Father started in on my buffalo. He soon had it all skinned and butchered. He said he had been all ready to go home when he discovered I was missing. He had thought I was with my grandfather, while Grandfather thought I was with him. All that time I was having a hard job all by myself. When we reached home it made me very proud to be able to give my stepmother the skin and kidney. And she was pleased that I had done so well.

My father called the old man of the camp, who always

acted as herald, to announce that 'Ota Kte' (or 'Plenty Kill') had shot his first buffalo, and that 'Standing Bear,' his father, was giving away a horse.

This was the first and last buffalo I ever killed, and it took five arrows to complete the job.

CHAPTER VI

MY FATHER'S TRIP TO WASHINGTON

ALTHOUGH we were free to do as we pleased, there were no idlers in our camp, no lazy ones. We were like the birds, flying hither and thither. When the men had nothing else to do, they went hunting, which kept our stomachs filled. The women were kept busy making moccasins, clothing, and playing games. There was no gossiping.

As our food supply was now beginning to run low, we started to move camp again. This time we went farther south in Nebraska.

Our scouts, who had gone out to locate the buffalo, came back and reported that the plains were covered with dead bison. These had been shot by the white people. The Indians never were such wasteful, wanton killers of this noble game animal. We kept moving, fully expecting soon to run across plenty of live buffalo; but we were disappointed. I saw the bodies of hundreds of dead buffalo lying about, just wasting, and the odor was terrible.

Now we began to see white people living in dugouts, just like wild bears, but without the long snout. These people were dirty. They had hair all over their faces, heads, arms, and hands. This was the first time many of us had ever seen white people, and they were very repulsive to us. None of us had ever seen a gorilla, else we might have thought that Darwin was right concerning these people.

Outside these dugouts we saw bale after bale of buffalo skins, all packed, ready for market. These people were taking away the source of the clothing and lodges that had been provided for us by our Creator, and they were letting our food lie on the plains to rot. They were to receive money for all this, while the Indians were to receive only abuse. We thought these people must be devils, for they had no sympathy. Do you think such treatment was fair to the Indian?

But some of you may say, 'Oh, the plains had to be cleared of the buffalo, and that was the only way.' That may all be very true; but did you ever stop to think of the thousands of Indians who had to go hungry in consequence of this wholesale slaughter? Why not look at it this way: Suppose a man had a farm with lots of cattle, and it was thought a good idea to build a town on his farm. Should you consider it right if other people had gone in and shot and killed all the farmer's cattle without paying him for the slaughter? No, you would not consider such a proposition fair or just. They would first have to pay the farmer for destroying his herds, so he could buy clothing and food for his family.

When we camped at this place where the dugouts were built, I remember that our mothers told us to hurry and go to sleep, or the hairy men would 'get us.' We knew they carried long sticks which made a great noise, with which they killed our buffalo. These 'sticks' we called 'maza-waken,' or 'holy iron.' These people cared nothing for us, and it meant nothing to them to take our lives, even through starvation and cold. This was the beginning of our hatred for the white people. But still we did not kill them.

Shortly after this, a delegation of men from our reservation started off for Washington, D.C., to see the 'Great Father.' These men could not speak English, and they all went in Indian regalia. My father was one of this number. They had a man along with them to act as interpreter, but he did not know very much.

When they reached Washington, they were shown around by the Senators and fed. Then they were given an audience with the 'Great Father.' Their grievances were laid before him in broken English, and he promised to right all the wrongs.

Then they were asked what they would like for presents.
Some of the men wanted guns and bullets, and they got
them. My father wanted cowboy boots, a Prince Albert
coat, high silk hat, and stiff-bosomed shirt, with cuffs on.
After getting all these things, and before the Indians left
for home, President Hayes presented each man with a
large round silver medal. It bore the picture of George
Washington and the date 1876 on one side. On the reverse
was a white man's hand clasping the hand of an Indian,
with the words 'Peace and friendship' underneath, also
the peace pipe and tomahawk crossed. There was a hole
through the medal and a red ribbon attached, so the men
could hang them around their necks.

While the Indians were at Washington, they were
treated very courteously and promised everything; but
these promises were never kept. They were broken — like
all the other promises the white man ever made the Indian.

Soon the Indians started for the West again, very happy
in the thought that they were going to have everything
they wanted. But my father was so dressed up that he
could not remove his boots all the way back to Dakota.
When he got home, we children did not recognize him at
all as he started to walk to his tipi. As he went inside, we
children all ran to see who the white man was who had
just gone into our tipi.

There sat my father. He asked one of his wives to pull off
his boots, as his feet were very tired. She got hold of one
foot and dragged my father all around the tipi. 'Are you
getting like the white people that you must wear such
crazy shoes that you cannot get them off?' she asked
Father. His silk hat he had hung on the tripod of the bed.
We children stood at the tipi door and peeped in at him.
He looked so funny to us — more like a real curiosity. He
even had kid gloves and a cane, but with all this white
man's stylish make-up, he still wore his long hair.

Mother started to get him something to eat, which he

seemed to enjoy. After supper, and when it came time to go to bed, Father kept on his stiff-bosomed shirt. He felt too dressed up to remove it. Mother told him she did not see how he expected to get any sleep wearing that board in front of him.

The next evening he dressed up to go to the council that was to be held. He stuck an eagle feather in the left side of his silk hat. This feather bore three red stripes, 'like a third liberty loan.' It signified that he had been wounded three times.

Whenever a man returned from Washington and attended a council, he was expected to come dressed up. This was a sort of 'badge,' to prove that he had really been to Washington. I think Father satisfied them that he had been there!

A few days after, the novelty of wearing white men's clothes began to wear off, and Father began to get careless about wearing them. One day two of my sisters noticed the silk hat in the tipi, and they decided it would be a fine thing to carry water in to make mud images. So they took the hat and went down to the creek. They filled it with water, and each took hold of the hat on the side and carried it to a place where they were going to make their mud playthings. The mud was a sort of adobe, like the soil in some parts of California. We called it 'gumbo.' The girls made mud clam shells, putting two of them together. They threw these into the water, and as they floated downstream, they would throw stones at them. These mud shells would burst and make quite a little noise when hit.

CHAPTER VII

RATIONS: A WAR–PARTY: WILD HORSES

ABOUT this time I was beginning to be old enough to notice what was going on around me. I observed that the Government was trying to pay us back for some of the land they had taken away from us. They had made an agreement with the Sioux that they would pay for the land by issuing rations and annuity goods. It makes me laugh nowadays to recall those times, because the Government did such foolish things and they always issued goods at the wrong time.

When it came to drawing rations, this was left for the women to attend to. Some bands put up their tipis near the agency, while others lived fifteen or twenty miles distant. It was not very hard for those who lived close in to draw their rations, but it was a hardship on those who lived at a distance. They had to go on horseback. In each tipi occupied by a single person, one hundred pounds of flour, one beef on the hoof, and a certain number of pounds of other staple goods were allowed. In case there was more than one person in the tipi, they were allowed just the same amount.

The women did not take home all they received. They took only what they liked. What did not suit them was unceremoniously dumped over the nearest bank.

One of the most foolish rations issued to the Indians was the flour in hundred-pound sacks. We had never seen flour, and as we ate no bread we did not understand its use. Most of the women did not know what to do with it. The Government failed to send teachers along with the flour to instruct our women in the making of bread. Consequently, when the women received the sack of flour, they carried it to the nearest high bank, cut open the sack, and dumped the flour out into the dirt. The sack was then shaken out and carried home. It made nice shirts for the boys, and I have seen many of the youngsters wearing these sack shirts. The sacks bore the trade-mark of the full figure of an Indian standing with a bow and arrow in his hand, all ready to shoot.

Then the Government issued plugs of tobacco. A certain amount of this went to each tipi. In some of these tipis the only occupant might be an old woman, living alone. What could she do with plug tobacco? The Indians did not care for this kind of tobacco, anyway, as it was too strong for them.

When we were ready to move camp, we boys were always wandering around to see if we could find anything that was lost. We observed some strange-looking things lying on the ground, strewn about. Investigation proved it was plugs of tobacco which had got wet from the rain. They would swell and burst open.

Green coffee was also issued to us. The women discovered that it had to be roasted before it could be used, but they had no mills in which to grind it after it was roasted. So they would put it in a buckskin bag, lay the bag on a stone, and pound it with a stone hammer. We had no name for this drink, but it was so black and bitter we thought it was some sort of medicine the white people had sent out to us. We finally gave it the name of 'pejuta sapa' or 'black medicine.' That is the Sioux word for coffee to-day.

When we first got this coffee, I recall going home to see my own mother. Every time I visited her, she always fixed such nice things for me to eat. She had just received the coffee, and, as she wanted to give me a real treat, she made some coffee or 'pejuta sapa' for me, and added plenty of pepper to it. Although I did not like the taste, I drank it because I wanted to please my mother, and she thought the more bitter it was, the better it would be for me. But my mother and stepmothers soon learned to use all these things sent to us by the whites as they should be prepared.

One day my father brought home a small keg of syrup, and my stepmother gave each of us children some of it from a goat-horn spoon. I tasted it with the tip of my tongue, not knowing whether I should like it or not. It was so sweet and good that I did not want to eat it all up right away; but it did not take long to disappear, and then I licked the spoon and wanted more.

After that, whenever Father took a skin to the trader we were all anxious to see him coming home, as we really expected him to bring another keg of syrup. One day he really did bring another keg, and we children all were happy. He carried it into the tipi to his wives, and they both began to get busy making fried bread. This was one of the first things the Sioux learned to make with the flour. The bread was made of flour, baking powder, salt and water, rolled out like doughnuts and fried in grease.

Of course we were very happy to see all these preparations being made. We stood about outside the tipi watching the work. Of course we were waiting for an invitation to have a piece of the fried bread with some syrup on it. But we met with a great disappointment. My father had invited some grown men over. They opened the keg of syrup and consumed most of the fried bread. Of course we all got a little, but not as much as we wanted. We did not know that syrup was for grown folks, and we were quite shocked to see the way the men pitched into it.

We also received bacon from the Government, but we had never seen any smoked pork, and it had a funny yellow look on the edges. One whole side was apportioned to a tipi, but the women cut off all the yellow and threw it over the bank.

The first sugar we ever received was maple sugar. The old men asked what this sweet stuff was. When it was interpreted to them, they understood that it came from the maple tree. So they called this sugar the 'juice of the wood.' After we began receiving white sugar, we had to have another word for that, so it was called 'can-hanpi' or 'white juice of the wood,' while the maple sugar was known as 'can-hanpi-zizi,' or 'yellow juice of the wood.'

We kept getting more and more sweet stuff, and we liked the taste of it. But this sort of food was not good for us, although we tried to eat everything that was sent to us. We received apples, plums, cakes, pies, and plenty of 'sweet talk,' but none of this was really good for us. When they thought they had things coming their way by their sweet talk, then they turned around and harmed us. When we tried to protect ourselves, they called us 'savages,' and other hard names that do not look good in print.

Then the missionaries came. They told us not to fight any more. But along with them came the bootleggers. These men sold us poisons to take away our senses. The pale-faces called this poison by various names, but the Indian had only two names for it. At first when the men drank this stuff, they could see different things. Then they found the minister using it in the church in the communion service. This gave them the idea that it was 'holy water.' So to this day the name for 'liquor' in the Sioux tongue is 'mini-waken' or 'holy water.' The men who sold this drink always were near the missionaries of all denominations. The white man's name of 'fire-water' is not used in our tribe, but is simply the name given by the whites for whiskey. I really think they gave it the right name, as it can stir up more fire than anything else.

Now I noticed for the first time the fort at Red Cloud Agency. When I came back to Spotted Tail Agency, we also had one there. Sometime after, when I went to school, and was able to read and write, it made me feel very bad to have those forts there. I read a treaty made by the Government with the Sioux in 1868, the year of my birth, and I learned the Government had no right to build forts on the reservation. But as soon as a white agent came to an agency, a fort was the first thing that was considered necessary. If they thought the Indians were so wild in those days that they had to have forts, it seems to me the United States ought to start building forts all over the country very quick, because the white race is surely getting pretty wild nowadays.

While the agency was running, and the Indians were drawing rations and annuity goods, the Spotted Tail Indians thought they would go after the Poncas for a change. They had no reason for bothering this tribe, but they just did not like them. The old feeling that they were enemies had not yet left them. Again, seeing so many soldiers about did not serve to quiet the nerves of these Indians.

Everybody was getting ready and a certain number were going. My father told me he would take me along on this expedition, and I was very happy. Here was the chance for which I had been waiting! My own mother knew nothing of this, but my two stepmothers were very nice to me about it. They were busy making extra moccasins and other things to take along. Finally all was ready and off we started.

Although I was just a youngster, I was very much pleased and I felt real big and brave. The first time we made camp everybody was very good to me, as I was the only boy along with the expedition. They knew my father was very brave and would stand by them. We kept on moving toward the Missouri River, or the 'mud water,' as we called it.

The third time we made camp, my father talked to me as follows:

'Son, I wanted you to come with me, because I wanted you to do something of great bravery or get killed on the battle-field. I have made my war-bonnet to fit over your head. I will like to see you wear this, and ride your race horse into the enemy's camp. You will not carry anything but a long stick in your hand. I will take you as near as possible to the camp of the enemy the night before.

'Early in the morning some one will come out of the lodge. Then I will let you go after that person. Touch this man with your stick, then ride through the camp as fast as your horse can run. I will be behind you, and, if you pass through without any harm, you will be the youngest man that has ever done such a thing, and I will be proud of you. But if the enemy is ready to shoot you (as they nearly always are) and you fall in their midst, keep your courage. That is the way I want you to die. I will be with you, my son.'

This made my heart beat so loud I could hear it, and the tears came into my eyes; but I was willing to do my father's bidding, as I wanted so much to please him.

The fourth time we camped, my father and I went away off from the party and started hunting antelope. He soon killed one and brought it into camp whole. He roasted the whole side of the ribs, and when it was cooked and we were just sitting down to eat, we observed that some of our people had been stopped back quite a way. We could see that there was some excitement at the camp, so we got on our ponies and rode over to learn the cause of it.

There we found one of the old chiefs who had been following us for the last four days. He was bringing the pipe of peace to us. This meant that we had to turn back. At that time we believed if the pipe of peace was offered us and we did not accept it, some great calamity would overtake us. As my father was a firm believer in the pipe, we had to go home.

The excitement we had seen in the distance was caused by one of the young men, who had tried to shoot the old chief when he saw him coming with the pipe. He told the chief he had broken up a strong war-party.

I was very much disappointed and felt ashamed for

having to turn back without even seeing an enemy from a distance. But my father had spoken, and his word was law, and we had to turn back, although it made me very much chagrined that I had to go home without having taken a chance of getting killed.

When we reached home, two of our men were missing. We had not thought they would disobey the mandate of the pipe, but they did. It was a long time after that one of these men came home and related what had happened. He and the other young man had decided they would fight the Poncas alone. They met them and the other man was killed. This survivor had also been badly wounded. Some soldiers were passing and they picked him up and took him to the fort at Greenwood, Yankton Agency. There they kept him until he was well enough to travel, when they sent him home. But he was very badly crippled.

I was about nine years of age when all this happened.

It was a short time after I had come home from the war-path, without being wounded, that we all started for the northern part of Nebraska on a buffalo-hunt. In those days this was a wonderful hunting country, and it all belonged to the Sioux. As we were making ready for this buffalo-hunt, some one reported that there were some wild horses near. This at once changed our decision. Everybody wanted horses.

An old man went around the camp calling out that everybody was going, and that we were all to wait for one another. Some of the men rode to the creek near by, my father among them. Soon I noticed these men returning with long willow sticks. The one my father brought was about fifteen feet long.

When the bark is peeled off and the willow is straightened, it does not take long to dry. It is also a very light wood. While father was preparing his stick, my grandfather was getting some buffalo-hide ropes, some long, some short, some heavy and some light in weight.

My father took a strip of buckskin and tied it to the end of the stick. He then tied another buckskin string about four feet below the first. Then he took a long, braided rawhide rope, made it into a loop, and tied this to the second string. The first string was also attached to the loop about halfway around.

Everybody was getting ready, but I was watching my father. When I asked him if I could go with the men, he said: 'Why, certainly I want you to go. Watch how this is done and learn all you can. Some day you will be big enough to do all these things.'

The entire camp seemed to be going, women and all. All the men who carried sticks, whether long or short ones, rode swift running-horses. They were dressed as if after buffalo. They wore no feathers.

Some white people have the idea that Indians wear feathers all the time — in fact, I imagine they have an idea that we go to bed with them on. We wore feathers only when we were going to dress up — just as the white people put on their evening clothes for a party or dance.

Two of the young men rode ahead to reconnoiter. Soon they came back and gave us our instructions. Some of the men were to ride two or three miles away, opposite to where the horses were feeding. Some were to go to the south and others to the north. All the men carrying sticks were to remain on the east side.

I rode my little black mare this time, and I remained on the east side with my father. I was watching every move he made. I noticed that every little while he would whip up his running-horse, to 'warm him up,' as a white man would express it. Whenever my father did this, I imitated him.

Then he took me over to a spot where we could see the wild horses grazing. There were forty or fifty of them, all busy eating the green grass. Among them was one animal which would raise his head very high very often and look all around in a very proud way. My father pointed out this particular animal to me. 'Do you see that horse with his head in the air?' he said to me. 'Well, that is a stallion — the leader of the herd.'

We all remained behind the hill, but one man on foot kept watch. Finally the party which had gone over to the west side of the animals came riding up over the hill. As soon as the wild horses saw them, they started running to the north. They were making good time up the side of the hill in that direction, when suddenly the party of men which had gone to that side made their appearance. The animals stopped in affright and started running back down the hill and toward the south. But the party on the south side headed them off from that direction and the horses turned toward the east, where our party were in wait for them, running right into our midst.

The animals had already run quite a distance and were not very fresh for a long chase. Our men with the sticks were all ready for them; our horses were fresh and anxious to go, so our men whipped up and gave chase. I rode my black pony and kept right behind my father. As we went up a hill and down on the other side, I observed that my father was after a buckskin horse, a very pretty animal. It was a good runner in spite of the fact that it had already covered considerable ground, but as we went up another hill and down on the other side, my father was very close behind the wild horse.

He was fixing the stick and getting the rope all ready as we rode along. I was not paying much attention to what the other riders were doing, as I wanted to watch my father, because, as I have said before, he was my ideal. So I whipped up my pony to keep as close as possible and not miss any of the excitement.

As we reached the foot of the hill, my father raised his stick and threw it over the wild horse's head. Then he urged his own horse faster until he was almost alongside the other animal. The loop was wide open, and it went down to the horse's neck. Then he gave the stick a jerk, which broke the buckskin strings which tied the rawhide rope to the stick. Father then threw the stick away, which left the loop free. It tightened around the wild horse's neck, and he had the animal at the other end of the long rope. By this time the wild horse was about 'all in' and not able to run so fast.

Father then took the end of the rope in his hand and threw it over the head of his own horse, well down on the neck, at the same time running his own horse away from the captured animal. When the loop tightened, the wild horse began to choke. It finally stopped, breathing heavily, staggered a bit, and then fell. Father quickly dismounted, ran over, and formed a halter of the long rope which he fastened to its nose.

He then went to his own horse, tied up its tail and backed him over to the head of the wild horse. The halter rope he first tied to the tail of his own horse, brought it around the shoulders and back to the tail again. This would make the pull all on the shoulders.

Just about this time the wild horse jumped to its feet, but now he was tied to another animal and was pulling against his own nose instead of the neck. On the way home I tried to figure out how all this was accomplished.

My father tied these two horses together in a very few minutes, and we were bringing an extra animal home in a very short time. As soon as we reached camp, two other men helped my father throw the wild horse down. They worked fast, while it was tired out. Then they took an extra heavy rawhide rope that had the hair on. Now I was to learn something again, as heretofore I had never understood why they made some ropes and left the hair on them. Using this rope, the men tied the legs of the wild horse, being careful to keep the hairy side of the rope next to the skin, as in this manner the animal could not kick or strike and skin its leg, as the hair was soft. They tied all four legs and then let the horse get on its feet.

The horse seemed somewhat amazed. Although it was very tired, it tried to kick, but soon discovered that kicking was out of the question. We boys finally approached and began to pat the horse. We felt quite safe in doing this, as long as its legs were tied. Finally two or three of us climbed on its back, taking turn about, then petted the animal more. Soon it knew it would not be harmed, and, before the day was over, the horse did not try to kick any more.

The next day its legs were untied, but it was fastened to another horse. Then a young man got on its back and rode it around the camp, tied to the other animal. By this method the wild horse learned not to be afraid. Soon it became very tame, and would run, trot, or gallop alongside the other animal. In two or three days we had a fine family horse instead of a wild one.

This was the way I was taught to catch wild horses, although I never had any actual experience at it; but I did enjoy that day with my father and the other men when we went on the wild-horse chase.

Even though I never had the opportunity of catching any wild horses, I can at least say that I know how it is accomplished. It was my father's wish that I learn all about our people and their way of living, and to learn all I could while I was young.

CHAPTER VIII

CUSTER'S LAST FIGHT AND THE DEATH OF CRAZY HORSE

WE were living at Spotted Tail Agency, where Pine Ridge Agency is now located. All the men were going north to visit the Northern Sioux. My father and several other chiefs thought it would be a good plan for them also to go along. My father did not take either of his wives with him. They remained at home with us children, and we did not worry about him, as we were having a good time.

But after he had returned from the north, he told about killing the 'Long Hair.' This was the name given to General Custer by the Sioux. I asked him to tell me about it. He did not care to talk much about this, as it was considered a disgrace for us to kill a white man.

This is the story of Custer's last fight, as my father related it to me:

'We chiefs were all counciling, when a few men ran into the village with the news that the soldiers were coming. We ran out, not prepared for war. But the soldiers were already shooting into our village. Some of the men wanted to fight right away, as the soldiers had killed one boy. But Crazy Horse, one of the greatest chiefs the Sioux ever had, said, "No, wait till I ride up to them first to see what is the matter."

'He got on his horse and rode in front of the soldiers' line, from one end to the other. The command was given, and all the soldiers commenced shooting at Crazy Horse. After he rode past them and they did not wound him, he rode back to the Sioux and told them to go on. The Sioux did not need to be urged, as the soldiers had some wonderful horses that the Indians wanted. They rode into the soldiers with their war-clubs, knocked them on the head, and took away their horses.

'But when we rode into these soldiers I really felt sorry for them, they looked so frightened. They did not shoot at us. They seemed so panic-stricken that they shot up in the air. Many of them lay on the ground, with their blue eyes open, waiting to be killed.

'In a few minutes every one was killed, all but one man. He had a very fine horse and had started away. Several of our chiefs started after him, but his horse was much faster and better than the Indian ponies, and he was gaining ground. We were beginning to talk of turning back, when this man pulled out his six-shooter, pointed it to his head, and fired. The horse without the rider was not so hard to catch, so one of our men got it.

'We men got off the field, as it was no honor to be seen on a battle-field with these weak victims as our adversaries. But the women and boys killed the soldiers who were not dead. They stripped the bodies, and the boys got some good clothes.'

This was all that was ever mentioned about Custer being killed. In all the years I was at home, I never heard this battle spoken of in a bragging way.

About the year 1877 I saw a great many Indians move in to Spotted Tail Agency from the north. Who these people were and what they came for, I did not know; but it seemed to me they were very poor. Their tipis were very small, and their clothes were not good. We boys went over to watch them fix up their camp.

The next day my father invited one of the men to our tipi. He had very dark skin and light brown hair, which was of a fine texture and not like the black, coarse hair that Indians usually have. He was a little man of slight build. He did not carry anything with him, and he was dressed very poorly. There was nothing 'fancy' about him in any way.

This man did not talk very much, and what he did say was in a quiet tone — just a few words to my father, but perhaps they were words of importance. I was running in and out of the tipi, but did not pay any attention to what the man was saying, but I wondered who he was.

One of my stepmothers saw me watching the stranger, and probably realized that I was curious to know who he might be. So she called me to one side and said, 'Son, that man is my cousin, "Ta-sun-ke Wit-ko" or "Crazy Horse."' The father of Crazy Horse was a brother of my stepmother's mother. In Indian relationship they were brother and sister. But Crazy Horse was only a relative of mine through the law.

Crazy Horse did not stay at our tipi long. After the meal was over he went away on horseback, as their camp was two miles away. We were then at Beaver Creek, where Spotted Tail Agency was established. After Crazy Horse had left, my father began talking to one of his wives in an undertone. He said to her, 'Now when I am gone, have your cousins keep the horses near. It will really be better if they build a fence, for then they can keep all the horses inside. During the night, be on the lookout and be careful.'

That was all I heard, but it gave me a queer feeling, as if something unforeseen was going to happen. The next morning two of my uncles and my grandfather were busy making a fence of willow trees. When evening came, I saw them get all the horses together and drive them inside this corral. All the other people who were living near by began to tie their horses close to the tipi.

Early the following morning, some men rushed into our camp with the news that Crazy Horse had been killed by the soldiers over at Red Cloud Agency (Fort Robinson). Everybody was excited. People rushed out and got their horses saddled up, and then got extra pack-horses. The women were busy getting together all the things they wanted to keep. Some of them even began to tear off pieces of their tipis.

My father had not yet come home, but we were all ready to run away with the rest. But where could we run to? We were like sheep in a slaughter pen, not knowing which way to go to escape the guns of the soldiers. Then I heard a man say: 'Wait here until Standing Bear comes home. It is true that Crazy Horse has been killed. They are bringing his body here. Maybe that is where Standing Bear is now.' I was glad we were going to wait for my father.

There was a man in our camp named 'Bawling Bull.' He was a very large man; but he was what we call a 'horse dreamer.' He had never touched a horse in his life. His wife had been busy making a travois for him to ride in, in case we had to make a run. As I now look back at that day, it is funny; but if any one had been in camp with us at the time, it would have made a great difference. It was a terrible feeling for us children to have our enemies so near, knowing that they had shot women and children before and feeling that we could expect no mercy now.

Some young men went up the hill to see what the others were going to do. They reported the camp of the northern Indians empty — which was the one Crazy Horse had belonged to. When this was reported to us, the people of our band became very much worried. They wondered if the soldiers had chased them. All sorts of thoughts went through their minds at that time. We afterward learned that, as soon as Crazy Horse was killed, Sitting Bull took charge of his people and ran north with them into Canada.

Finally my father came home. His two wives and their mother had cut their hair short. This meant that they were in mourning for Crazy Horse, their nephew and cousin. They were all crying when my father came in. As soon as it was noised about that Standing Bear was at

home, every one ran to our tipi to learn what we were to
do and to find out all the news. Then my father told them
all about the trouble. Said he:

'We were all outside the prison [guardhouse] at Fort
Robinson. Crazy Horse had been invited in, and he took
with him a friend by the name of Little Big Man. These
two were constant companions. They entered the prison
together, while we waited outside.

'Soon we heard some trouble in the prison. It was loud
talking and it disturbed us. The father of Crazy Horse
and some of his friends ran in. It was not long until we
saw the old man and his friends bringing out the body of
their son, and he was dying. He had been pierced with a
bayonet in the hand of a common soldier. His father and
friends carried the body from the spot where he fell. Why
had they tried to kill him? He had done no harm. They
had invited him in, and then had stabbed him.

'When his father brought him out into the open, the old
man said, "If my son had known this was coming, the
bayonet of the soldier would never have pierced his body;
but he was taken unawares."

'The Red Cloud and Spotted Tail people then stepped
forward, and, because they were jealous of him, they began
to get ready to shoot at the dying body of Crazy Horse.
But I stood over his body and protected him. I held my
gun all ready to shoot any man who dared fire a shot, as
that was a cowardly act. When they saw I meant to shoot
any one, they stopped. Then I wrapped Crazy Horse in
my blanket and left him in the care of his father. They
were preparing a travois when I left, and they are going
to bring his body here.

'But we will not leave this place; we will not run away.
To-morrow morning I am going to see our father [the
Agent] at the agency. Then I will have a talk with him.'

By this time everybody began to cool down. Those who
had been singing brave-songs stopped while my father was

talking to them. They knew they could depend on him to stand by his race.

We all waited patiently for the family of Crazy Horse to bring in his body. My stepmothers and their mother were all in mourning, and were crying most of the time. Soon we saw them coming in the distance. They had his body on a travois and were moving slowly.

Some of his friends remained loyal to their dead leader. They did not run away with Sitting Bull into Canada. They all moved in with our band, with their relations, but they remained at a distance, because they had a dead body with them.

We waited for them to lay the body away, but they did not build up a bier for him as had been done for other great chiefs. I think it was because they did not want their son touched by hands that were jealous of him.

I want you to remember that all the celebrated Indians who have big names in the white man's histories and stories were not the ones we considered important men. Their prominence was due either to getting into the show business, or to selling things that did not belong to them personally, or trading it to the white people for little money. When a Sioux committed a crime and was detested by his own people, then he usually went over to the whites, thinking to protect himself. But the white men who came West in those days were not friends of the Indian — any more than they had been friends among their own race.

Crazy Horse was the greatest chief the Sioux ever had. I make this claim because he was a wonderful man. He never was wounded in his life until he came to meet his death. Crazy Horse was always in the front ranks when there was a fight, but an arrow or bullet had never pierced his body. Not even any horse that he ever rode was wounded. That is how this celebrated Indian chief came to be called 'Crazy Horse.' He never cared to dress up in gaudy clothes, but was a very plain man. In battle he did not wear a full war-bonnet, but simply the full body of a hawk on the left side of his head. Over his shoulders he wore a red cape, which was his full dress.

In the battle of the Little Big Horn, Crazy Horse rode to meet the soldiers first. He rode before them from one end of the line to the other. The soldiers were all in a line, shooting at him, but they did not harm his body. Many times he repeated this, but neither he nor his horse was wounded. So they called him 'Ta-sun-ke Wit-ko,' or 'Crazy Horse.' Right after the killing of Long Hair (General Custer), when the white people began to make a fuss, Crazy Horse took his band and ran away across the border into Canada.

Then Spotted Tail, Red Cloud, my father, and some other chiefs went up into Canada after Crazy Horse. They were bringing the pipe of peace with them, just for him. This was with the understanding that if Crazy Horse accepted and smoked the pipe, the United States Government was to appoint him head chief over all the other chiefs of the Dakotas. They would then take him to Washington to see the Great White Father, or President of the United States.

All the people of the Red Cloud and Spotted Tail Agencies did not like this idea, especially Spotted Tail and Red Cloud themselves. So they were against Crazy Horse, and he was in danger from both factions, but he did not know it. He trusted both sides — and then they killed him.

CHAPTER IX

A BOY SCOUT

SHORTLY after the killing of Crazy Horse, my father came home one day with a new gun and a six-shooter. He told me to take good care of these because they belonged to the soldiers, but that I could use them if I cared to. Needless to say, I did! I strapped that six-shooter right onto my belt. There was a fine holster in which to carry the gun, and I felt as proud as a peacock to be sporting a real six-shooter, just like a young man, although I was but ten years of age at that time.

I was very anxious to try the six-shooter to see how well it would shoot. So I got a few of the boys together and we went out rabbit-hunting. I did not care whether we shot any rabbits or not, for the loud report of the gun was all I wanted. It was like your Fourth of July to me. The other boys stood around to listen to the noise, and I could see that they were anxious to shoot the gun. So I gave each one a chance, and we had a real picnic.

Soon after this we were compelled to move toward the Mini Sose or Mud Water River, which the white people call the Missouri. The Spotted Tail Agency was located there. We were now supposed to go to the old Ponca Agency, which was located below the Yankton Agency on the west side of the river, the Yankton Agency being located on the east side. We heard the Red Cloud Agency was to be moved also. They were following the Big White River to the Missouri.

Our first move from Beaver Creek was not very far. There I saw lots of cattle (or spotted buffalo as we called them) being driven alongside our camp. There were also a great lot of wagons with blue boxes on them. These were dragged six or eight miles. Then I learned that these cattle were for us to eat as we moved along, and that the wagons were loaded with rations. So we were not worried, as we had plenty to eat, and were not in any hurry about getting to our destination.

It was now late fall and getting very cold, and finally snow began to fall. We were pretty well used to the hard winters, so we did not mind this very much. Even though the Government was compelling us to move, they were beginning to treat us very nicely at this time. General Custer had been killed for trying to take our land from us by force; so now the Government was trying another plan. Our Indians knew this, and acted quite independent. Whenever the camp moved, the Indians chose the place to stop, and when they moved again, the agent did not have very much to say to them, for he knew better. We went either on horseback or on foot; but we had very fine times in those days.

When we came to the Little White River, where Rosebud Agency is now located, that country was full of game. The deer were so plentiful that they often ran right through our camp. I had plenty of good times here with my six-shooter. I never killed a deer with it, but as long as it made a loud report I was satisfied.

Shortly after this my father told me I had been selected to act as a scout for the soldiers. Then I began to notice that several of the young men among us were carrying six-shooters just like mine. I think I was the youngest scout the United States Government ever employed — and I did not even know I was a scout!

The idea of moving our band was because the Government had several men scheming to get our land away from us. It appears that if they could persuade enough of the Sioux to keep these two agencies on the west side of the Missouri River, from the mouth of Big White River down to the mouth of the Niobrara, then the Government would jump in with some sort of agreement to be signed. Then some of the crooked chiefs among our people who were standing in with the whites would be given some 'fire-water,' calico, and promises, and after they were good and drunk they would sign off what did not belong to them alone. This would be done without the knowledge of the other chiefs. As long as there were enough chiefs present to obtain the necessary signatures, it made no difference to the Government whether they were drunk or sober. The agreement would be signed and the Sioux would lose their land. This happened more than once.

When we got to the Missouri River, we discovered that it was no place for us. It was nothing like the place on Little White River; but the Commissioners tried to argue the chiefs into the belief that this land was very good for farming; but what did we care — or know — about farming at that time? We did not need to. Everything necessary for our comfort and needs grew wild in our own land. Why move us here where there was nothing? We wanted plenty of game, wood, and water.

Now that we were at the Missouri River and found it was not the place for us to stay, we tried to be contented for the winter. The parents of Crazy Horse moved away from us a short distance. They built up a tripod to which they fastened the body of their son, wrapped in a blanket and covered with a skin. In the old Indian days, a dead body was never allowed to touch the ground, but was fastened to a tripod. We wondered when they were going to put the body of Crazy Horse away, but we never asked questions. It was their son, and they had the right to do as they thought best with his body.

We remained here for the winter. Then one day my father said he thought it would be much better if we moved to where the Poncas formerly camped. They were at a place called 'Opa Wojula,' or 'Planting Creek.' At this place there was plenty of wood and good water. So we moved there. At this place we found many white men's houses.

One day several of us boys went to one of these houses on our ponies, just out of curiosity. At first we sat on our ponies at some distance, but as we grew more courageous we went closer and peeped in through the windows, from beneath our blankets.

The Poncas who had lived there had moved farther down the Missouri River, between Sioux City and Omaha, Nebraska. Some of these people settled in Nebraska and called themselves 'Omahas.' But those who went on down into Oklahoma called themselves 'Poncas.' But they were all of the same tribe.

When they left these houses some of our mixed bloods moved in. While we boys were examining the different houses, I came across some relatives of ours. They were very nice to me, inviting me to get off my pony and come inside for something to eat, and it was quite a treat to see the inside of a white man's house.

While I was talking with them, a strange-looking man entered. He was dressed in a long skirt, like a woman, but he was a man. He shook hands with every one, even including myself. As he shook my hand he also patted me on the shoulder. All the time I was trying to figure out whether it was a man or a woman, as I had never seen any one dressed this way before.

This man with the skirts started talking to the mixed bloods, but I could not understand a word of his talk. Then one of the mixed bloods told me: 'Plenty Kill, this Holy Man likes you, and he wants you to come and stay with him a few days. You will have to tell your father about this; so next time you come, bring your father with you.'

So I went home and told my father all about this 'Wicasa Waken,' or 'Holy Man,' with the skirts, and what he had said to the mixed bloods about me. Then my father said: 'We will go to-morrow and I will see what this Holy Man wants of you. Perhaps he wants to give you something.'

Early the next morning Father and I started away to visit Louis Bernard, the mixed blood with whom I had talked. When we reached his house, Louis sent for the Holy Man, who presently came in and talked with my father, through Louis, who could speak both Indian and the white man's language.

The Holy Man said to my father, 'I like your son, and I want him to stay with me a few days.' Then Father asked the interpreter if he thought it would be all right for me to stay with this Holy Man. Louis said, 'Yes, it will be all right.' So Father took my six-shooter and said I could stay. He led my pony back to camp, but I remained with this Holy Man. He fixed some nice things for me to eat, and I waited for him to motion me to sit down.

As we sat down to a table I was all ready to eat right away, but the Holy Man did not begin to eat at once. He sat there a minute, making some motions with his hands. Whatever he did, I imitated him, not understanding what it meant. I realized later that he was blessing the food for us. When night came, he fixed a place for me to sleep. I got into bed, but he motioned for me to get out and kneel down with him. I did, but watched him all the time. He clasped his hands and by motions gave me to understand that I was to do the same. Then he moved his lips and I did the same. He was praying, but I did not know how to pray his way.

Next morning he took me to another building, which had crosses made of wood inside and out. There were many other people in this house. There were seats all around the inside, like an Indian council. The Holy Man motioned me to sit down. Soon more people began to come in. They were mostly mixed bloods in their blankets;

but a few were white people. The Holy Man then came out with another man. They both talked, and I observed that the Holy Man had a cup or bowl which was very shiny. There was water or some sort of liquid in it, and in his other hand he had something like a whisk broom. As he walked near the people, he started sprinkling them with this fluid which he sprayed about with the little broom. He got ready to throw some on me, but I covered my head with my blanket and did not get wet.

Next day he took me to the Missouri River and we got into a boat and were carried to the other side. Here we got into a wagon with a driver, and were carried to the Yankton Agency, near the present town of Greenwood, South Dakota.

It was evening when we reached Greenwood, and was getting very dark. The Holy Man secured a boat and we got in. The water was very rough, but a white man was to row us across the river. The waves were very high, and both men were frightened and commenced to yell. I was all ready to swim in case the boat went down.

When we got across, we left the boat and went on to a fort. This post was located on the Missouri River just below Chamberlain, South Dakota. The Holy Man visited all the soldiers. He talked to several men with brasses on their shoulders. Then we went through long halls with beds along the sides. I stayed close behind the Holy Man, just like a little puppy following its master. After we had made the rounds of this place, he shook hands with all the men and we came out again.

It was now very dark, but we went back to the boat, where the white man was waiting to row us back to the other shore. The waters had calmed down and we had no trouble; but I was very glad when we got across in safety.

Next morning the driver of the wagon brought us back to the place we had started from with him. Then we took the boat home to our own shore. When we reached the

Holy Man's house, I sneaked out and ran home to my father. That was the first and last time I was with this Holy Man.

My people were all very glad to see me, and of course wanted to know what I had been doing while I was away, and if the Holy Man had given me anything. I told my father and my stepmothers about the trip. My grandfather happened to be there and heard my story. He listened to my experience and then said, 'Maybe that man with the woman's dress tried to drown you in the Mud River.' My grandfather did not like the idea of this strange man taking me away on a trip like that without the knowledge of my parents.

Then Father said: 'I did not think this man would take you away on a trip like that. He only told me he liked you and wanted you to stay with him a few days. He will never see you again.'

Since then I have often thought that my father went to the Holy Man's place and told him something, because he never came to look for me again.

While I was away I had left my six-shooter with my father. One of my reasons for hurrying home was because I wanted that pistol. So this was the first thing I asked for after relating my experience. Father then said he had returned both the six-shooter and the rifle because they belonged to the soldiers. It was certainly a disappointment to me to come home and not have my six-shooter again.

Then my father told me in two days more I was to go to the soldiers and they would give me some money. I inquired what I was to receive money for, and Father said it was because I had been a scout for the Government for a whole winter. This came as quite a surprise to me, as I did not know I had been working for the Government.

So on the second day I got on my pony and rode up to the fort at the old Ponca Agency. I found a crowd of

people there, so I sat on my pony some distance away
watching everybody. Once in a while an old man would
come out of a house and call a name, and the person whose
name was called would go into the house and in a little
while come out with some green paper and silver money
rattling in his hands.

Presently the old man came out again and asked, 'Is
Ota Kte here, Standing Bear's son?' But I kept quiet
and stayed back until every one urged me to go into the
house. So I slid off my pony and went in, because I
did not want any of my people to think I was afraid of
the white soldiers.

When I entered the place, there sat a soldier with stripes
on his shoulders. Another soldier sat beside him. All the
other men in the room were white men, and they had big
books in front of them. The man with the stripes seemed
to be the 'big man.' He looked at my name, and then he
sized me up. The man sitting next to him counted out
some money. The other men in the room were white
traders who had given the Indians goods on credit, knowing they were scouts for the Government and had money
coming to them.

When my name was called and the man was counting
out the money, all these traders were looking through
their books to see if there was any account against me.
They shook their heads from side to side like a 'sunsunla,'
or donkey. Then the money was pushed toward me, but
I did not touch it. Then the interpreter said to me, 'Take
it, it all belongs to you.' So I put my blanket against the
edge of the table and scooped the money in. As I was
ready to leave, the interpreter said something to the two
men with the books, and they replied to him, whereupon
he said to me, 'All right, go on.'

When I got outside, and before starting for home, I saw
some Indians going into a store, so I followed them in.
They were all busy buying calicoes, blankets, shawls,

paints, and various other things; but I was looking at the candy and apples. But as I did not know how to use the money I did not buy anything. I finally came out, jumped on my pony, and rode back to camp.

After I arrived at our tipi there sat my grandfather, my father, and my two stepmothers. My father was sitting on a blanket between his two wives, and they were all eating. I turned my pony loose and went in. My father raised his head and asked, 'Son, did you get the money?' I answered by pouring it all out into the blanket. Everybody in my family was so happy to get this money; but to this day I do not know how much I got.

CHAPTER X

MY FATHER'S STORE: THE FIRST WAGONS

AT this time my father was accounted a great man in his tribe and a chief who had the welfare of his people at heart. But he saw that the white men were pushing toward the West, and that sooner or later they would occupy the whole country. He realized that fighting would not get the Indian anywhere, and that the only recourse was to learn the white man's ways of doing things, get the same education, and thus be in condition to stand up for his rights. My father was a smart man and he looked ahead, and so right here was his turning point.

He took the money the Government had just paid me and started off on a trip. He was gone about ten days, and then he returned all dressed up. He wore a collar, a necktie, a stiff shirt, and even carried a watch and chain. Then he told his wives he had bought lots of things and was going to open a store. He said the goods would arrive in a few days.

Shortly after, a big wagon drove up, drawn by four packing-buffalo (or oxen). We called the oxen 'pete-wa-quin' or 'packing-buffalo.' All the goods in the wagon, as well as the wagon itself and the oxen, belonged to my father. The man who brought the goods was also leading a beautiful horse.

My elder sister, Zintkaziwin, wanted this horse, but Father told her he had bought the animal for me. She wanted it very badly, however, so I let her have it, as I had one of my own, and did not care. She saw so many pretty things in the wagonload of goods that she went wild over them — just as the girls of to-day act. But I did not hang around to watch anything. I took my bow and arrows and went out to hunt birds.

When I returned from my hunt I was very hungry. My two mothers were extra good to me on this occasion, although I did not realize it at the time. I afterward learned that it was because I had been a scout and had earned all these things that they were enjoying so much; but I never thought at that time of claiming anything myself.

The man who brought all the load now went away, and one of my stepmother's cousins and I were to take care of these packing-buffalo. He was a big young man, so we drove these packing-buffalo with our ponies. They soon became used to going alongside the animals, and we did not have any trouble with them at all.

By this time it was early spring, and the whole tribe were getting ready to move back to where Rosebud Agency is located to-day. My stepmother got another of her cousins to drive the oxen as we were moving along. His name was High Pipe. Before we started to move, my father bought another wagon and hitched it behind the other one, like a trailer.

High Pipe got all ready to drive. As it was spring he wore no blankets, having on only leggins and moccasins. His shirt-tail was hanging out, and his long black hair was worn in two braids. Over his shoulder he carried a long blacksnake whip. He did not wear a hat.

At that time I could not see anything very funny in the picture presented by this big Indian as he drove that team of oxen; but now, when I think of it, I have to laugh. The dress he wore and his equipment in general were enough to make even a white man smile. I imagine he thought he occupied a very important position.

While we were making this journey I observed that the agent had furnished a four-mule team to carry Spotted Tail's goods. In addition he had a team of beautiful white horses and a new top buggy to ride in. When we got back from the Missouri River to the place where Rosebud is now located, we learned that Spotted Tail was allowed to draw credits for fifty dollars from each store on the reservation. A short time later the Government built a two-story frame house for him to live in at the agency. I think this building is yet standing. All this he received from the Government. The other Indians began to wonder how it was that Spotted Tail received all these favors, as nobody else was accorded such generous treatment; but they were kept in ignorance for some time.

When we arrived at our destination the parents of Crazy Horse still had the travois covered with the skin; but they did not build up a tripod at this time. One day we heard that the parents had opened this bundle which was supposed to contain the body of their son, and there was nothing but rags inside! What had they done with the body and where was it buried? Nobody could tell. It was a secret of Crazy Horse's family. His body was put away without the knowledge of anybody, and where it now reposes no man knows. He was a great man, a good chief, and a wonderful leader. He never had a picture taken in all his life, and his burial place is unknown to any one. Such was the end of one of the greatest men in our tribe.

After our arrival, my father bought a big square tent in which to open his store. Finally the Government erected a sawmill on Little White River, and my father asked the agent if he would have some lumber sawed for him if he would bring in the logs. The agent promised that he would, so my father got some of his friends to go to the timber with him. I did not know anything about this until I saw him bring home some rough lumber from the mill.

After all the lumber was cut, my father sent for one of his cousins from the Pine Ridge Agency, named Lone Wolf, who came and helped him put up a building in which to run the store. They also built racks on which to dry skins which the Indians brought and traded in for goods.

In those days I thought that anything my father did was

all right, but as I look back at it now, things seem very different. He really did some funny things while trying to learn the white man's ways. For example, when he and Lone Wolf built the store, I recall that my father wore one of those little derby hats, and had a blanket tied around his waist, fastened with a belt. This made plenty of pockets to hold the nails.

Lone Wolf did not wear a hat, but he tied his long braids back so they would not be in the way when he drove nails. He had his blanket tied around his waist just like Father. Both wore leggins and moccasins. While Father had his long hair, he did not forget his dignity, but wore an eagle feather on the side of his little derby. Those two men worked upon the roof of the store in their 'fifty-fifty' clothes, not realizing how funny they looked.

After they had finished the store, they built a counter and put up some shelves. Father had no scales, but that did not worry him any. He sold so many cups of sugar for a dollar. Fifty cents was the smallest coin in use there at that time.

You white people who have 'kept store' know there are always certain customers who do not pay cash, but want credit. It was the same with the Indians. But the manner of my father's bookkeeping would have made you laugh. He never had a day's education in his life (from the white man's standpoint), but he tried to learn. If Running Horse came to the store and wanted credit for ten dollars, Father let him have the amount. Then he would get out his 'books' and draw a man's head with a running horse above it. In front of the man's face he would draw ten straight lines. If Running Horse came back and paid five dollars on account, then Father would cross off five of the lines.

Running Horse needed no receipt for the money he paid, as it would not be collected again. Crossing out five of the straight lines meant that he had been given credit for five dollars. Father did not need to look through a lot of books to determine what Running Horse owed him. When the other five dollars were paid, Father just crossed out all the lines. There were no receipts given. If Running Horse, or any other Indian, wanted credit in those days, they got it. They did not need to bring any security. Their word was as good as gold; they were still honest and uneducated.

I recall that when the Indians would trade in skins, my grandfather would take his sharp butcher knife and cut out all the fat that had been left on the hide. After the skins had been cleaned properly and dried out, the hides would be hauled away to some place on the Missouri River. Then, when Father returned, he would have more goods with him for the store.

When he went away to attend a council, or for any other purpose, he depended upon me to take care of the store. I would watch out for things very closely — until I had had my fill of candy and ginger snaps, then 'keeping store' would become monotonous. I would then tell one of my stepmothers that I was going out. But my father never scolded me for this, because I was the oldest son.

When it came time to issue annuity goods to the Spotted Tail Indians, the Government hauled them out about a mile and a half above the agency on Rosebud Creek. Here all the tipis were put up in a circle, and all the goods were placed in the center of this ring. We were advised that the goods were not to be distributed until the next day. There were many large boxes and several bales of blankets piled high. Several young men were appointed to watch over these goods through the night. They built a fire, and some of the wives of the chiefs cooked nice things for them to eat while they were on duty. We smaller boys went over and climbed up on the bales of blankets and boxes, and thought we had a great time; but it never entered our heads to take anything.

Next day a big council was held, and some good young men were elected to open the boxes and bales. These youths had to be honest, and it was considered a great honor to be appointed on this 'committee.' Some of their relatives were so proud that they gave away a horse to express their pleasure that one of their young men had been chosen.

Four other men were appointed who carried clubs. It was their duty to see that nobody interfered with these young men while they were distributing the goods among the Indians.

After the boxes were all opened and the bales of blankets cut, the young men started to distribute the goods. There were yards and yards of blanket goods in blue, black, green, and yellow. The blankets were measured off by one of the young men who would hold out his arms as far apart as possible. The length from finger tip to finger tip, twice, made a good-sized blanket. Each man was entitled to one of these.

While these blankets were being distributed an Indian named Paints-His-Ear-White wanted to exchange a black blanket for a blue one. He tried to make this exchange himself, when he was observed by one of the 'policemen' named High Bear, who walked up and knocked Paints-His-Ear-White down. He lay there for several minutes stunned, but when he came to he went right home without waiting to get anything. This was his punishment for disobeying orders.

Then the men were called upon to go to the office of the agent. Here a slip was issued to each man which entitled him to a wagon. But the wagons were at some place down the Missouri River and the Indians must go after them. My father got one of these slips, so one of my uncles and I went after the wagon. On the way we met several of our relatives, all on the same errand. Some men took their whole families. They were all riding their ponies to the place, not realizing the job they would have to get back home with those wagons.

It was a trip of fifty miles, so we made two camps before we reached the place. The Government had shipped these wagons by steamboat to a place called Black Pole, with sets of harness for each. This was the nearest point to the agency. Red Cloud's people came about twice the distance we did, but they were glad enough to do it in order to secure the wagons.

When the Indians reached Black Pole, they all camped in a circle. The wagons had not been assembled, but the different parts were all tied together. The harness was all in gunny sacks. There were some white men there putting the wagons together. When one was ready they would call out, 'This wagon goes to' (calling some one's name). Then the party would come with his relatives and friends to get the new wagon. The white man handed him one box of axle grease and two sets of harness. Then one of the Indians would get hold of the tongue of the wagon and the others would push.

After each man had got his wagon over to the camp, he would try to harness up his little ponies to it, with those great big collars which hung way down on their shoulders. The Government knew we had no work horses at that time, yet they sent out those big sets of harness, expecting the Indians to use them on little Indian ponies. This was only another of the foolish expenditures of money made by the Government. Other parts of the harness would have to be cut down, but of course they could not cut down the collars, and many of the Indians put a blanket around the pony's neck to hold the collar in place.

I was very anxious for my father's name to be called, because I wanted one of those beautifully colored wagons. The boxes were all painted green and the wheels red. They were Studebaker wagons, and were very fine, strongly built ones.

Finally one of the white men called out, 'This wagon goes to Standing Bear.' My uncle and I went over and pulled it out of the way, then greased the axles. We did what the white men told us, and it did not seem hard to my uncle. But as I look back and recall how those little ponies looked in those big collars, I have to laugh.

You must remember that this was the first time the Indians had ever tried to use a wagon, and their little ponies had never been harnessed. The poor animals seemed dumbfounded at the strange treatment, and most of the Indians were puzzled to know how they were going to get those wagons home. The ponies pulled and pulled, but the man who had forgotten to grease the axles could not understand what was the matter.

Then the white man came over and told some of the men they must grease their wagons before they tried to drive home. The Indians were all very willing to listen and take advice, so one man got very busy on this job of greasing his wagon, not knowing where to begin. Finally he greased the box all over, and then started in on the wagon spokes. When my uncle and I saw this, we rushed over and laughed at him. However, he was good-natured about it, and had his wife bring some rags to wipe the wagon off.

Then somebody explained to him about greasing the axles. The white man removed the nut that held the wheels in place and showed the Indian how to lift up the wagon a little and pull out the wheel just far enough to show the axle. He thought he understood it very well now, so he got hold of the wheel and gave it a jerk, and off came the wheel and knocked him flat, and the wagon tipped up until one end was on the ground. This man certainly had an awful idea about the ways of civilization.

Finally the man got all four axles greased, and then he loaded up his rations and harnessed his four ponies. But he did not understand about putting a cross-line between the left front pony and the rear right one. He just harnessed them up 'straight.' Then he mounted his wagon, as proud as a king, but when he started up his ponies, they divided in the center, and the front ponies came back to look at him.

We all turned in and helped him make another start. The ponies did their best at pulling, but they were too small to haul a wagon loaded with twenty-five hundred pounds. They were used to carrying packs on their backs, but dragging a wagon behind them was a different proposition, and they could not understand it. However, the man got started away from Black Pole at last and was doing fairly well, until he came to a hill down which there was quite a steep grade. Here the ponies became frightened, and so did the Indian. Finally he got down, unharnessed the ponies, and started to ride home on the back of one of them, driving the others. That Indian had had all the wagon he wanted, and he just left it there standing beside the road. All his rations were in it, but he was completely disgusted. He had had enough of 'civilization' for one day.

That man never went back for his wagon. Some one else got it, but the owner didn't care. The agent never said anything to him about the matter. I expect maybe he thought it was a dangerous topic, so he kept quiet.

Some time after this, my father got another wagon, so that made two for us. Then he thought he would take a load of hides down the Missouri River and get more stocks of goods for the store. He told me to drive one team and he would take the other. Both wagons were loaded with dried hides. These were spotted buffalo (or cow) skins. As it was a heavy load, we camped about eleven miles east of the agency on what was known as Antelope Creek. At that time no one lived in that part of the country, and it was very wild.

We were traveling along, trying to reach the Keya Paha, or Turtle Butte Creek, which was straight across the plains. A short distance ahead of us was a small hill. Suddenly over the top of it came four wild-looking cowboys. They were about half a mile distant, and they were on the same road with us.

When Father saw them he stopped his team and came behind his wagon. Noting this, I also stopped my team. When Father came around from behind his wagon I saw that he had his gun. He loaded it quickly to be all ready for trouble. Then he said to me, 'Son, those men do not look good to me. In case they shoot, then I shall have to fight. If I shoot two of them, then you remain with me, but if you see I am shot first, then you unhitch that black horse and ride back as fast as you can. If these men were Indians, it would be all right for you to help me fight, but I do not want you to be killed by a white man. I am going to drive straight ahead, and you stay close behind me. When I stop, then you watch. Remember, if I am wounded, you go back home.'

Then Father got on his wagon again, carrying his gun across his arm. His horses were trotting now, and I was close behind him. When these men came within about a quarter of a mile of us, they turned their horses in another direction.

I think they must have seen that my father was ready for them, and possibly they thought I was another man with a gun. So they went on their way without molesting us. If they had known I was just a small boy, there might have been a different ending to this story — or it might never have been written at all!

After this little scare, we went on about six miles and camped; but Father did not trust these men. After we had eaten our supper, we hitched up and went off the road about a mile and a half, for the night.

I went to sleep at once, like any healthy youngster, but I do not think my father slept at all that night. Every time I awakened, there he sat with his gun fully loaded.

How glad I was when it came daylight and we cooked our breakfast. Then we harnessed up and came back to the road again. Here Father got down and examined the road to see if there were any tracks of these cowboys following us, but there were none. He told me to be on the lookout all the time on this trip, and it was quite exciting, because it seemed as if we were really on the war-path.

We arrived at the Missouri River safe, and there we met some Indians who were just getting ready to leave. Father told them about our experience with the wild-looking cowboys, and what a rough-looking bunch they were and seemed to be looking for trouble. This report seemed to disturb them quite a bit, and after a short consultation among themselves, they asked my father if they could wait for us and accompany us back. He said yes, and, to tell the truth, I felt safer for having these extra men along with us.

When we arrived home we learned that during our absence some bad white men had come into camp and stolen many ponies from some of the Indians. They told Father about what time this happened, and then he came to the conclusion that the men we had seen were out on a pony-stealing excursion and had taken their animals. It was just about such a time as they would have required to reach our camp from where they met us on the road, between Antelope Creek and Turtle Butte Creek.

I have often wondered what they might have stolen from us if they had known my father was alone.

CHAPTER XI

AN INDIAN TRIANGLE

EARLY in the spring of 1878 the different bands of the Sioux had moved around the agency. Some had moved in very close so as to be among the first to draw rations. Here they were all waiting. It was suggested that we have a big dance and everybody went home and dressed in his best clothes. After the people had returned, some one suggested that it would be a good idea to dance in front of one of the agency stores. This always drew a crowd, and the traders would come out and make the dancers presents in the shape of paints, calicoes, and boxes of soda crackers.

The Indians liked this idea very much, and they went around to the different stores collecting all they could. At length one of the old men of the tribe announced that there was to be a ball game the next day, in which everybody could play. The 'Loafers' were to play against the 'White Thunder's' band. The 'Loafers' were a bunch of the Spotted Tail Indians who always hung around the agency. We called them Wa Klure, or loafers, because that was all they did.

The following day there was quite a crowd at the agency. We went across the creek where the Episcopal Church stood. There were no houses there at that time. We started playing about noon, and the game lasted until perhaps two o'clock. I was in the game playing on the White Thunder's side. Finally I became tired and quit.

Then I thought I would go and visit my mother. To reach her place I had to follow a path which wound around the creek. As I was walking along I noticed some one was coming behind me. I looked around and observed a woman walking very fast. I ran ahead a bit and then slowed down, for I was not sure whether she wished to catch up with me or go on ahead.

Just as I came around a bend in the path, a man jumped out from behind a bush, with a gun in his hand, and he pointed it right at me. I stopped short. The man had a rather bad look in his eye and I was undecided what he meant to do. He wore a piece of white cloth around his head and had on a gray blanket. He carried a belt of cartridges around his shoulders instead of around his waist. For a second I thought he was going to shoot me down, but he pointed the gun to one side of me. I then noticed that he was after the woman behind me, and not myself.

As soon as the woman saw him, she turned and ran as fast as she could. The man ran after her. Just as he passed me he shot at her, but missed. I could not tell where the bullet struck, but the man began loading his gun again as he ran. The woman was now screaming loudly for help, and several of the men who had been playing ball came running toward her.

The man with the gun caught up with the woman, and I had a terrible feeling that he was going to shoot her down now. Instead, he just grabbed her by the arm. Just at this time the other men arrived and pulled the man away from her. They took his gun away and shot the charge into the air.

Then I ran on to where my mother lived and told her what I had seen, but I did not know either the man or woman. I remained until after dark, and in the evening the White Thunder's band held a council, and the woman was present. We boys remained outside to hear what the chiefs had to say.

It appeared that the woman was the wife of the man who had shot at her, and she had run away from him and did not want to return. White Thunder spoke first. He said, 'We must return this woman to her husband.' Swift

Bear spoke next, as he was the leader of my mother's band. Others also made talks. One of them said, 'I will furnish a pony for her to go back.'

When the woman heard the decision of the chiefs, she began to cry. She did not want to go back to her husband, but that was the ruling of all the chiefs. During this hearing no questions were asked and no sides were taken. The woman had simply run away from her husband, and the chiefs decided she had to go back, as he was a good man.

The next day I saw the two bands of White Thunder and Swift Bear taking this woman over to the agency. They took some ponies and other things along. Then they had the agent send for her husband. The agent gave him the ponies and other things the Indians had brought. That meant if he accepted the presents he must take his wife back, be good to her and forgive her. He accepted the presents and left with her.

That afternoon I thought I would visit some of my relatives who lived about six miles from the agency on the Little White River. I concluded to walk, as it was a beautiful day and the birds were singing and I meant to enjoy my little trip on foot.

Soon I observed some one in front of me. There were two pack-ponies and some extra animals, which a young man was driving, and a woman was riding a pony and leading another which dragged a travois. At this point there was a small footpath that led over a hill. I concluded to take this footpath, so as not to frighten their ponies by running past them.

Just as I got to the top of the hill, there lay the same man who had pointed his gun at me the previous day! His wife was going back home with a young man, who was a friend of her husband's. He looked at me just about as he had the day before, and I started off on a dead run! I don't know whether he recognized me or not, but I remembered him.

The name of the man whose wife had left him was White

Man's Horse, of Red Cloud's band. The name of the man who had stolen his wife was Mr. Eleven, and he belonged to the White Thunder and Swift Bear band, located at Spotted Tail Agency.

Mr. Eleven went from Swift Bear's band to stay with White Man's Horse, who was a distant relative. He remained quite awhile, taking care of the ponies. The wife of White Man's Horse fell in love with him, and they ran away to the Rosebud Agency together.

So the chiefs got her to return to her husband. She saw the folly of her ways, went home, and they made up. This all happened when I was ten years old, but they are still living together on Wounded Knee Creek, at Pine Ridge Agency.

You see we were not infallible in those days. The Indians had their little 'triangle affairs,' but they were much better taken care of than by the white man's method. The chiefs always gave presents, from the one who was at fault to the other, who was to forgive and forget. If they could not do this, then they were not to go back together again. There was no great scandal written up in the papers about either party. It was up to them to do just as they thought best, and they lived happy, whether they were together or living apart.

CHAPTER XII

THE SUN DANCE

It was about the middle of the summer of 1879 that I saw the last great Sun Dance of the Sioux. The Brules were holding the dance about six miles southwest of Rosebud Agency, on the place where old Chief Two Strikes's band now have their allotments. As I started for Carlisle Indian School in the fall of 1879, I cannot say whether this was the last dance held or not.

I have read many descriptions of this dance, and I have been to different tribes which claimed they did the 'real thing,' but there is a great difference in their dances from the Sun Dance of the Sioux.

The Sun Dance started many years before Christopher Columbus drifted to these shores. We then knew that there was a God above us all. We called God 'Wakan Tanka,' or the 'Big Holy,' or sometimes 'Grandfather.' You call God Father. I bring this before you because I want you to know that this dance was our religious belief. According to our legend, the red man was to have this dance every summer, to fulfill our religious duty. It was a sacrificial dance.

During the winter if any member of the tribe became ill, perhaps a brother or a cousin would be brave enough to go to the medicine man and say, 'I will sacrifice my body to the Wakan Tanka, or Big Holy, for the one who is sick.' Or if the buffalo were beginning to get scarce, some one would sacrifice himself so that the tribe might have something to eat.

The medicine man would then take this brave up to the mountain alone, and announce to the Great Spirit that the young man was ready to be sacrificed. When the parents of this young man heard that he was to go through the Sun

Dance, some of his brothers or cousins would sacrifice themselves with him as an honor.

If some young man of another band had the desire to go through the Sun Dance, some of his friends or relatives might offer to dance with him. Sometimes as many as thirty or forty braves went into the dance.

As soon as the women heard that there was to be a Sun Dance in their band, they began making all the things which were necessary for the ceremony. They placed beautiful porcupine-quill-work on the eagle-bone whistles which the men carried in their mouths during the dance, as well as beautiful head-dresses for the dancers. These were made from porcupine-quill-work. The dancer wore a piece of buckskin around the waist, hanging down like a skirt. This also had pretty quill-work decorations. Soon all the things were ready for the dance.

When the chiefs learned this dance was coming, they called a meeting and selected a place they thought as best suited to hold it. They then sent word to the other bands to get ready.

The main band would move to the place selected, and the other bands would come in one at a time, the boys and warriors mounted on ponies. They would all keep together until they were very near, when they would make an imitation charge on the camp, just as if it were an enemy camp.

After this 'attack' they would all go up to a hill near by. Four men were then chosen who were to lead the parade. The warriors would now have a chance to show their beautiful war-ponies and good clothes. Then they would all parade into the village. Just about the time the parade was over, the rest of the camp would be moving in. The women would then be very busy erecting the tipis.

After the various bands had all arrived, there were some special tipis put up for those who were going to dance. These tipis were not erected in one place, but were sometimes considerably scattered. I have seen a camp of this sort which was a mile and a quarter in diameter. There were from four to six of these special tipis for the dancers. Everybody was allowed to go, and there was always plenty to eat in these tipis.

The first day all the people collected at the center of the camp and some scouts were selected to go out and look for the cottonwood pole which was to be used in the dance. After being chosen, these scouts retired to their tipis and dressed in their best clothes, mounted their war-ponies, and rode into the circle. Their parents gave away ponies and other pretty things as a token of respect that their sons had been chosen to act as scouts.

Among these scouts were one or two of the old-timers, who were to act as leaders. A fire was now built in the center of the circle, and the scouts rode their ponies around this fire three times, and, after the fourth time, they were off! They rode their ponies at full speed. All those on horseback rode as fast as they could and encircled the scouts as they went on.

The scouts would be gone about a half-hour. On their return they would come to the top of a hill and stop. The others in the camp would once more mount their ponies and ride out to meet the scouts. Then they would turn about and race back to the center of the circle, where they would wait for the scouts to ride in.

One of the old-timers would then relate how they had found a pole which was considered good enough to be used in the dance. Then everybody got ready to go to the place where the pole had been found.

All the various lodges of the tribe now gathered in the timber near the place where the pole was located. There was the White Horse, Bull, Fox, and Short Hair lodges. As each separate tribe had its form of ceremonies, each selected some of its people to go to the tree and 'chop it.' They did not really chop the tree, but just simply touched it. As they touched the tree, they gave away ponies or anything they wanted. They stayed here a long time, as they had plenty to eat all the time they were in the timber. If they knew a man who had plenty of ponies, they would select one of his children to come forward and touch the tree, and then he would give away a pony.

After all had finished their ceremonies, some one cut the tree down. There were about twenty men to carry this pole. They had long sticks which they put under it, and two men to a stick to carry it. Everybody was carrying something. Some carried forked branches, others limbs of the tree, etc. They had no one to order them around, but every one did his share toward this religious dance.

As the twenty men lifted the pole, they walked slowly toward the camp. The rest of the tribe trailed along behind. They stopped three times, and each time a medicine man howled like a wolf. The fourth time they stopped, all the men and boys raced their ponies as fast as they would go, trying to see who would be first to reach the center of the camp. Here they found the effigy of a man made from the limbs of trees. Each tried to be first to touch this. There would be plenty of dust as these men and boys rode in to attack this wooden man. Sometimes two ponies would run together, and then some one was likely to be hurt.

At last the men came in with the pole. Then the lodges had some more ceremonies to be gone through with, while some of the men started to dig the hole in which to set the pole. Others would get busy arranging forked poles in a circle. This circle was to serve as our hall.

When the hole was ready, all the men from the different lodges got together to help erect the pole, which was sometimes sixty or seventy feet long. They tied two braided rawhide ropes about the middle of the pole, on which some brave was to hang. Other ropes were to be used to hoist the pole into place. These hoisting ropes were tied in such a way as to be easily removed, after the pole was in the right position. We had no stepladders nor any men with climbers on to go up and untie any ropes that might be left up when the pole was in place.

When all was ready, some of the men used forked poles, some held on to the ropes, and others got hold of the pole. It required about forty men to do this work properly. The pole must be raised and dropped in the hole at one operation, and with no second lifting. Some pushed, others pulled, while the men with the forked sticks lifted. As the pole dropped into the hole, everybody cheered.

There was a strong superstition regarding this pole. It was believed that if the pole dropped before it was set into the hole, all our wishes and hopes would be shattered. There would be great thunder-storms and high winds; our shade or council hall would be blown away, and there would be no Sun Dance. On top of this, it was believed that the whole tribe would have a run of bad luck.

Consequently, when this pole was being erected, every man used all his strength to ward off any accident or mishap. We were taught to believe that if all minds worked together, it helped a great deal. We were taught this by our parents, and we had strong faith in it.

The pole was always a cottonwood tree, as I have previously stated. No other tree would do. It was not always a straight tree, but there was always a branch which extended out from the main trunk. This would be about thirty or forty feet up. This branch would be cut off about four feet from the trunk. On the top of the pole, branches with leaves on would be left.

They made a bundle of branches from the tree which were wrapped in bark and tied together. This bundle was placed in the branch which had been cut off about four feet from the trunk. When this bundle was in place, it looked not unlike a huge cross, when viewed from a distance.

From this cross-piece hung something which resembled

a buffalo and a man. These effigies were cut from rawhide and were tied up with a rawhide rope. They were suspended about ten feet down from the bundle of wood or the cross-piece. Both were painted black, the paint being made from burned cottonwood mixed with buffalo fat.

Sometimes there was a small bundle of sticks painted in a variety of colors. At the end of each, a small bag made of buckskin and filled with tobacco was hung. All this was suspended to the cross-piece. Under the pole were many little bags of tobacco, tied on little sticks, as a prayer offering to the spirit.

About ten feet to the west of this cross lay the skull of a buffalo on a bed made of sagebrush. The horns were attached to this skull and it was laid facing the east. Behind the skull, about two feet, were two forked sticks stuck in the ground, with another stick across them. Against this the pipe of peace rested, with the stem pointing toward the east.

The real meaning of having the effigy of the buffalo hanging from the cross was a prayer to the Wakan-Tanka, or Big Holy, for more 'pte,' or buffalo meat. The effigy of the man meant that in case of war we were to have victory over our enemies.

When the main big pole was all completed, the men bent their energies toward the dancing-hall, or shade, as it should rightfully be called. All the forked poles were placed in a double circle, about fifteen feet apart, with an opening left toward the east. Long sticks were laid from one forked pole to another in the inner circle as well as the outside circle. We used no nails in those days, and anything that was to be fastened must be bound with rawhide or tied with bark. In this case, we peeled off the bark of the willow trees and used that to fasten the poles together. Then the longest tipi poles would be brought in, and laid from the inner to the outer circle. The outside wall was made from entwined branches, and on top would be laid the largest tipi coverings, which made a fine shade. This 'shade' was about one hundred and fifty feet in diameter, with a depth of about fifteen feet. It was considered a great honor to have one's tipi covering chosen for this purpose.

After the shade was completed, if any one wanted to give a piece of buckskin, or some red or blue cloth, as an offering to the Great Spirit, he took a long stick and put a cross-piece on it, from which was suspended his offering. These pennants were hung all around the dance-shade. It quite resembled a great convention hall. Several beds of sage-brush were made for the dancers. Sometimes a big dance would precede the Sun Dance. This dance was known as 'owanka ona sto wacipi,' or 'smoothing the floor.' It was, in fact, a sort of 'house-warming' affair, and was for the braves and young men only. Each carried a weapon and wore his best clothes. The crowd came in from all the different bands in the camp, forming in lines like soldiers as they appeared. Sometimes there were as many as fifteen abreast.

Then an old chief came forward with a scalp-lock tied to a pole. He danced before the others, facing them. When he danced backward, the others danced forward, and *vice versa*. When the old chief led them toward the pole, those carrying guns shot at the buffalo and the effigy of the man, hanging from the pole.

While this dance was in progress, different medicine men were in the tipis with the young men who were to do the Sun Dance. From each tipi came six, eight, and sometimes ten from a band to dance. There was a leader, who carried a pipe of peace; the others followed one by one. They wore buffalo robes with the hair outside, and quite resembled a band of buffalo coming to a stream to drink.

After these Sun Dance candidates reached the shade from their tipis, they did not go in immediately, but marched around the outside three times. After the fourth time, they went in and took their places. Then the medicine man came forward and took charge of four or eight of the dancers. Four of them must be painted alike. They put on beautiful head-dresses richly ornamented with porcupine quills. Their wrists were wound around with sagebrush, and the eagle-bone whistles they used were likewise decorated.

This was a very solemn affair. These men were to dance for three or four days, without food or water. Some of their relatives cried; others sang to praise them and make them feel courageous.

The singers were now in their places. They used no tom-tom, but sat around a large buffalo hide which lay flat on the ground, using large sticks to beat upon the dried skin.

The braves started dancing as soon as the sun started to rise. They stood facing the sun with both hands raised above their heads, the eagle-bone whistles in their mouths, and they blew on these every time the singers hit the skin with their sticks. All day long they stood in one position, facing the sun, until it set.

The sunflower was used by the Sioux in this dance. They cut out a piece of rawhide the shape of a sunflower, which they wore on a piece of braided buckskin suspended around the neck, with the flower resting on the breast. At that time I did not realize the significance of the sunflower, but now I know it is the only flower that follows the sun as it moves on its orbit, always facing it.

The dance would be kept up until one of the participants fainted, then he was laid out on one of the sagebrush beds. On the second day of the dance a young man who had started it would come into the shade. First he would walk all around the hall so that all could see him. Then he went straight to the pole. He was giving himself for a living sacrifice. Two medicine men would lift the young man and lay him down under the pole. An old man would then come forward with a very sharp-pointed knife. He would take hold of the breast of the young brave, pull the skin forward, and pierce it through with his knife. Then he would insert a wooden pin (made from the plum tree), through the slit and tie a strong buckskin thong to this pin.

From the pole two rawhide ropes were suspended. The candidate would now be lifted up and the buckskin string tied to the rawhide rope. The candidate was now hanging from his breasts, but the rope was long enough for him to remain on the ground. Although the blood would be running down from the knife incision, the candidate would smile, although every one knew he must be suffering intense pain.

At this point the friends or relatives of the young brave would sing and praise him for his courage. Then they would give away ponies or make other presents. The singers now began to sing and the young brave to dance. The other dancers were behind him, four in a line, and they accompanied his dancing. These dancers always stood in one spot while they danced, but the candidate danced and at the same time pulled at the rope, trying to tear out the wooden pin fastened through his breasts.

If he tried very hard and was unsuccessful, his friends and relatives possibly could not bear to see him suffer any longer; so they would give away a pony to some one who would help him tear loose. This party would stand behind the dancer and seize him around the waist, while the candidate at the same time would throw himself backward, both pulling with all their strength. If they could not yet tear the candidate loose, an old man with a sharp knife would cut the skin off, and the dancer would fall beneath the pole. Then he would be picked up and carried to a sagebrush bed. Occasionally a man with a very strong constitution, after tearing loose, would get off his bed and resume the dancing. I have often seen these braves with their own blood dried to their bodies, yet going on with the dance.

This brave candidate fasted three or four days; taking no food or water during that time, instead of the forty days the Saviour did. The candidate had his body pierced beneath the cross. I learned all about this religion in the natural way, but after learning how to read the white man's books I compared your religion with ours; but religion, with us Indians, is stronger.

Many things were done during this dance which were similar to what I have read about Christ. We had one living sacrifice, and he fasted three or four days instead of forty. This religious ceremony was not always held in the same place. We did not commercialize our belief. Our medicine men received no salary. Hell was unknown to us. We trusted one another, and our word was as good as the white man's gold of to-day. We were then true Christians.

After the dance was over, everybody moved away, going where he pleased. It was a free country then. But afterward, if we ever returned to that sacred spot where the pole was yet standing, with the cross-piece attached, we stood for a long time in reverent attitude, because it was a sacred place to us.

But things have changed, even among the white people. They tear down their churches and let playhouses be built on the spot. What can be your feeling of reverence when you think of the house of God, in which you worshiped, being used to make fun in?

As I have many times related in my story, I always wanted to be brave, but I do not think I could ever have finished one of these Sun Dances.

CHAPTER XIII
GOING EAST

WE had spent our summer in playing games, and now it was the fall of the year 1879. My father had his store well stocked, and we were getting along splendidly. It was about the latter part of September, and the days were nice and cool — just the time to play hard and not feel too warm.

A little boy named Waniyetula, or Winter, and I were playing between my father's store, and the agency. He was a distant cousin of mine, but we always called each other 'brother.' The agency was perhaps a quarter of a mile from our tipi.

Suddenly we observed a great many people gathered around one of the agency buildings, and our curiosity was at once aroused. I said, 'Let us go over and see what they are looking at.' So we ran as fast as we could. Reaching the building, we looked in through one of the windows and saw that the room was filled with people. Among them were several white men and we noticed one white woman.

When they saw us peeping in at the window, they motioned for us to come inside. But we hesitated. Then they held out some sticks of candy. At this, we ran away some little distance, where we stopped to talk over this strange proceeding. We wondered whether we had better go back again to see what the white people really wanted. They had offered us candy — and that was a big temptation. So we went back and peeped in at the window again. This time the interpreter came to the door and coaxed us inside. He was a half-breed named Charles Tackett. We called him Ikuhansuka, or Long Chin. We came inside very slowly, a step at a time, all the time wondering what it meant.

There we saw two Indian boys dressed in white men's

clothes. They had been educated somewhere. They were both Santee Sioux, from the Mud or Missouri River. With their new clothes on they looked like white men.

Then the interpreter told us if we would go East with these white people and learn the ways of the white man, we could be all dressed up, as these Indian boys then were. He told us the white man, whose name was Captain R. H. Pratt, had asked him to tell us this.

However, all this 'sweet talk' from the interpreter did not create much impression on me. We had heard this same sort of 'sweet talk' many times before, especially when these interpreters were paid by the Government for talking.

My mind was working in an entirely different channel. I was thinking of my father, and how he had many times said to me, 'Son, be brave! Die on the battle-field if necessary away from home. It is better to die young than to get old and sick and then die.' When I thought of my father, and how he had smoked the pipe of peace, and was not fighting any more, it occurred to me that this chance to go East would prove that I was brave if I were to accept it.

At that time we did not trust the white people very strongly. But the thought of going away with what was to us an enemy, to a place we knew nothing about, just suited me. So I said, 'Yes, I will go.' Then they said I must bring my father to the agency first, as they wanted to talk the matter over with him.

In the excitement of talking to these white people, we had forgotten all about the promised candy, so we did not get any. I ran home, and when I entered, my people were all eating. My father was sitting between his two wives, and all the five children were there. So I sat down with the others and started telling my father about the white people at the agency. The children listened to what I had to say. There were my sisters, Zintkaziwin and Wanbli Koyake-win, my two brothers, Wopotapi and Nape Sni, and my little sister, Tawahukezanunpawin. As I talked, I ate but little. I was so anxious to get back to the agency again.

After the meal, my father and I went back where the white people were. They were very nice to him, and shook hands. Then they told him, through the interpreter, about the proposed trip East. Father listened to all they had to say, then he turned to me and asked, 'Do you want to go, son?' I replied, 'Yes.'

I do not remember whether I was the first boy to sign up, but they wrote my name in a big book. At that time I was entered as 'Ota Kte, or Plenty Kill, son of Standing Bear.' After my name was in the book all the white people shook hands with me and said something in the white man's language which I did not understand.

Then my father and I came away together and started for home. He never spoke a word all the way. Perhaps he felt sad. Possibly he thought if I went away with these white people he might never see me again, or else I might forget my own people. It may be he thought I would become educated and betray them; but if he felt any of these fears, he showed no sign of it.

The next day my father invited all the people who lived near by to come to his place. He got all the goods down off the shelves in his store and carried them outside. Then he brought in about seven head of ponies. When all the people were gathered there, he gave away all these things because I was going away East. I was going with the white people, and perhaps might never return; so he was sacrificing all his worldly possessions. Some of the other chiefs also gave away many things.

The day following, the agent told the Indians he had some Government teams ready to take all the children who were going away. My father said he would much rather take me himself as far as possible. Then my sister Zintkaziwin gave herself up to go with me, doing this as an honor.

My father had a light spring wagon, and they loaded this up with a small tipi, some bedding, cooking utensils, and whatever might be needed on the trip. We were to drive to the place where a steamboat was to carry us part of the way. When we were ready to start, I looked over to the spot where my ponies were grazing. How happy they were — and I was leaving them, perhaps never to return! My heart went out to the little animals as I stood there looking at them.

Then I asked my father if I might ride one of the saddle-ponies from Rosebud Agency to Black Pole, a distance of fifty miles, where we were to board the steamboat. He gave me permission, although I knew at the end of the journey my pony and I would have to part for many a long, lonesome day.

About halfway to Black Pole we camped for the night. At this point we met many other Indian boys and girls who were also going East with the white people. Some rode in Government wagons; others came on their ponies as I had done. Many drove their own wagons.

Early the next morning we were all on the road again, my sister riding in the wagon with her mother and father. We were now making the last lap of our journey from the reservation to the steamboat, and it would be only a short time that my pony and I would be together. We did not know where we were going, only that it 'was east somewhere.'

At last we reached Black Pole. Our tipis were pitched again, as we had to wait the arrival of the boat. However, none of us were in a hurry. Here we had such a good time! We ran, shouted, and played, trying hard to crowd in all the fun possible before we were separated from our people. We waited three days, and then were told that the boat would arrive the following day.

But at this point my sister suddenly experienced a change of heart. She concluded that she did not want any white man's education. However, that really suited me very well, because I figured that she would have been a lot of extra trouble for me. I knew that I could take care of myself all right, but if she were along and anything happened to her, I would be expected, of course, to look out for her, as she was younger than I — and a girl, at that!

Finally the boat arrived. They put a little bridge way out to the shore. It was now just about sundown. Then the Indian boys and girls who were going away were lined up, and as their names were called they went on board the boat. Even at this point some of the children refused to go aboard, and nobody could compel them to. So my sister was not the only one who had 'cold feet,' as the white people say.

When my name was called, I went right on the boat without any hesitation. By the time all the children were aboard, it was getting quite dark. So they pulled in the little bridge, while the parents of the children stood lined up on the shore and began crying. Then all the children on the boat also started to cry. It was a very sad scene. I did not see my father or stepmother cry, so I did not shed any tears. I just stood over in a corner of the room we were in and watched the others all crying as if their hearts would break. And mind you, some of them were quite young men and women.

Bedtime at length came, but I did not see any nice bed to sleep in that night. We were scattered all over that big room, the boys on one side and the girls on the other. We rolled up in our blankets and tried to go to sleep; but riding in a steamboat with a paddle-wheel at the back which made lots of noise was an experience we were not used to, and it kept us awake.

Along in the night, when we were all supposed to be asleep, I overheard some big boys talking quietly. They were going to get ready to jump off the boat. When I got the drift of their conversation, I jumped up and saw three

big boys going down the stairway. The boat appeared not
to be moving, so I followed after the three boys to the floor
below. There I saw a lot of men bringing cordwood onto
the boat. The three boys were standing at the edge of the
boat waiting for a chance to jump off and take to the woods.

I remained back at the foot of the stairway watching to
see what they would do. Then the larger of the boys said
to the others: 'Let us not try it this time. I understand
they are going to put us off the boat to-morrow anyway,
and if they do, we will have a good chance then.' So they
started back to their blankets on the floor and I got into
mine. But I could not get to sleep, because I was wondering where we were going and what was to be done with us
after we arrived.

It did not occur to me at that time that I was going away
to learn the ways of the white man. My idea was that I
was leaving the reservation and going to stay away long
enough to do some brave deed, and then come home again
alive. If I could just do that, then I knew my father would
be so proud of me.

About noon the next day, the interpreter came around
and told us we must get ready to leave the boat. Finally it
stopped close to the shore and they put out the little
bridge and we all got off. We walked quite a distance until
we came to a long row of little houses standing on long
pieces of iron which stretched away as far as we could see.
The little houses were all in line, and the interpreter told
us to get inside. So we climbed up a little stairway into
one of the houses, and found ourselves in a beautiful room,
long but narrow, in which were many cushioned seats.

I took one of these seats, but presently changed to another. I must have changed my seat four or five times before I quieted down. We admired the beautiful room and
the soft seats very much. While we were discussing the
situation, suddenly the whole house started to move away
with us. We boys were in one house and the girls in an-

other. I was glad my sister was not there. We expected every minute that the house would tip over, and that something terrible would happen. We held our blankets between our teeth, because our hands were both busy hanging to the seats, so frightened were we.

We were in our first railway train, but we did not know it. We thought it was a house. I sat next to the window, and observed the poles that were stuck up alongside the iron track. It seemed to me that the poles almost hit the windows, so I changed my seat to the other side.

We rode in this manner for some distance. Finally the interpreter came into the room and told us to get ready to leave it, as we were going to have something to eat. Those who carried bundles were told to leave them in their seats. Some of the older boys began fixing feathers in their hair and putting more paint on their faces.

When the train stopped at the station there was a great crowd of white people there. It was but three years after the killing of Custer by the Sioux, so the white people were anxious to see some Sioux Indians. I suppose many of these people expected to see us coming with scalping-knives between our teeth, bows and arrows in one hand and tomahawk in the other, and to hear a great war-cry as we came off that Iron Horse. The Sioux name for railroad was Maza Canku, or Iron Road. The term 'Iron Horse' is merely a white man's name for a moving-picture play.

The place where we stopped was called Sioux City. The white people were yelling at us and making a great noise. When the train stopped, we raised the windows to look out. Soon they started to throw money at us. We little fellows began to gather up the money, but the larger boys told us not to take it, but to throw it back at them. They told us if we took the money the white people would put our names in a big book. We did not have sense enough then to understand that those white people had no way of discovering what our names were. However, we threw the money all back at them. At this, the white people laughed and threw more money at us. Then the big boys told us to close the windows. That stopped the money-throwing.

The interpreter then came in and told us we were to get off here. As we left the little house, we saw that there were lots of what we took to be soldiers lined up on both sides of the street. I expect these were policemen, but as they had on uniforms of some sort, we called them soldiers. They formed up in a line and we marched between them to the eating-place.

Many of the little Indian boys and girls were afraid of the white people. I really did not blame them, because the whites acted so wild at seeing us. They tried to give the war-whoop and mimic the Indian and in other ways got us all wrought up and excited, and we did not like this sort of treatment.

When we got inside the restaurant, there were two long tables with white covers on. There was plenty of fine silverware and all kinds of good food. We all sat down around the table, but we did not try to eat. We just helped ourselves to all the food, scooping it into our blankets, and not missing all the lump sugar. The white people were all crowded up close to the windows on the outside, watching us and laughing their heads off at the way we acted. They were waiting to see how we ate, but we fooled them, for we carried everything back to the iron road, and inside the little houses we sat down in peace and enjoyed our meal.

Then the train started up again, and we traveled all that night. The next day we reached Sotoju Otun Wake, which, translated into Sioux, means 'smoky city' or your great city of Chicago. Here we saw so many people and such big houses that we began to open our eyes in astonishment. The big boys said, 'The white people are like ants; they are all over — everywhere.' We Indians do not call the

Caucasian race 'white people,' but 'Wasicun' or 'Mila Hanska.' This latter means 'long knife.'

At Chicago we waited a long time. Pretty soon they brought us in all kinds of food. They did not try to feed us at a table again. After the meal was finished, the interpreter told us we were going to have a little dance and enjoy ourselves. We had no tom-tom with us, so they brought a big bass drum from some place. We were in a big room — possibly it was the waiting-room of the station but there were no seats in it. Here the big boys had a good time, and we little fellows looked out the windows and watched the wagons going by. A few white people were allowed to come inside and watch the dance, while there was a great crowd outside.

In the evening we were all loaded on to another iron road, traveling all night, the next day and then another night came. By this time we were all beginning to feel very restless. We had been sitting up all the way from Dakota in those straight seats and were getting very tired. The big boys began to tell us little fellows that the white people were taking us to the place where the sun rises, where they would dump us over the edge of the earth, as we had been taught that the earth was flat, with four corners, and when we came to the edge, we would fall over.

Now the full moon was rising, and we were traveling toward it. The big boys were singing brave songs, expecting to be killed any minute. We all looked at the moon, and it was in front of us, but we felt that we were getting too close to it for comfort. We were very tired, and the little fellows dozed off. Presently the big boys woke everybody. They said they had made a discovery. We were told to look out the window and see what had happened while we were dozing. We did so, and the moon was now behind us! Apparently we had passed the place where the moon rose!

This was quite a mystery. The big boys were now singing brave songs again, while I was wide awake and watchful, waiting to see what was going to happen. But nothing happened.

We afterward learned that at Harrisburg, Pennsylvania, the train turned due west to Carlisle, which placed the moon in our rear. And to think we had expected to be killed because we had passed the moon

CHAPTER XIV

FIRST DAYS AT CARLISLE

At last the train arrived at a junction where we were told we were at the end of our journey. Here we left the train and walked about two miles to the Carlisle Barracks. Soon we came to a big gate in a great high wall. The gate was locked, but after quite a long wait, it was unlocked and we marched in through it. I was the first boy inside. At that time I thought nothing of it, but now I realize that I was the first Indian boy to step inside the Carlisle Indian School grounds.

Here the girls were all called to one side by Louise McCoz, the girls' interpreter. She took them into one of the big buildings, which was very brilliantly lighted, and it looked good to us from the outside.

When our interpreter told us to go to a certain building which he pointed out to us, we ran very fast, expecting to find nice little beds like those the white people had. We were so tired and worn out from the long trip that we wanted a good long sleep. From Springfield, Dakota, to Carlisle, Pennsylvania, riding in day coaches all the way, with no chance to sleep, is an exhausting journey for a bunch of little Indians.

But the first room we entered was empty. A cast-iron stove stood in the middle of the room, on which was placed a coal-oil lamp. There was no fire in the stove. We ran through all the rooms, but they were all the same — no fire, no beds. This was a two-story building, but we were all herded into two rooms on the upper floor.

Well, we had to make the best of the situation, so we took off our leggins and rolled them up for a pillow. All the covering we had was the blanket which each had brought. We went to sleep on the hard floor, and it was so cold! We had been used to sleeping on the ground, but the floor was so much colder.

Next morning we were called downstairs for breakfast. All we were given was bread and water. How disappointed we were! At noon we had some meat, bread, and coffee, so we felt a little better. But how lonesome the big boys and girls were for their far-away Dakota homes where there was plenty to eat! The big boys seemed to take it worse than we smaller chaps did. I guess we little fellows did not know any better. The big boys would sing brave songs, and that would start the girls to crying. They did this for several nights. The girls' quarters were about a hundred and fifty yards from ours, so we could hear them crying. After some time the food began to get better; but it was far from being what we had been used to receiving back home.

At this point I must tell you how the Carlisle Indian School was started. A few years previously, four or five tribes in Oklahoma had some trouble. They were Cheyennes, Arapahoes, Comanches, and Wichitas. There was another tribe with them, but I have forgotten the name. The Government arrested some braves from these various tribes and took them to Virginia as prisoners. Captain Pratt was in charge of them. He conceived the idea of placing these Indians in a school to see if they could learn anything in that manner. So they were put into the Hampton School, where negroes were sent. They were good-sized young men, having been on the war-path already, but old as they were, they were getting on splendidly with their studies.

That gave Captain Pratt another idea. He thought if he could get some young Indian children and educate them, it would help their people. He went to the Government officials and put the proposition up to them, and asked permission to try the experiment. They told him to go ahead and see what he could do, providing he could get any Indians to educate. Captain Pratt was not at all sure he could do this.

He had nothing prepared to start such a school, but the Government gave him the use of some empty buildings at Carlisle, Pennsylvania. He brought some of the Indian prisoners from Virginia with him, and they remained in the Carlisle Barracks until Captain Pratt could go to Dakota and return with his first consignment of 'scholars.' Carlisle School had been a soldiers' home at one time; so at the start it was not built for the education of the Indian people.

I had come to this school merely to show my people that I was brave enough to leave the reservation and go East, not knowing what it meant and not caring.

When we first arrived at Carlisle, we had nothing to do. There were no school regulations, no rules of order or anything of that sort. We just ran all over the school grounds and did about as we pleased.

Soon some white people began to come in from near-by towns to see us. Then we would all go up on the second floor and stand against the railings to look down at them. One of our boys was named Lone Hill. He watched the people closely, and if he saw a negro in the crowd he would run inside and put his war-shirt on. Then he would come out and chase the negro all over the grounds until he left. How the people laughed at this!

For some time we continued sleeping on the hard floor, and it was far from being as comfortable as the nice, soft beds in our tipis back home. One evening the interpreter called us all together, and gave each a big bag. He said these were to be our mattresses, but that we would have to fill them ourselves with straw. He said, 'Out behind the stable is a large haystack. Go there and fill these bags all full.'

So we all ran as fast as we could to the haystack and filled our sacks as quickly as possible, pushing and scuffling to see who would get finished first. When the bags were all full, we carried them to one of the big rooms on the second floor. Here the bags were all laid out in a row. We little fellows certainly did look funny, lugging those great bags across the yard and upstairs.

That night we had the first good sleep in a long time. These bags were sewed all around, and in the center there was a slit through which they were filled with the straw; but there was nobody to sew the slit up after the bag was filled. We had no sheets and no extra blankets thus far — nothing but the blankets we had brought from the reservation.

The next day we played back and forth over these bags of straw, and soon it began to filter out through the slits. Presently it was scattered all over the floor, and as we had no brooms with which to sweep it up, you can imagine the looks of the room at the starting of our school!

Although we were yet wearing our Indian clothes, the interpreter came to us and told us we must go to school. We were marched into a schoolroom, where we were each given a pencil and slate. We were seated at single desks. We soon discovered that the pencils made marks on the slates. So we covered our heads with our blankets, holding the slate inside so the other fellow would not know what we were doing. Here we would draw a man on a pony chasing buffalo, or a boy shooting birds in a tree, or it might be one of our Indian games, or anything that suited our fancy to try and portray.

When we had all finished, we dropped our blankets down on the seat and marched up to the teacher with our slates to show what we had drawn. Our teacher was a woman. She bowed her head as she examined the slates and smiled, indicating that we were doing pretty well — at least we interpreted it that way.

One day when we came to school there was a lot of writing on one of the blackboards. We did not know what it meant, but our interpreter came into the room and said, 'Do you see all these marks on the blackboard? Well, each word is a white man's name. They are going to give each one of you one of these names by which you will hereafter be known.' None of the names were read or explained to us, so of course we did not know the sound or meaning of any of them.

The teacher had a long pointed stick in her hand, and the interpreter told the boy in the front seat to come up. The teacher handed the stick to him, and the interpreter then told him to pick out any name he wanted. The boy had gone up with his blanket on. When the long stick was handed to him, he turned to us as much as to say, 'Shall I — or will you help me — to take one of these names? Is it right for me to take a white man's name?' He did not know what to do for a time, not uttering a single word — but he acted a lot and was doing a lot of thinking.

Finally he pointed out one of the names written on the blackboard. Then the teacher took a piece of white tape and wrote the name on it. Then she cut off a length of the tape and sewed it on the back of the boy's shirt. Then that name was erased from the board. There was no duplication of names in the first class at Carlisle School!

Then the next boy took the pointer and selected a name. He was also labeled in the same manner as Number One. When my turn came, I took the pointer and acted as if I were about to touch an enemy. Soon we all had the names of white men sewed on our backs. When we went to school, we knew enough to take our proper places in the class, but that was all. When the teacher called the roll, no one answered his name. Then she would walk around and look at the back of the boys' shirts. When she had the right name located, she made the boy stand up and say 'Present.' She kept this up for about a week before we knew what the sound of our new names was.

I was one of the 'bright fellows' to learn my name

quickly. How proud I was to answer when the teacher called the roll! I would put my blanket down and half raise myself in my seat, all ready to answer to my new name. I had selected the name 'Luther' — not 'Lutheran' as many people call me. 'Lutheran' is the name of a church denomination, not a person.

Next we had to learn to write our names. Our good teacher had a lot of patience with us. She is now living in Los Angeles, California, and I still like to go and ask her any question which may come up in my mind. She first wrote my name on the slate for me, and then, by motions, indicated that I was to write it just like that. She held the pencil in her hand just so, then made first one stroke, then another, and by signs I was given to understand that I was to follow in exactly the same way.

The first few times I wrote my new name, it was scratched so deeply into the slate that I was never able to erase it. But I copied my name all over both sides of the slate until there was no more room to write. Then I took my slate up to show it to the teacher, and she indicated, by the expression of her face, that it was very good. I soon learned to write it very well; then I took a piece of chalk downstairs and wrote 'Luther' all over everything I could copy it on.

Next the teacher wrote out the alphabet on my slate and indicated to me that I was to take the slate to my room and study. I was pleased to do this, as I expected to have a lot of fun. I went up on the second floor, to the end of the building, where I thought nobody would bother me. There I sat down and looked at those queer letters, trying hard to figure out what they meant. No one was there to tell me that the first letter was 'A' the next 'B' and so on. This was the first time in my life that I was really disgusted. It was something I could not decipher, and all this study business was not what I had come East for anyhow — so I thought.

How lonesome I felt for my father and mother! I stayed upstairs all by myself, thinking of the good times I might be having if I were only back home, where I could ride my ponies, go wherever I wanted to and do as I pleased, and, when it came night, could lie down and sleep well. Right then and there I learned that no matter how humble your home is, it is yet home.

So it did me no good to take my slate with me that day. It only made me lonesome. The next time the teacher told me by signs to take my slate to my room, I shook my head, meaning 'no.' She came and talked to me in English, but of course I did not know what she was saying.

A few days later, she wrote the alphabet on the blackboard, then brought the interpreter into the room. Through him she told us to repeat each letter after her, calling out 'A,' and we all said 'A'; then 'B,' and so on. This was our real beginning. The first day we learned the first three letters of the alphabet, both the pronunciation and the reading of them.

I had not determined to learn anything yet. All I could think of was my free life at home. How long would these people keep us here? When were we going home? At home we could eat any time we wished, but here we had to watch the sun all the time. On cloudy days the waits between meals seemed terribly long.

There soon came a time when the school people fixed up an old building which was to be used as our dining-room. In it they placed some long tables, but with no cover on. Our meals were dished up and brought to each plate before we entered. I very quickly learned to be right there when the bell rang, and get in first. Then I would run along down the table until I came to a plate which I thought contained the most meat, when I would sit down and begin eating without waiting for any one.

We soon 'got wise' when it came to looking out for the biggest portion of meat. When we knew by the sun that it was near dinner time, we would play close to the dining-room, until the woman in charge came out with a big bell in her hand to announce that the meal was ready. We never had to be called twice! We were right there when it came meal-time!

After a while they hung a big bell on a walnut tree near the office. This was to be rung for school hours and meals. One of the Indian boys named Edgar Fire Thunder used to sneak around the building and ring the bell before it was time to eat. Of course we would all rush for the dining-room, only to find the doors locked. Nobody seemed to object to this boy playing such pranks, but we did not like it.

We were still wearing our Indian clothes. One of the Indian prisoners was delegated to teach us to march in to the dining-room and to school. Some of the boys had bells on their leggins, which helped us to keep time as we stepped off.

One day we had a strange experience. We were all called together by the interpreter and told that we were to have our hair cut off. We listened to what he had to say, but we did not reply. This was something that would require some thought, so that evening the big boys held a council, and I recall very distinctly that Nakpa Kesela, or Robert American Horse, made a serious speech. Said he, 'If I am to learn the ways of the white people, I can do it just as well with my hair on.' To this we all exclaimed 'Hau!' — meaning that we agreed with him.

In spite of this meeting, a few days later we saw some white men come inside the school grounds carrying big chairs. The interpreter told us these were the men who had come to cut our hair. We did not watch to see where the chairs were carried, as it was school time, and we went to our classroom. One of the big boys named Ya Slo, or Whistler, was missing. In a short time he came in with his hair cut off. Then they called another boy out, and when he returned, he also wore short hair. In this way we were called out one by one.

When I saw most of them with short hair, I began to feel anxious to be 'in style' and wanted mine cut, too. Finally I was called out of the schoolroom, and when I went into the next room, the barber was waiting for me. He motioned for me to sit down, and then he commenced work. But when my hair was cut short, it hurt my feelings to such an extent that the tears came into my eyes. I do not recall whether the barber noticed my agitation or not, nor did I care. All I was thinking about was that hair he had taken away from me.

Right here I must state how this hair-cutting affected me in various ways. I have recounted that I always wanted to please my father in every way possible. All his instructions to me had been along this line: 'Son, be brave and get killed.' This expression had been moulded into my brain to such an extent that I knew nothing else.

But my father had made a mistake. He should have told me, upon leaving home, to go and learn all I could of the white man's ways, and be like them. That would have given a new idea from a different slant; but Father did not advise me along that line. I had come away from home with the intention of never returning alive unless I had done something very brave.

Now, after having had my hair cut, a new thought came into my head. I felt that I was no more Indian, but would be an imitation of a white man. And we are still imitations of white men, and the white men are imitations of the Americans.

We all looked so funny with short hair. It had been cut with a machine and was cropped very close. We still had our Indian clothes, but were all 'bald-headed.' None of us slept well that night; we felt so queer. I wanted to feel of my head all the time. But in a short time I became anxious to learn all I could.

Next, we heard that we were soon to have white men's clothes. We were all very excited and anxious when this was announced to us. One day some wagons came in, loaded with big boxes, which were unloaded in front of the office. Of course we were all very curious, and gathered around to watch the proceedings and see all we could.

Here, one at a time, we were 'sized up' and a whole suit handed to each of us. The clothes were some sort of dark heavy gray goods, consisting of coat, pants, and vest. We were also given a dark woolen shirt, a cap, a pair of suspenders, socks, and heavy farmer's boots.

Up to this time we had all been wearing our thin shirts, leggins, and a blanket. Now we had received new outfits of white men's clothes, and to us it seemed a whole lot of clothing to wear at once, but even at that, we had not yet received any underwear.

As soon as we had received our outfits, we ran to our rooms to dress up. The Indian prisoners were kept busy helping us put the clothes on. Although the suits were too big for many of us, we did not know the difference. I remember that my boots were far too large, but as long as they were 'screechy' or squeaky, I didn't worry about the size! I liked the noise they made when I walked, and the other boys were likewise pleased.

How proud we were with clothes that had pockets and with boots that squeaked! We walked the floor nearly all that night. Many of the boys even went to bed with their clothes all on. But in the morning, the boys who had taken off their pants had a most terrible time. They did not know whether they were to button up in front or behind. Some of the boys said the open part went in front; others said, 'No, it goes at the back.' There is where the boys who had kept all their clothes on came in handy to look at. They showed the others that the pants buttoned up in front and not at the back. So here we learned something again.

Another boy and I received some money from home. His name was Waniyetula, or Winter, and he was my cousin. We concluded we might as well dress up like white men; so we took all our money to the interpreter and asked him if he would buy us some nice clothes. He promised he would.

We did not know the amount of money which we handed over to him, but we gave him all we had received, as we did not know values then. He took the money and went to town. When he returned he brought us each a big bundle. We took them and went into an empty room to dress up, as we did not want the other boys to see us until we had the clothes on. When we opened the bundles, we were surprised to see how many things we had received for our money. Each bundle contained a black suit of clothes, a pair of shoes and socks, stiff bosom shirt, two paper collars, a necktie, a pair of cuffs, derby hat, cuff buttons, and some colored glass studs for our stiff shirt fronts.

We were greatly pleased with our purchases, which we examined with great curiosity and eagerness. As it was nearly time for supper, we tied the bundles together again and took them into one of the rooms where an Indian prisoner was staying, asking him to keep the bundles for us until the next day. We had to talk to him in the sign language, as he was from a different tribe. The sign language, by the way, was invented by the Indian. White men never use it correctly.

We felt very proud of our new purchases and spent most of that evening getting off by ourselves and discussing them. We found out later that our wonderful clothes cost all together about eleven dollars. The interpreter had bought the cheapest things he could get in the town of Carlisle.

All the next day we were together. We kept our eyes on our disciplinarian, Mr. Campbell, because we wanted to see how he put on his collar. We were studying not very far away from him and we watched him constantly, trying to figure out how he had put that collar on his shirt.

When evening came at last, we carried our bundles up to the second floor where we could be alone. Here we opened the things up and started to dress up. While we were thus engaged, in came the prisoner with whom we had left the bundles the night before. We were glad, in a way, that he had come in, because he knew more about how the clothes ought to be worn than we did, and he helped us dress.

Just as we were through, the bell rang for supper. The other boys were already in line. We came down the outside stairway, and when they observed us, what a warwhoop went up! The boys made all kinds of remarks about our outfits, and called us 'white men.' But our teachers and the other white people were greatly pleased at our new appearance.

We had only two paper collars apiece, and when they became soiled we had to go without collars. We tried our best to wear the ties without the collars, but I guess we must have looked funny.

It was now winter and very cold, so we were supplied with red flannel underwear. These looked pretty to us, but we did not like the warmth and the 'itching' they produced. I soon received some more money from my father, and another boy named Knaska, or Frog, and I bought us some white underwear. This was all right, but we did not dare let any one else know it, as the rules were that we had to wear the red flannels. So every Sunday morning we would put the red ones on, because they held inspection on Sunday morning. Captain Pratt and others always looked us over that day very carefully; but as soon as the inspection was through, we would slip into our white underclothes and get ready to attend Sunday School in town.

All the boys and girls were given permission to choose the religious denomination which appealed to them best, so they were at liberty to go where they pleased to Sunday School. Most of us selected the Episcopal Church. I was baptized in that church under the name of Luther.

In our room lived a boy named Kaici Inyanke, or Running Against. While not exactly bad, he was always up to some mischief. His father's name was Black Bear, so when the boy was baptized he took his father's name, while his Christian name was Paul. He is yet living at Pine Ridge Agency, South Dakota. More than once Captain Pratt had to hold Paul up. He would play until the very last minute and then try to clean his shoes and comb his hair, all at once seemingly. On this particular Sunday Paul rushed in and was so busy that he did not get half finished. He had combed his hair, but had applied too much water, which was running down his face, while one of his shoes was cleaned and the other was dirty.

We had been taught to stand erect like soldiers when Captain Pratt, Dr. Givens, and others entered the room for inspection. First, Captain Pratt would 'size us up' from head to foot, notice if we had our hair combed nicely, if our clothes were neatly brushed, and if we had cleaned our shoes. Then he would look the room over to see if our beds were made up right, often lifting the mattresses to see that everything was clean underneath. Often they would look into our wooden boxes where we kept our clothes, to see that everything was spick and span.

Paul Black Bear had not been able — as usual — to finish getting ready for inspection, and when Captain Pratt looked at his feet, Paul tried to hide the shoe that was not polished, by putting it behind the other one. Captain Pratt also noticed the water running down his face. We all expected to see Paul get a 'calling down,' but Captain Pratt only laughed and told Paul to do better next time.

At Carlisle it was the rule that we were not to be permitted to smoke, but Paul smoked every time he had a chance. One day he made a 'long smoke' and stood by one of the big fireplaces, puffing away very fast. All at once he got sick at the stomach and fainted. We had to drag him out of the fireplace and pour water on him.

One day our teacher brought some wooden plates into the schoolroom. She told us they were to paint on. She gave me about half a dozen of them. We each received a small box of water-colors. I painted Indian designs on all my plates. On some of them I had a man chasing buffalo, shooting them with the bow and arrow. Others represented a small boy shooting at birds in the trees. When I had them all painted, I gave them back to the teacher. She seemed to be well pleased with my work, and sent them all away somewhere. Possibly some persons yet have those wooden plates which were painted by the first class of Indian boys and girls at Carlisle.

About this time there were many additions to the school from various tribes in other States and from other reservations. We were not allowed to converse in the Indian tongue, and we knew so little English that we had a hard time to get along. With these other tribes coming in, we were doing our best to talk as much English as we could.

One night in December we were all marched down to the chapel. When the doors were opened, how surprised we were! Everything was decorated with green. We all took seats, but we could not keep still. There was a big tree in the room, all trimmed and decorated. We stretched our necks to see everything. Then a minister stood up in front and talked to us, but I did not mind a thing he said — in fact, I could not understand him anyway.

This was our first Christmas celebration, and we were all so happy. I saw the others were getting gifts from off that tree, and I was anxious to get something myself. Finally my name was called, and I received several presents, which had been put on the tree for me by the people for whom I had painted the plates. Others were from my teacher, Miss M. Burgess, and some from my Sunday-

School teacher, Miss Eggee. I was very happy for all the things I had received.

I now began to realize that I would have to learn the ways of the white man. With that idea in mind, the thought also came to me that I must please my father as well. So my little brain began to work hard. I thought that some day I might be able to become an interpreter for my father, as he could not speak English. Or I thought I might be able to keep books for him if he again started a store. So I worked very hard.

One day they selected a few boys and told us we were to learn trades. I was to be a tinsmith. I did not care for this, but I tried my best to learn this trade. Mr. Walker was our instructor. I was getting along very well. I made hundreds of tin cups, coffee pots, and buckets. These were sent away and issued to the Indians on various reservations.

After I had left the school and returned home, this trade did not benefit me any, as the Indians had plenty of tinware that I had made at school.

Mornings I went to the tin shop, and in the afternoon attended school. I tried several times to drop this trade and go to school the entire day, but Captain Pratt said, 'No, you must go to the tin shop — that is all there is to it,' so I had to go. Half school and half work took away a great deal of study time. I figure that I spent only about a year and a half in school, while the rest of the time was wasted, as the school was not started properly to begin with. Possibly you wonder why I did not remain longer, but the Government had made an agreement with our parents as to the length of time we were to be away.

A short time later, some boys, myself among the number, were called into one of the schoolrooms. There we found a little white woman. There was a long table in front of her, on which were many packages tied in paper. She opened up one package and it contained a bright, shining horn. Other packages disclosed more horns, but they seemed to be different sizes.

The little white woman picked up a horn and then looked the boys over. Finally she handed it to a boy who she thought might be able to use it. Then she picked out a shorter horn and gave it to me. I learned afterward that it was a B-flat cornet. When she had finished, all the boys had horns in their hands. We were to be taught how to play on them and form a band.

The little woman had a black case with her, which she opened. It held a beautiful horn, and when she blew on it it sounded beautiful. Then she motioned to us that we were to blow our horns. Some of the boys tried to blow from the large end. Although we tried our best, we could not produce a sound from them. She then tried to talk to us, but we did not understand her. Then she showed us how to wet the end of the mouthpiece. We thought she wanted us to spit into the horns, so we did. She finally got so discouraged with us that she started crying.

We just stood there and waited for her to get through, then we all tried again. Finally, some of the boys managed to make a noise through their horns. But if you could have heard it! It was terrible! But we thought we were doing fine.

So now I had more to occupy my attention. In the morning I had one hour to practice for the band. Then I must run to my room and change my clothes and go to work in the tin shop. From there I had to run again to my room and change my clothes and get ready for dinner. After that, I had a little time to study my lessons.

Then the school bell would ring and it was time for school. After that, we played or studied our music. Then we went to bed. All lights had to be out at nine o'clock. The first piece of music our band was able to play was the alphabet, from 'a' to 'z.' It was a great day for us when we were able to play this simple little thing in public. But it was a good thing we were not asked to give an encore, for that was all we knew!

After I had learned to play a little, I was chosen to give all the bugle calls. I had to get up in the morning before the others and arouse everybody by blowing the morning call. Evenings at ten minutes before nine o'clock I blew again. Then all the boys would run for their rooms. At nine o'clock the second call was given, when all lights were turned out and we were supposed to be in bed. Later on I learned the mess call, and eventually I could blow all the calls of the regular army.

I did these duties all the time I was at Carlisle School, so in the early part of 1880, although I was a young boy of but twelve, I was busy learning everything my instructors handed me.

One Sunday morning we were all busy getting ready to go to Sunday School in town. Suddenly there was great excitement among some of the boys on the floor below. One of the boys came running upstairs shouting, 'Luther Standing Bear's father is here!' Everybody ran downstairs to see my father. We had several tribes at the school now, many of whom had heard of my father, and they were anxious to see him.

When I got downstairs, my father was in the center of a large crowd of the boys, who were all shaking hands with him. I had to fight my way through to reach him. He was so glad to see me, and I was so delighted to see him. But our rules were that we were not to speak the Indian language under any consideration. And here was my father, and he could not talk English!

My first act was to write a note to Captain Pratt, asking if he would permit me to speak to my father in the Sioux tongue. I said, 'My father is here. Please allow me to speak to him in Indian.' Captain Pratt answered, 'Yes, my boy; bring your father over to my house.'

This was another happy day for me. I took my father

over to meet Captain Pratt, who was so glad to see him, and was very respectful to him. Father was so well dressed. He wore a gray suit, nice shoes, and a derby hat. But he wore his hair long. He looked very nice in white men's clothes. He even sported a gold watch and chain. Captain Pratt gave father a room with Robert American Horse, in the boys' quarters. He allowed the boys to talk to him in the Indian tongue, and that pleased the boys very much. Here Father remained for a time with us.

CHAPTER XV

SCHOOL LIFE: THE LAST OF THE HEAD CHIEFS

WHEN my father arrived at Carlisle School, he had two presents for me — some silver dollars and a gold watch and chain. There was a little cross-piece in the center of the watch chain to fasten through my vest button. How proud I was to receive this watch! When any of the boys or girls looked at me, I always took out that watch and looked at it, imagining I could tell the time! At that day I did not know how to tell the time by looking at a watch or clock. And those silver dollars — how they did jingle in my pocket!

Then my father wanted me to go downtown with him, so Captain Pratt gave his permission. When we reached the town, my father asked if there was anything I wanted; if I did, just to say so. But I thought he had done pretty well by me already, and I told him there was nothing I wanted. However, he bought some fruits and candy, which we carried back to the school.

Captain Pratt was very kind to my father during his stay with me, and took him to Boston, New York, Baltimore, Philadelphia, and Washington. I did not go with him, but a mixed blood named Stephen Moran accompanied them as interpreter. My father was greatly pleased that he was given an opportunity to visit these great cities.

After he returned from the trip, he spoke to me in this wise: 'My son, since I have seen all those cities, and the way the Long Knife people are doing, I begin to realize that our lands and our game are all gone. There is nothing but the Long Knives (or white people) everywhere I went, and they keep coming like flies. So we will have to learn their ways, in order that we may be able to live with them. You will have to learn all you can, and I will see that your brothers and sisters follow in the path that you are making for them.'

This was the first time my father had ever spoken to me regarding acquiring a white man's education. He continued:

'Some day I want to hear you speak like these Long Knife people, and work like them.'

This was spoken to me by my father in the Dakota tongue, but it meant so much to me. He was so serious in his conversation along this line that I felt quite 'puffed up.' I wanted to please him in everything — even to getting killed on the battlefield. Even that I was willing to endure.

But now he had seen so many white people, all working, that he knew the days of the old Indian life had passed. My father was a very bright man, although he never had a single day's education, such as I was getting, in all his life; but he always tried to learn all he could wherever he was.

Just before returning to the West, he was invited into our Chapel to listen to the service. He asked me what it was, and I told him it was the white man's religion which was discussed in that room. He came in and sat with us boys. During the preaching he sat very reverently and listened attentively to all that was said, although he could not understand a single word. His attention to the service pleased Captain Pratt exceedingly.

When my father was ready to depart, he was presented with a well-made top-buggy and a set of harness, all of which were made there at the school. I was delighted at seeing my father so well treated and recognized. Other chiefs had visited us, but my father was the first Indian to receive such courteous recognition and agreeable presents.

Doubtless they wished to convince him that I was a boy they were pleased to have in the school. The school people were glad to have had him with us, as he was so neat and clean, and conducted himself in such a gentlemanly manner, even if he was an Indian right off the reservation. I there learned that it paid to do whatever was asked of me, and to do it without grumbling; also that it pays to obey your parents in all things.

There was one boy in school whom Captain Pratt was anxious to have returned to the reservation, so he asked my father if he would take the boy along with him. Through the interpreter Father was told that none of the teachers in the school could do anything with the boy — he did not try to learn anything, nor seem inclined to want to. But Father said, 'No, you brought him here to teach him. Why don't you do it?'

'That is true,' replied Captain Pratt, 'but we can do· nothing with him. If you will take him home, we will pay you for your trouble.'

Finally Father agreed to do this. Captain Pratt gave permission to a few of us to accompany Father and the boy to the train, in the town of Carlisle. After they had departed, I came back to the school more determined than. ever to learn all the white people's ways, no matter how hard I had to study.

Toward the summer of 1881 we were doing splendidly in the school. Some of the boys were learning the tailoring trade, and they started to make uniforms for the pupils. The suits were of blue cloth, with two narrow stripes of red down the seams of the trousers. How proud we were when our uniforms were completed and we donned them. About that time our band was able to play a few pieces, and we marched to the bandstand in our new uniforms and made a splendid showing with our music.

After the school closed for the summer vacation, some of the boys and girls were placed out in farmers' homes to work through the summer. They were scattered through two counties of the State — Bucks County and Columbia County. Two of our teachers were from those counties and knew the people who had taken in our boys and girls.

Those who yet remained at school were sent into the mountains for a vacation trip. I was among this number.

When we reached our camping place we pitched our tents like soldiers, all in a row. Captain Pratt brought along a lot of feathers and some sinew, and we made bows and arrows. Many white people came to visit the Indian camp, and seeing us shooting with the bow and arrow they would put nickels and dimes in a slot of wood and set them up for us to shoot at. If we knocked the money from the stick, it was ours. We enjoyed this sport very much, as it brought a real home thrill to us.

We were presented with straw hats such as the farmers in that section wore. Sometimes in the morning we would go out picking wild fruit — strawberries, cherries, and plums. After our stomachs were full, we would fill our hats and carry the fruit back to camp. We were always obliged to return to camp for meals. This was impressed upon us, but I do not recall that any boy was ever punished for being late at meal time!

We each had a tin cup and plate, knife, fork, and spoon, which we were required individually to wash and care for. When the bell rang for meals, we quickly formed in line, each with his tin cup and plate. The cook ladled out each one's portion, which was supposed to be all the helping we could expect. However, this did not exactly suit some of the boys — myself among them — who never seemed to get filled up. So we got together and did some scheming.

Robert American Horse, Julian Whistler, Clarence Three Stars, and I lined up one morning with the others. After we had received our portions from the cook, we ran to our tents. Here two of us emptied our plates into the plates of the others. Then we wiped off our plates and ran back to get in line again. After receiving a second helping without being detected, we hustled to the tent again, where we divided the six portions among the four of us! In that manner we got plenty to eat. All through the vacation we had a fine time. Many people called at our camp, at Captain Pratt's invitation, to see how we were getting along. They were quite surprised to see how we were acquiring the white man's ways.

After the vacation trip was over and we were again in school, we began studying hard. When we came to take up geography, it was a great puzzle to us all. We had been taught to believe that the earth was flat, with four corners. Our teacher, however, told us it was round, and that it did not stand still, but was moving all the time, which was the reason we had day and night, as well as the four seasons. She brought a ball into the schoolroom. It was painted in several colors, and with it she explained how the earth revolved.

After this lesson was over, we boys got together for a talk. We could not exactly believe this story that the earth revolved on an axis, and turned upside down. How could we stick to the ground like flies if we were standing on our heads!

One day an astronomer came to the school and gave us a talk. He explained that there would be an eclipse of the moon the following Wednesday night at twelve o'clock. We laughed and laughed over this, not believing a word of it. When the day arrived, we were filled with a wonderful curiosity to see if the man spoke the truth. We were allowed to remain up to view the eclipse. Sure enough, it happened! The moon was eclipsed, and after that, we readily believed everything our teacher told us about geography and astronomy.

When we really had settled down with a determination to master the white man's language, several of us had an idea that some morning we would awaken and discover that we could talk English as readily as we could our own. As for myself, I thought if I could only be permitted to sleep in a white man's home, I would wake up some morning with a full knowledge of the English language.

We did not realize that we must learn one word at a time.

We slept in large dormitories. Each boy had a black enameled bed, a chair, and a wooden box, the latter serving as a trunk. The rooms were now kept very clean by the boys. The beds were fastened together by two catches attached to the legs, which clamped to the sides of the bed to hold them in position. When these catches were loosened, the bed did not drop down quickly unless one sat on it.

Paul Black Bear discovered this arrangement of the beds. One night when the boys were all downstairs, he sneaked up into the dormitory and unfastened several of the catches. When the boys occupying them crawled into bed, there was a grand crash! Paul thought this was a great joke on us, but we soon learned to examine our beds before getting into them. However, this boy was so full of jokes that he would even wait until we were asleep and then go around and unfasten the catches, and as soon as the occupant turned over, down would go the bed again.

One day we were told that we were to have night shirts to sleep in. We wondered why they gave us so many clothes to take care of. Upon our first arrival we had only the clothes on our backs — leggins, moccasins, thin shirt, and blanket. Now we had full suits, red flannel underwear, shoes, hats — and now it was going to be night shirts to sleep in!

We were curious as to what they would look like. When they arrived, we discovered that they were long — just like a woman's dress! We had already been advised that we must not go out on the grass after the dew fell or we might catch cold and die. But the night we got those night shirts we felt like angels. So most of the boys skipped out from the dormitory after the bugle had blown for 'lights out.' They ran around through the grass until some one heard the office door open. Then everybody knew that Captain Pratt was coming, and a grand rush was made for the dormitory, not even stopping to wipe one's feet! We expected a scolding the following morning, but the incident was never mentioned.

Shortly thereafter, Chief Spotted Tail came to visit the school. He had three sons, one daughter, and a granddaughter there. When he arrived he did not get such a reception as had been accorded my father. He was shown all around, but he did not like the school, and told Captain Pratt that he was going to take all his children back to the reservation with him.

Spotted Tail was accompanied by an interpreter from the reservation, and the Captain told the chief that he was at liberty to take his own children home, but that he must leave his granddaughter. So Spotted Tail got his children together, including the granddaughter, and went to the depot, arriving just as the train was pulling in. When the train started, the chief took the granddaughter aboard into the car with him, and the agent was obliged to take her along.

During the early part of 1881, while we were still in school, news came that Chief Spotted Tail had been assassinated. Of course we imagined he had been killed by the white people, and we began to think of war again. The big boys told us, 'If the Indians go on the war-path now, we will all be killed at this school.' However, this suited me, as I was willing to die right there, just as I had promised when leaving home.

But we soon were advised that Spotted Tail had been shot and killed by an Indian named Crow Dog. The occurrence was as follows: You will recall that I have stated, in Chapter X, that Spotted Tail had received a nice team of horses and a top-buggy for himself and family; how the Government had furnished him an extra team to haul his gifts home. And he had also been given a fine two-story frame house, and then allowed credit at each of the trading stores.

At that time everybody wondered why he received such favors which nobody else enjoyed. But it was soon learned that he had sold a strip of land in northern Nebraska without the knowledge or consent of the other chiefs. The land was not his, but was the hunting ground of all the Sioux.

When this knavery was discovered, several of the chiefs wanted to shoot Spotted Tail immediately, but my father interceded. One night one of the men was all prepared to kill him, but after my father had cautioned him and advised against it, he cooled down. When Spotted Tail saw that nobody took any action against him, he doubtless began to imagine that all the Sioux tribe was afraid to do anything to him, and he began to get too smart. He got the agent to come to Carlisle School with him, and then took all his children home. After that he induced the wife of a crippled Indian to live with him. This was going a bit too far, so the chiefs held a council. They all knew this crippled man needed his wife, so one man was chosen to go to Spotted Tail and tell him he must return the woman to the lodge of the cripple.

But Spotted Tail only replied, 'I will not return the woman, and you can tell those other chiefs that I will do as I please. The Government is behind me, and is my friend.'

The messenger returned and told the chiefs what Spotted Tail had said. The other chiefs decided that he could not do as he pleased, even if he did think so. A council to send some delegates to Washington was called shortly after, and Spotted Tail was expected to be present. Several men were waiting for the chance to kill him.

But Crow Dog was too swift for the others. He lay in wait for Spotted Tail on the road that led to the council hall. When the chief came driving along, with one of his old wives, Crow Dog stood up, threw off his blanket, and shot Spotted Tail right out of the seat of the wagon, killing him instantly.

The crippled man received his wife back. Swift justice

had overtaken the man who had sold the land of his people without their consent or knowledge — a man who wanted to keep friendly to the whites himself, and yet keep his people in ignorance of his duplicity. Spotted Tail played a wrong game. Dishonesty never paid any one yet.

One day one of the schoolboys named Wica-karpa, or Knocked-It-Off, complained that he did not want to go to school. He was the son of White Thunder. He said he preferred to stay at home and do some drawing. He did not make any complaint, but was allowed to stay out. The next day he complained that he felt sick, and he was again allowed to remain away from school. The following day he died.

Of course his father, Chief White Thunder, was very angry that he had not been notified that his son was even sick, and he stopped off at the school, en route to Washington, where he was going with the expectation of being appointed head chief at Rosebud Agency. White Thunder said he wanted the body of his son sent home, but if the school authorities would not do that, they might at least place a headstone over his grave. Neither request was ever granted.

That was one of the hard things about our education — we had to get used to so many things we had never known before that it worked on our nerves to such an extent that it told on our bodies. When this boy became sick, nobody knew anything about it. He had merely said that he did not feel like going to school that day. Nobody expected he would die within two days' time. His father could not believe such a thing possible, as at home the boy had always been so strong and well.

When White Thunder returned to Dakota from his Washington trip, he told the Sioux that he had been selected by the Great Father to be head chief at Rosebud Agency. When the son of Spotted Tail heard this, he became very angry, as he had expected to take his father's place. Taking two of his friends, Thunder Hawk and Long Pumpkin, he went to the tipi of White Thunder when he was not at home and took his wife away. When White Thunder discovered this, he plotted for revenge.

He went over to Spotted Tail's place, got his wife, and then appropriated several of Spotted Tail's best horses. He took the animals home and staked them out in front of his tipi. According to Indian custom this was an open challenge for the son of Spotted Tail to come and get the horses, if he was man enough.

Early the following morning Spotted Tail's son and his two friends went up to the camp of White Thunder. Hiding in the brush near by, they waited until White Thunder came out of his tipi with his blanket still around him, when they shot him down and ran away.

The youngest brother of White Thunder, who was in the lodge, heard the shooting and came running out with his gun. He gave chase and shot Long Pumpkin in the leg. The other two men made their escape. Long Pumpkin is yet alive, but he walks lame.

That was the end of our 'head chiefs,' and we have had none since.

We heard all this news while we were at school, even though it was a long time getting to us. Sometimes we felt that we were in a very tight place, miles away from our homes, and among white people, where we felt that at the least show of trouble we would all be killed; but we were always ready.

CHAPTER XVI

RECRUITING FOR CARLISLE: A TRIP TO WASHINGTON

ABOUT this time Captain Pratt thought it would be a good idea to send some of the more advanced of the Indian boys and girls back to the reservation, in order to show the Indians there that we were really learning the white man's ways. By doing this, he also hoped to induce more of the Indian children to come to the school. He asked me if I would like to go, and I said "Yes," not knowing that any one else was going with me.

But when the day arrived to start, there were Maggie Stands Looking, Robert American Horse, and myself. Miss Burgess, our teacher, was also going with us, and we were to be her interpreters. Although we knew but little of the English language, we were ready to do anything for Miss Burgess.

This was in 1882. We passed through Yankton Agency, or Greenwood, as it is called to-day, and thence to Fort Randall. Here we met old Chief Sitting Bull and his followers. They had their tipis arranged in a circle, like a regular camp, but soldiers, with guns on their shoulders, were marching around the camp constantly. We did not talk much with the old chief, but Miss Burgess, through an interpreter, had quite a little conversation with him. We youngsters did not even realize the fact that here were our people, held prisoners by these white soldiers, merely because they had tried to protect themselves and their families!

Our teacher hired a team and engaged a driver to take us across country to the railroad station where we were to take the cars for Thatcher, Nebraska. It was quite a late hour when the train arrived and we all climbed inside, a very tired party. It was a chair car we occupied, and every chair was filled with cowboys, all sound asleep. One of them had been drinking quite heavily, and he started to insult our teacher. He first asked me for a match. I saw that he was drunk, so did not answer him. At this he became abusive, and my teacher, seeing trouble ahead, told the man that I could not understand English. He then tried to engage her in conversation. At this, Robert American Horse started up as though he were going to make trouble for the cowboy, and the only thing that prevented him was the fact that the man's station was reached, and he had to leave the train.

Arriving at Thatcher, we went by team to the Rosebud Reservation. Our people were all delighted to see us, of course. I was soon put to work in the blacksmith shop, making stovepipes and elbows, as a demonstration of my education acquired in the school. All the Indians came in to watch me, and they were very proud of my work.

Robert American Horse and Maggie Stands Looking were taken over to Pine Ridge Agency, where their people lived. Robert was a blacksmith by trade, while Maggie was considered a very good housekeeper. We were all very sincere in our desire to show what we had learned, in order to interest more of the children to go back to Carlisle School.

But so many had died there that the parents of the Indian boys and girls did not want them to go. Consequently it was hard work to engage students. As many of the parents had not even been notified when their children were taken sick, and knew nothing until they were dead and buried, it is easy to understand their hesitation in not wanting their children to leave the reservation. They had not been treated fairly or justly in the matter.

This was not due to any negligence on the part of Captain Pratt, but the carelessness of the Indian agent at the reservation — or his laziness. When he received a notice that one of the Indian children was sick at Carlisle, instead of trying to notify the parents, he would lay the letter aside in his desk, waiting for the parents of the sick child to come in to the agency for something. Then, if he happened to think of it, he would give them the letter. This made less work for the agent, but plenty of trouble for the school.

We three who had been sent home knew all about this, as our parents had talked it over with us, but we worked hard to show that we were all right and to create a good impression upon the other Indians, who seemed greatly pleased with my work, and would go away talking about my improved appearance and the trade I was learning. While they were proud of me, yet they were afraid to send their children away, fearing they would never see them again.

To settle the matter it was decided to hold a big council. I was delegated to speak. I felt very important, as many leading chiefs were to be present. Of course I had to address them in the Sioux tongue. I told them all about the training we received in the East; how we were taught to read, write, spell, count, and keep our rooms clean and neat; how we were treated at Christmas time and the gifts we received.

After I had finished talking, my father arose and told of his visit to Carlisle, laying particular stress on the kindness he had received from Captain Pratt, and what an improvement the children had shown in learning and acquiring the ways of the white people. He recounted his trips to the various large cities and what a numerous people the whites were. He then said: 'You all see my son, and how nice he looks. Most of you have seen his work and know how well he does it. I know this learning of the white man's way is good for my children; so I am sending his two brothers and a sister back with him, so they can also learn. When he is ready to return, my daughter,

Zintkaziwin, and my two sons, Totola and Wopotapi, are all going with him.'

Then several of the Indian people arose and said their children could also go. It was a very proud day for me that I was able to influence the Indians in this manner. When we were all ready to start back for Carlisle, there were fifty-two boys and girls in the party. After we were on the cars, we told the children not to be afraid of anything they saw or heard, consequently they were not as frightened as we had been on our first trip East. It was quite a task for our teacher to start out with so many boys and girls, none of whom, excepting myself and the two who had come from the school, could speak a word of English. But we acted as interpreters and did the best we knew how, and we experienced no trouble.

Captain Pratt was greatly pleased when we arrived home with so many students. The children started right in to learn, and soon were doing nicely. Then one day the Captain sent for me again to come to his office. He said he wanted more students for our school, and asked if I would be willing to return alone to the reservation to get them. I replied, 'Yes, I will be glad to do so.'

Shortly after this interview I was told to get ready to start back to Dakota. Word had been telegraphed ahead that some one was coming from the East to get more children for the Carlisle School, and of course the Indians were expecting to see either a man or a woman. I knew nothing about a telegram having been sent. The thing uppermost in mind was that I was assigned to induce more children to learn the ways of the white men; but the responsibility of getting them back to the school did not worry me in the least.

When I arrived at the reservation, my father was very glad to see me again. The agent sent out word for all the people to gather at the agency, as there was to be a council to determine how many children were going back to the school.

The night the council was held, my father and I went together. All the Indians began to gather, and soon the council room was filled. Then I arose to talk to them.

At this point a man named Sitting Around came forward. He let his blanket drop down, and I saw that he had his gun with him, and was wearing only a breech-cloth. His body was painted all over in spots of white. His hair was cut short, which indicated that he was in mourning. His only daughter had died in our school, and she passed away so suddenly that this man could not believe she was dead.

Anger showed in his eyes as he stepped toward me. His fist was closed, and he tapped me on the chest with these words: 'My nephew, if any one else had come from that school for more children — any one but you — I would have killed him right here.'

I could see, by the flash in his eye, that he meant what he said. After he had finished speaking, he drew his blanket around him and left the council.

Then Sorrel Horse, one of our brave old men, arose and addressed the council. 'You women afraid of soldiers, don't send any more of our children to school to die. If the soldiers should come and try to force us to give up our children, I will fight them alone, if you women are afraid of them.'

Such a remark coming from a man having the influence of Sorrel Horse, was like a wet blanket before the council. It closed the mouths of the others, and the council broke up right there, before either the agent or myself had a chance to explain matters. It made me feel very bad; but my business was to get more scholars for the school, and I determined not to get discouraged too quickly.

So the following morning I followed the Indians to their camp alone. It was about six miles from the agency, on the Little White River. Here I got them all together again; but old Sorrel Horse was there, and made the same sort of speech. But now I was prepared and determined to have my say and explain.

I arose and said it was true that many of the children had died at school; but that now everything was fixed up better. We had a good medicine man who knew how to take care of us. He looked after our health, and instructed us in the various kinds of white man's food — what to eat and what to leave alone; dressed us according to the climate and looked after our welfare in general, so that now we were much better prepared to give all the children good attention in every way.

After I had explained all this in a very earnest manner, the Indians began to soften toward me. Finally various ones came up and told me to write down the names of their children, and for quite a time I was kept very busy enlisting them. When I had finished I had more than fifty names. So I was very proud when the time came for me to start back to Carlisle again with all these boys and girls. We reached the school in good season and without anything of note occurring on the way. Captain Pratt was greatly pleased that my efforts had borne such good fruit.

So things progressed. Captain Pratt was always very proud to 'show us off' and let the white people see how we were progressing. Sometimes we were drilled for days before starting out to an invitation for dinner, so that our deportment should all be correct and proper.

I recall one night in particular when we were invited to an entertainment in a big hall. Captain Pratt and some of our teachers were to take part, while several of the pupils had recitations and others were to sing. During the programme, some one in the audience asked Captain Pratt to have one of the Indian boys sing a song in the native tongue. Several of the older boys were thereupon asked to give a song, but they felt too bashful. Then he turned to

me with 'Luther, I wonder if you will sing an Indian song
for us?' So I sang a love-dance song. This pleased the
audience greatly. Finally an old man who looked like
Santa Claus to me, got up and asked to hear some of the
children speak in the Sioux tongue.

Now in school we were not allowed to converse in the
Indian tongue, but here was an old man making a formal
request which Captain Pratt did not wish to refuse. So
he asked several of the boys to speak a few sentences in
the Sioux language, but they all refused. Then he turned
to me again with a request that I say something in my
native tongue. I was never afraid to talk, so I arose and
said, '*Lakota iya woci ci yakapi queyasi oyaka rnirapi kte sni
tka le ha han pe lo*,' which, interpreted into English, means,
'If I talk in Sioux, you will not understand me anyhow.'

But I did not understand exactly how to interpret this
properly at that time, so I was pleased when there was
a clapping of hands, so I could sit down again. Just then
the old man stood up again, and while I was shivering in
my shoes for fear of what he might again ask me, he said,
'Can that boy interpret what he said into English?' I
knew I had to say something, so I replied that it meant,
'We are glad to see you all here to-night.' This seemed
to satisfy the audience, and Captain Pratt also seemed
pleased — but I knew I had told a lie, and that did not
'set' exactly right. However, I smothered my conscience,
for the sake of my school, on that occasion and let it pass.

Shortly after this, my father came to visit the school
again, but this time I did not get as many presents as
before. My oldest sister and two brothers were now in the
school, and Father had to divide the presents among us.
He did not remain very long, as he was simply on his way
to Washington on business. Captain Pratt came to me
and said I was to accompany him as interpreter.

Now I was greatly pleased of the opportunity to visit
Washington, but did not like the idea of acting as inter-

preter, for the reason that I did not think I was well quali-
fied for the work just then, as I did not know very much.
Captain Pratt, however, was quite sure I could fill the bill,
after what I had said in the hall. He said he was going
along with us, and that he would use language which they
would understand in case I got 'stuck.' It pleased me that
he was going to speak to the big men at Washington for my
father, and soon we started.

When we reached that city, my father did not try
to see the Grandfather (or President). He went right to
the Commissioner of Indian Affairs.

'You want us to learn the white man's ways, and be
farmers, do you not?' he asked.

Said the Commissioner, 'Yes, that is why we are trying
to educate your children.'

'Then,' answered my father, 'I am here to ask one favor
of you. The little ponies with which we are trying to do
farm work, are too small for such work, and I want to ask
that you will put one or two big stallions at each agency, so
we can breed some big horses. We will have to have bigger
horses if we are expected to do farm work.'

The Commissioner replied, 'That is a very sensible
speech, Standing Bear. Your people shall have what you
ask for.'

All this conversation was spoken by my father in the
Sioux tongue. Then I repeated it to Captain Pratt in
broken English to the best of my ability, and he interpreted it to the Commissioner.

My father was very proud to think that he could depend
on me for the sake of the whole tribe. I will say that the
breeding stallions were sent to the different agencies, as
promised, and even to-day at each agency there are
breeding stallions furnished by the United States Government.

Whenever my father went to Washington he did not
complain, but in just a few words he would explain what

was wanted for the benefit of the Sioux Nation, or the Indians as a whole. He was always treated very well, and whatever he asked for the authorities knew was just and right. This happened over forty years ago, but the Sioux Nation is yet reaping the benefit of my father's efforts. Other chiefs went there also, but they talked a whole lot, but said nothing; then they came home and also received nothing.

On the occasion of this visit to Washington, and after we had finished all the business my father came for, Captain Pratt said he would take me through the Smithsonian Institution. My father had been through before when in Washington. The man who showed us about talked to Captain Pratt a great deal, but I could not understand all they were saying for some time. But at length Captain Pratt told me to tell my father that the man wanted to make a bust of me as the first Indian boy to enter Carlisle School. He said it would be finished in marble, like many others we had seen in the building.

I explained all this to my father. He was greatly puzzled, and told me to ask the man how it would be done. The man explained that first my face would be greased all over. Then tubes would be put in my nostrils to breathe through, after which plaster of paris would be put all over my face and head, and left there a while to harden. Then it would be broken off very carefully, so as not to spoil the impression of my head.

My father was quite shocked at the idea of my head being covered with plaster of paris to be left on until it hardened; while the idea of my having to breathe through those tubes throughout the process was too much for him! So he said, 'No, it cannot be done.' Captain Pratt felt disappointed at his refusal, as he thought it would be a good thing for the school if there was a bust of me in the Smithsonian Institution; but we did not realize that it might not be appreciated by all at the time.

Now our business in Washington was finished, so Captain Pratt and I started back to Carlisle; but my father went right on through to South Dakota. He had asked for what he wanted, and it had been promised him. Now he was anxious to get home to see if the promise was to be fulfilled.

CHAPTER XVII
THE CARLISLE BAND IN NEW YORK

AT the school we were now beginning to practice our music every day. We were told we were going to New York City to play before thousands of people, and must have our clothes neat and clean, so as to create a good impression. Our bandmaster was very strict with us, making us drill daily.

Finally the day came when we were to leave for New York. The band boys were dressed in their best; several of the girls were to accompany us. We were all ready to start, but at the last minute our bandmaster did not show up. So we went on down to the train, thinking he might meet us there, but he did not appear.

So we boarded the cars and went to Philadelphia, and from there by boat to New York. Here we were lined up in a park. I believe it was City Hall Park. As our bandmaster did not appear, Captain Pratt came to me and asked me if I thought I could lead the band. Then we discovered that we were to play at the opening of the Brooklyn Bridge, and were to march across it. I told him I would try. Poor Captain Pratt was greatly worried and wanted the school represented in the line of march.

We were instructed to keep playing all the way across the bridge. When the parade started I gave the signal, and we struck up and kept playing all the way across the great structure. So the Carlisle Indian band of brass instruments was the first *real American band* to cross the Brooklyn Bridge, and I am proud to say that I was their leader. This was on the 24th of May, 1883.

After that, I played in several of the big churches, notably, the Fifth Avenue Baptist Church. I led with my cornet in the hymn 'Old Hundred.' Then Captain Pratt took me to several other large churches in Philadelphia. It was there that I received my first Holy Communion. This was on an Easter morning in the Episcopal Church, and I was the first Indian boy to be thus honored.

As my three years were now drawing to a close, I began to realize more than ever what the education of the white man would mean to me. Time had slipped by very fast. In many of my vacation trips I had been entertained in some very nice homes. I spent some time in the home of Senator James of Brooklyn. He was a very fine man, and was so good to me. He had a splendid wife and two lovely daughters, and they all tried hard to be good to me; but I could not understand all they were talking about, and it made me feel out of place. The daughters had some pictures taken with me, but those which I took home were destroyed in a fire. Should Senator James or any of his family ever read this little incident, I trust they will write to me — providing they remember the Indian boy who was a guest in their home in Brooklyn.

Captain Pratt was a very hard-working man; he was always busy. But one day he took a notion to go fishing. Quite a little party of us started away from the school. When we reached the stream, we were told to have a good time while Captain Pratt fished. All the boys ran around and played; but I remained near Captain Pratt. He was a very smart man, and I wanted to learn all I could before my stay at the school was up. He always talked on interesting topics, and all this helped me with my English.

Now Captain Pratt had forbidden any of the Indian boys smoking. He said it was 'very bad' for us. He told us how it 'injured the lungs and stomach,' and that smoking was attended with great danger to one's health.

But all at once, while I was loitering a little distance away, I saw the Captain pull a cigar from his pocket, and soon there was a cloud of smoke puffing skyward like a steam engine. He had forbidden us to smoke, as he said it was a very bad habit. I felt that I did not want any one to see him doing anything bad, so I remained away until he had finished his cigar.

When Saturday came and we were all assembled in chapel, it was the custom for any boy or girl who had done anything that was wrong through the week to come forward. On this occasion there were some few small offenders, and as usual there was the report of tobacco smoking among the scholars. Then Captain Pratt had the offenders come up on the platform, while he spoke to them of the dangers of tobacco smoking! And the man who knew so much about the evils of the weed smoked himself!

Some boys would have thought, 'Well, if my teacher smokes, so can I.' But to me the thought of tobacco was very repulsive, as it seemed to be a habit which once formed was not easily put away. I wondered what there was about it which seemed to hold the smoker in its grasp. I could see nothing good in it, and believed my teacher when he said it was very harmful. So right then and there I made up my mind never to touch tobacco, as it was not good for my constitution. And I have never smoked, although I am now fifty-eight years of age.

I considered that I 'had one' on Captain Pratt, but as he had been good enough not to speak of our 'night shirt party' (which we were all sure he had witnessed), I never spoke to him about seeing him smoke, until we were both pretty well along in years. But of this later.

Some time after this incident, the Secretary of the Interior, accompanied by the Commissioner of Indian Affairs, with quite a large party, came to visit the school. As this was getting to be a common sight, we did not pay much attention to them. But shortly after they arrived, all the Sioux scholars were called into the chapel. I would state here that at this time there were between thirty-five and forty different tribes of Indians represented at the school.

When everybody was seated, the Secretary of the Interior, the Honorable Henry M. Teller, got up to talk. He said:

'Now, boys and girls, when we took you away from your homes, we promised your parents that we would send you back to them at the end of three years. The three years are up. How many of you would like to go home right now — hold up your hands?'

Of course all raised their hands, they were so pleased to go. But I did not raise mine. I would like to have done so, but the words of my father seemed to come to me: 'Son, learn all you can of the ways of these Long Knives (white people) as they are so thick in our country.' So I wanted to be brave and stay to please my father.

Mr. Teller observed that I had not raised my hand, so he said, 'I see that one of the boys did not raise his hand. Stand up, boy.'

I did so.

Then he said, 'Don't you want to go home and see your parents and come back again?'

'But I have been home twice since I came here,' was my reply.

This was a somewhat unusual answer, so he turned to Captain Pratt for a possible explanation. Then Captain Pratt told Mr. Teller how I had been home twice on business for the school, and had brought more scholars East.

Mr. Teller then turned to me again.

'So you want to stay here, do you?'

'Yes, sir,' I replied.

Then Robert American Horse said he would also like to stay. This brought others to their feet. Maggie Stands Looking, Frank Twist, Clarence Three Stars, and one other boy I cannot remember. This made five Sioux who wished to remain in the East. Thereupon Mr. Teller remarked.

'Very well; in a few days all the Sioux will be ready to

start for home, excepting these four boys and one girl, who may remain here at the school.'

When the day of departure came, how happy those boys and girls appeared to be at the thought of going home! Of course I wanted to go very much myself, but my father was depending on me to learn everything I could of the white man's ways, and I was determined to be brave and 'stick it out.' Captain Pratt gave us permission to accompany the party as far as Harrisburg, about eighteen miles from the school. I refused to go with the others, as there was a pain in my heart which did not make me feel very well at the thought of remaining behind in the East.

When all the others had left, there I was — the only Sioux among a thousand scholars from between thirty-five and forty different tribes from all over the United States! It seemed to me that everybody noticed me, and when I entered the dining-room that noon, I felt as if all eyes were upon me.

When everybody was seated, Captain Pratt asked me to stand up. He then complimented me on my bravery in remaining to learn more. I was only a little boy of fourteen at the time, and this talk, together with the eyes of everybody fastened upon me, made me feel a little shaky at the knees. However, later in the day, after the others of my tribe had returned from Harrisburg, I felt better.

Now there was one thing I really wanted, and that was to have all my time in school, instead of working as a tinsmith half the day. I could not see that that trade was going to benefit me any, as the Government was already giving the Indians all the tinware they wanted. But Captain Pratt said that a trade was a good thing for a boy to learn. Then I asked if I could not go into the carpenter shop and learn that trade, in preference to that of a tinsmith. But Captain Pratt did not agree with me. I had made the big round tin ball for the top of the flag pole, and the people from Washington had seen the folding cups and other things I had made, and my work was considered good. However, what worried me was the thought that I might not be able to work at the trade after I returned home. But Captain Pratt could not understand why I wanted to make a change, and so the matter was dropped.

CHAPTER XVIII

AT WORK FOR WANAMAKER

Sometime later in the year we were all called into the chapel one Saturday evening. We supposed it was just for the usual prayer meeting at which Captain Pratt and our teachers always gave brief talks for our good. On this particular evening, Captain Pratt said:

'Now, boys and girls, you all know we have sent many of you out on farms for your vacation. You have all done very well; but now I have a request of a very different sort, for work which you have not before attempted. A man who owns one of the largest department stores in this country has sent me word that he wants two Indian boys to work in the store as clerks. We must send two of the best boys in the school. I am going to ask the teachers to help me select these two boys who will represent this school in John Wanamaker's immense Philadelphia store. Next Saturday about this time, we will be ready to tell you what boys are the ones chosen.'

Of course we were all excited, and everybody was wondering who these two boys would be. Who were the two best boys in Carlisle School? Who was good enough to work in such a large store as John Wanamaker's?

Among the boys there was considerable discussion over the question. Some of them suggested that we make bets as to who would be the winners. I had about fourteen cents in my pocket, so I bet this sum on a half-breed Creek Indian boy named Robert Stuart, a young man who was very well educated; in fact, he was one of the boys who had been brought up from the South before the Sioux boys and girls came to the school. He was the sergeant major in charge of the boys, so I thought it was 'sure money' to bet on him.

Saturday came at last, and we went into the chapel, a very excited crowd. I was positive of winning the fourteen cents, as I felt that Robert Stuart was the one best fitted for a clerkship in the store.

After the usual prayer meeting was over, Captain Pratt stood up on the platform.

'Boys and girls,' he said, 'I know you are all anxious as to which two boys are going to work in Mr. Wanamaker's store. I am sorry to say we have selected only one. Of course I want you to see this boy, so I will ask him to come up on the platform here so you can all get a look at him.'

He stopped talking and stood still for some seconds. Finally he said, 'Luther Standing Bear, please come forward.'

I was sitting pretty well back in the chapel. As I arose everybody turned to look at me. It seemed as if I was walking on air. My feet did not seem to touch the floor!

When I reached the platform and faced the audience, all clapped their hands. I braced up and tried to stand like a soldier as we had been taught. Captain Pratt put his hand on my shoulder and continued:

'My boy, you are going away from us to work for this school, in fact, for your whole race. Go, and do your best. The majority of white people think the Indian is a lazy good-for-nothing. They think he can neither work nor learn anything; that he is very dirty. Now you are going to prove that the red man *can* learn and work as well as the white man. If John Wanamaker gives you the job of blacking his shoes, see that you make them shine. Then he will give you a better job. If you are put into the office to clean, don't forget to sweep under the chairs and in the corners. If you do well in this, he will give you better work to do.'

All this time I was standing like a statue, my mind working pretty fast. Then Captain Pratt continued:

'Now, my boy, you are going to do your best. If you are a failure, then we might as well close up this school. You are to be an example of what this school can turn out. Go, my boy, and do your best. Die there if necessary, but do not fail.'

If I had been asked to make a speech, it would have been impossible to respond. I felt as if I should burst out crying. I was not so brave that night, after all. If I had not cared for my race, all the strong impressions would have had no effect upon me, but the thought of working for my race brought the tears to my eyes. You must remember that I was just a small boy at that time.

After Captain Pratt had finished, he asked all the school to say a silent prayer that I would not fail my people.

As we came out of the chapel and started back to our quarters, everybody was talking about my having received the appointment. Some were pleased, while others were very jealous of my good fortune. It did not dawn upon them that this meant very hard work for me to try and lift up a race of people before another race that had tried to hold us down.

The boys who had made bets were now busy paying each other off; but the thought of my losing that fourteen cents did not bother me in the least. My whole mind was full of the words Captain Pratt had spoken to me before more than a thousand pupils in the chapel. I went to my room and to bed, but sleep did not come very quickly. I prayed that I would be able to fulfill all the hopes of my school and race, and that it would please my father. Then I finally fell asleep.

Not an hour passed in the succeeding days that my mind was not dwelling on the thoughts of going to work in a big store. I was to prove to all people that the Indians could learn and work as well as the white people; to prove that Carlisle School was the best place for the Indian boy. Every thought that passed through my mind seemed to end in that expression of Captain Pratt's: 'To die there if necessary.'

About three days later, Captain Pratt sent for me to come to his office. 'Luther,' said he, 'we have been trying to decide on a boy to go with you, but we are unable to agree on one. Have you any friend or relative here whom you would like to be your companion in the city? You will be alone there, so it will be better if a boy who is agreeable to you goes along.'

I was told that I could choose my companion, so after leaving the office I began to look around to decide which boy I preferred. There was one from Pine Ridge named Clarence Three Stars who had a little trouble when he first came to the school, but was now trying hard to do his best. He was one of the boys who had remained over his allotted time to get more education. He and I were distantly related, but he was from Pine Ridge and I was from Rosebud. So I decided to ask this boy if he cared to go with me to Philadelphia.

I located him and told him that Captain Pratt had asked me to choose a companion to go along. 'Do you think you would like to go?' I inquired.

'Why, yes, I will go with you, Luther,' he said at once.

'But I don't want your answer right off,' I insisted. 'I want you to think it over. I will wait until this evening for your answer.'

That evening we met again and I asked him if he still thought he would like to go with me.

'Why, yes, I am going,' he replied.

So I reported to Captain Pratt that I had decided on Clarence Three Stars. He was pleased that I had made a selection. The news traveled through the school, and it was quickly learned that Clarence was to accompany me.

Finally the day came when we were to leave. I have often thought since that probably Captain Pratt had an idea that the only thing we could do well was to black shoes and sweep the floors; but I was determined that there should be something better in store than that.

My Sunday-School teacher, Mrs. Eggee, and the school physician, Dr. Givens, were to accompany us. Captain Pratt's last instructions were, 'If the manager asks you what you can do, tell him you are willing to try anything.' So we shook hands and parted.

My Sunday-School teacher sat beside me on the train and talked to me all the way to Philadelphia, encouraging me as much as she could. When we reached the city, we got off the cars and walked through the City Hall. On the east side of it stood John Wanamaker's great department store. It certainly looked big to us then!

Dr. Givens, Mrs. Eggee, Clarence Three Stars, and I entered the store, and inquired for the manager. We were directed to an office, where we were introduced by Dr. Givens to Mr. William Wanamaker, brother of Mr. John Wanamaker.

He shook hands with us. Then he turned to me and asked, 'My boy, what can I do for you?' I told him I was there to work, and was willing to try anything. Mr. Wanamaker tapped a bell and a boy answered. 'Ask Mr. Walker to come here,' said Mr. Wanamaker.

Mr. Walker shortly appeared and I was introduced to him. Said Mr. Wanamaker: 'Mr. Walker, take Luther Standing Bear to your department and put him to work.' So I said good-bye to my kind friends and followed Mr. Walker down to the basement.

Here I was turned over to a Mr. Pier, who was at the head of the invoice department. This was where I was to make my start. Mr. Pier was a very fine man, and I thought that working under him would be a pleasure.

Mr. Pier explained that I was to check off the goods as he called them off to me. Other men opened up large cases of goods and passed them to Mr. Pier. He would examine the contents of the boxes and show me the bills required for each, so that each bill could be checked off and the goods accounted for. It was quite necessary to be quick and accurate at this work. All day long boxes were coming down to this department, which had to be opened and the contents checked off. All the goods which came into the store had to pass through our hands first, the contents labeled with the cost price and selling price. I liked this work right from the start, as it was all very interesting to me.

I was so interested that I never thought about where I was to stay that night. But unknown to me, Dr. Givens had been hustling around to find me a boarding-place, and before quitting time, he came back and said he had found me a place to stay. It was a large boarding-school of soldiers' orphan boys, of which a Mrs. Cox was superintendent.

Here Clarence Three Stars and I were to board with white boys. A big wagon left the school every morning, carrying several of the boys who worked out. We were invited to ride with them. After the first few mornings however, I preferred to ride in the street cars, rather than listen to the rough, profane language which these boys used on their way to work. And these boys were supposed to be civilized, having had good teachers and good education, yet they used the vilest of language, to which I did not care to listen.

I liked my work and was getting along splendidly, but the language to which I had to listen used by some of the men in the basement was not to my liking. If one of them happened to hit his thumb with a hammer, how he would swear! And in those days bad language was not nearly so common as to-day.

Finally Clarence Three Stars began to worry. So one day I asked him what was the matter. He then told me he did not like his work. He had been put on the first floor. Said he:

'Luther, my work is not to my liking. I have to go through all the different departments collecting goods that are to be shipped out. I have to take them to the shipping department, and as I go behind the counters the clerks all call me "Indian," and I don't like it; it makes me nervous.'

'Well,' I replied, 'you are an Indian, aren't you?'

'Yes,' he said, 'but just the same, I don't like my job, and I am going to write to Captain Pratt to take me back into the school.'

'Don't do that!' I exclaimed. 'You know how he talked to us. You said you were willing to come to the city with me.'

'Well, I don't like this job, anyway,' Clarence retorted. 'If I can work in some other department I might stay, but I am going to write to Captain Pratt.'

He did write to Captain Pratt, who answered that he had better stay where he was and do his best — that he did not want Clarence to return to the school.

Clarence read the letter to me, then he said, 'Well, as long as Captain Pratt doesn't want me at the school, I will go back to the reservation.'

I did my best to persuade him to stay, but all to no use. He was determined to quit, regardless of the reputation of the school or the race we belonged to. So one day Clarence packed up and started for home, never even stopping off at Carlisle to say good-bye. And Captain Pratt never knew Clarence had left Wanamaker's store until he reached the reservation, when he was notified by letter.

With Clarence gone, I was more determined than ever to stay and make good. I worked all the harder, just to let them know that not all Indians are quitters. I learned fast, and did so well that finally Mr. Wanamaker gave me a better job. One day I was called up to the first floor where a little glass house was built. Mr. Walker took me inside. There were several large trunks there. Inside the trunks was considerable valuable jewelry. Mr. Walker instructed me that my new work was to put price tags on all this jewelry.

So every day I was locked inside this little glass house, opening the trunks, taking out the jewels and putting price tags on them. How the white folks did crowd around to watch me! They were greatly surprised to discover that John Wanamaker could trust an Indian boy with such valuables. At that time the white people seemed to have an idea that an Indian would steal anything he could get hands on — and some people yet have that opinion! I did so well at this work that soon I was given a better job with more pay.

I was placed in the bookkeeping department as an entry clerk. I did not like this office work so well, as I was put to work between a couple of young girls, and I felt very much embarrassed. I imagined all the time that they were talking about me behind my back. I wondered if they thought I carried a scalping-knife or a tomahawk in my clothes.

About this time the whole Carlisle School made a visit to Philadelphia. A meeting was held in a large hall, and Captain Pratt spoke of the work of the school, and how well all the Indian boys and girls were doing. Then John Wanamaker had me come up on the stage. He told the audience I was working for him and that I was a Carlisle boy. He stated that I had been promoted from one department to another, every month getting better work and more money, and that in spite of the fact that he employed as many as a thousand people in his establishment, he had never promoted any one as rapidly as he had me. That brought considerable applause, and Captain Pratt was very proud of me.

One evening while going home from work, I bought a paper, and read that Sitting Bull, the great Sioux medicine man, was to appear at one of the Philadelphia theaters. The paper stated that he was the Indian who killed Gen-

eral Custer! The chief and his people had been held prisoners of war, and now here they were to appear in a Philadelphia theater. So I determined to go and see what he
had to say, and what he was really in the East for.

I had to pay fifty cents for a ticket. The theater was
decorated with many Indian trappings such as were used
by the Sioux tribe of which I was a member.

On the stage sat four Indian men, one of whom was
Sitting Bull. There were two women and two children
with them. A white man came on the stage and introduced
Sitting Bull as the man who had killed General Custer
(which, of course, was absolutely false). Sitting Bull arose
and addressed the audience in the Sioux tongue, as he did
not speak nor understand English. He said, 'My friends,
white people, we Indians are on our way to Washington
to see the Grandfather, or President of the United States.
I see so many white people and what they are doing, that
it makes me glad to know that some day my children will
be educated also. There is no use fighting any longer. The
buffalo are all gone, as well as the rest of the game. Now
I am going to shake the hand of the Great Father at Washington, and I am going to tell him all these things.' Then
Sitting Bull sat down. He never even mentioned General
Custer's name.

Then the white man who had introduced Sitting Bull
arose again and said he would interpret what the chief had
said. He then started in telling the audience all about the
battle of the Little Big Horn, generally spoken of as the
'Custer massacre.' He mentioned how the Sioux were all
prepared for battle, and how they had swooped down on
Custer and wiped his soldiers all out. He told so many lies
that I had to smile. One of the women on the stage observed me and said something to the other woman, then
both of them kept looking at me.

Then the white man said that all those who wished to
shake hands with Sitting Bull would please line up if they

cared to meet the man who had killed Custer. The whole audience got in line, as they really believed what the white man had told them. It made me wonder what sort of people the whites were, anyway. Perhaps they were glad to have Custer killed, and were really pleased to shake hands with the man who had killed him!

I lined up with the others and started for the stage, not intending to say a word. But the woman who had first noticed me smiling from my seat, watched me all the closer as I came toward them. She grabbed me by the hand, not knowing exactly what to say and not knowing if I were really an Indian boy.

Finally she spoke in Sioux as follows: 'Niye osni tona leci,' which meant, 'How many colds (or winters) are you here?' I replied in Sioux, 'In winter we have so many cold days here that I do not know really how many colds I have been here.'

That sort of broke the ice, and she laughed, then the other Indians laughed. Then she asked me who my father was. I replied, 'Standing Bear of Rosebud is my father.' 'Why,' she exclaimed, 'then you are my nephew.' Then she called her brother, who was Sitting Bull, 'See who is here.' He was pleased to see me again.

Of course this caused some excitement among the crowd of white people. I had been working in the store so long that I had become lighter in complexion. All the Indians then crowded about me, forgetting all about shaking hands with the crowd of white people, who could not understand it. The white man who had spoken on the stage now came up to see what was the matter and why the Indians had suddenly left off shaking hands with the others. Sitting Bull beckoned him to come up, then he turned to me and said, 'Tell this white man we want you to go to our hotel with us to eat.'

So I interpreted what Sitting Bull requested, and the man said, 'Why, yes, you can come with them.' Then the

Indians packed up their things which decorated the hall
and were very anxious to get back to the hotel where
they could have a talk with some one who understood
them.

When we reached the hotel, Sitting Bull said to me that
he was on his way to Washington to shake hands with the
President, and that he wanted his children educated in
the white man's way, because there was nothing left for
the Indian.

He then asked me how far it was to Washington, and
in what direction it was. I told him that it was toward the
sunset, and that he was now in Philadelphia, a long way
east of Washington. Sitting Bull expressed much surprise,
saying, 'Why, we must have passed the place.' Then I
told him he certainly had.

Then the white man entered the room, and Sitting Bull
said to me again, 'Ask this white man when we are going to
see the President, and when we are going home.' The man
said to tell him, 'You are soon going home, and on the way
you may see the President.' As the man remained in the
room, I did not get a chance to tell Sitting Bull how the
white man had lied about him on the stage. And that was
the last time I ever saw Sitting Bull alive.

As I sit and think about that incident, I wonder who
that crooked white man was, and what sort of Indian
agent it could have been who would let these Indians
leave the reservation without even an interpreter, giving
them the idea they were going to Washington, and then
cart them around to different Eastern cities to make
money off them by advertising that Sitting Bull was the
Indian who slew General Custer! Of course at that time
I was too young to realize the seriousness of it all.

A few weeks after this incident a show came to Phila-
delphia having with them a few Sioux Indians. Of course
I went to see them. The name of one of the men was
Standing Elk. They had their wives and a couple of

children along with them. These Indians had no interpreter either. They were shown in a little side-show,
on a small stage. I stood there for a long time, but they
did not notice me. The children had a little box down
in front of the stage into which people would drop coins.
Then the children would shake hands with them.

There was a rope stretched across in front of the stage,
and finally I raised this rope and started for the platform.
One of the Indians remarked to another, 'Look at this
white boy coming up here.' I walked up and started to
shake hands with all of them. I suppose they thought I
was some crazy white boy who wanted to be noticed —
at least they talked that way. Then I started talking in
Sioux to them. I said, 'I recognize all you people, even
though you do not recognize me. You are all from Rosebud Agency, where I belong.'

Then one of the women exclaimed, 'Why, this is Standing Bear's boy.' And then they were so glad to see me!
They just grabbed me and held on to me, as Sitting Bull's
people had. Old Standing Elk was very sick, and he
wanted me to tell the white show manager that he wanted
to go home.

The man replied that they were all going back to the
reservation just as soon as they were through showing in
Philadelphia. That was the last time I saw Standing Elk
alive, and I was the last of our tribe to talk to him. The
next day he was so much worse that they took him to a
hospital instead of starting him home. The show went on
to New York. Nothing was ever again seen of Standing
Elk. To this day nobody knows what became of him.
His death was never reported; the hospital to which he was
taken was never located by his relatives, and his poor old
wife had to go home alone.

To get back to my work in the Wanamaker store: The
girl who worked next to me soon left her job to teach in an
educational school. Every Sunday we went out together,

and she would read to me. I thought a great deal of her, but I did not say anything to her about it.

One day Mrs. Cox, the superintendent of the boarding-school, sent for me to come to her office. A Mr. Louis was there with her. They asked me if I did not think it a good idea to get some Indian boys from the reservation and put them in school with the white boys, expecting that the Indian boys would learn faster by such an association. I agreed that it might be a good plan, so Mr. Louis went to Washington and got a permit to go to an Indian reservation for some children.

He went to Pine Ridge and brought back about sixty boys. Then at the school they discharged all but sixty of the white boys, leaving an equal number of both red and white. They had hoped the Indians would learn the English language faster by this arrangement. But lo and behold! the white boys began to learn the Sioux language! So they discharged all the white boys and kept the Indians.

Vacation time was coming and they were going to close the boarding-school for the summer, so I wrote to Captain Pratt about it. He answered that I could come back to Carlisle for the summer if I wished. But I wanted to continue with my work at the store, as I was interested in it. I wrote Captain Pratt that if I could locate a good boarding-place I would remain in Philadelphia. I tried very hard to find a suitable place, but when I would find something that seemed suitable, and the people discovered my nationality, they would look at me in a surprised sort of way, and say that they had no place for an Indian boy.

Finally I went to Mr. William Wanamaker with my trouble and told him of the difficulty I had to find a decent place to board. I told him I would have to go back to Carlisle. He said if that was my determination I could come back to the store any time I wanted to. So I prepared to return to Carlisle.

But when I got back to Carlisle, it was during vacation

time, and most of the students had gone out to work. There was no school and there were no studies. This was not the life I desired, and I became lonesome. Finally I told Captain Pratt I wanted to go home to my people. He objected.

'No, Luther,' he said, 'I want you to stay here. When school is open again, you may go to school a whole day instead of a half day, or you can take care of the wardrobe half a day if you prefer.'

But I said: 'No, I want to go home, but I want to go in the right way. Several of the boys have run away from you, but I do not want to do that.'

'All right,' said Captain Pratt. 'You may go, but I want you to promise that you will come back.

I answered that if I cared to come back I would do so.

Captain Pratt wrote a letter to the agent at Rosebud Agency. Then he gave me money for my ticket and five dollars extra for meals. I had some money of my own in addition.

So I said farewell to the school life and started back to my people, but with a better understanding of life. There would be no more hunting—we would have to work now for our food and clothing. It was like the Garden of Eden after the fall of man.

CHAPTER XIX

BACK TO DAKOTA: TEACHING AND MARRIAGE

MY trip was very lonesome, as I was all alone. When the train reached Valentine, Nebraska, my father was waiting at the depot for me. My only baggage was just a suitcase. It was early morning when I arrived, so we went to a lunch counter; but I was now too happy to eat much. I was home again!

My father had a team of pretty spotted ponies and a nice buggy, and I certainly did enjoy that morning ride. Our reservation was about thirty miles away, and there was a halfway house at White Lake. All along the road everything looked so beautiful to me — the flowers, the singing birds, the herds of cattle and horses.

At the halfway house we unhitched the team and ate some lunch. We rested about an hour and then resumed our journey. At last we came in sight of the agency. All our relatives had heard that I was coming home, and there was quite a gathering at my father's place to greet me. Some of them were very glad to see me; others hesitated about shaking my hand. I found out later the reason for this. It seems that some of the returned Carlisle students were ashamed of their old people and refused to shake hands with them; some even tried to make them believe they had forgotten the Sioux language.

All that evening I was busy telling my people all they wanted to know. I heard several of them remark that I looked more like a white boy, because my skin had become lighter from my work inside. It made me feel very proud to have them compare me to a white boy. The clothes I wore were the latest style at that time, and I felt quite 'swell' in them. But I have to laugh now at my appearance. I looked like one of these Jew comedians on the stage. I wore a black suit with a cutaway coat which had quite a tail, a small derby hat, a standing collar, and my cuffs stuck out about half an inch below my coat sleeves, and I had on one of those 'dirty-shirt hiders' known as a necktie at that time. All I lacked to resemble Charlie Chaplin was a cane.

My stepmothers had a very nice room fixed up for me. Father had observed how nice and clean our rooms were at the school and had tried to fix things like that. The following day I had intended to go and see my own mother. I spoke to my father about it, and then came the saddest news a boy can hear — my mother had passed away while I was in the East. My father had not informed me because he was afraid I would worry myself sick.

When I awoke the following morning there was no school discipline to follow out — nobody to tell me when to get up; I had no cornet to blow to arouse others. I felt that I was at last free. After I had eaten my breakfast, I thought of the letter Captain Pratt had given me to the agent, so I started for the agency.

The agent's name was Wright. I handed him the letter, and after reading it he said, 'All right, my boy, you can come back to work to-morrow. My daughter, Nellie Wright, is teaching here, and you will be her assistant.' I thanked him and went home.

Miss Wright was a very fine young lady, and was trying hard to keep up the education of the returned students; but we did not know very much. So she started a night school at the agency, but it did not last long. After working all day, few of us cared to study at night, so the night school plan was finally abandoned.

It was about 1884 that I started teaching school at the agency. At that time, teaching amounted to very little. It really did not require a well-educated person to teach on the reservation. The main thing was to teach the children to write their names in English, then came learning the alphabet and how to count. I liked this work very well, and the children were doing splendidly. The first reading books we used had a great many little pictures in them. I would have the children read a line of English, and if they did not understand all they had read, I would explain it to them in Sioux. This made the studies very interesting.

One day the agent sent for me to come to his office. A young white woman was there. The agent introduced us, and then told me she was going to teach at High Hawk's camp, located at a place called Cut Meat Creek. He said that as the young woman was going out there all alone, he wished I would accompany her, and stay about a week until she became accustomed to the Indians.

So the following day the Government team took us out to Cut Meat Creek, about twelve miles from the agency. We found there a little one-room schoolhouse, and there was a three-room house provided for the teacher's use. While this young woman was smart enough in books, she knew very little else. I really felt sorry for her, because she did not even know how to keep house.

At that time the Government furnished the Indians ginghams by the bolt, and the teacher was supposed to show the Indian girls how to make their own clothes. She was also expected to teach the Indian mothers how to keep house properly.

But this is the method she used in making the first dresses for the girls: The girl would stoop over; then the teacher would roll the whole bolt of gingham over her head, and with a piece of chalk mark the outlines of the girl's body, after which the goods were cut out. When the dress was finished, it was a most peculiar piece of dress-making.

When my week was up, I returned to the agency, but did not say anything about the clothes the teacher was making, or the slovenly manner in which she kept house. We Indians wondered how the whites taught their girls only through books. What would they do if left alone? How would they be able to cook for a family? Book learning is very good, of course, but it strikes me that domestic science is the best thing for all girls to adopt, regardless of wealth or position in life.

A great many peculiar and amusing experiences happened to me while I was teaching school and staying around the agency. My father was a gentleman, even though an Indian, and he was one of the chiefs of the Rosebud Agency. He was considered 'well fixed,' as he owned so many spotted horses. As I was his eldest son, had been educated, and was now at home working, the girls liked to be with me and did not seem to mind it that I gave my father my pay check every month. Nowadays a young man has to spend plenty of money on a young lady, although the girl may not know in what manner he earns it. So it happened that if one girl did not care to go with me, there were plenty of others who did.

My father saved some of the money from my check every month, and kept house on the balance. I do not know how much he spent, and I never asked, because he knew how to handle money, and I was not afraid to trust him.

One evening when I returned home from school, my father told me the 'black-dress man' (Catholic priest) wanted to sell his house, which stood about fifty yards from the dwelling the Government had erected for Chief Spotted Tail. My father thought it would be a good buy, and specified the amount which the priest asked for it; so I told him to buy it. He made the purchase in part cash and the balance in spotted horses and cattle.

The priest who had been occupying it then packed up all his belongings and moved away. My family now were very anxious to move into their first real 'white man's house.' There was no lack of helpers in moving into our new home. My father bought a nice new table, which was to be for me.

He had observed how the white people ate while visiting me at Carlisle, and he wanted me to have the same benefits at home. He told my stepmothers, my brothers and sisters how a table should be set. That evening when I returned from school, there was the nice table all ready for me. There was no cloth on it, but my little sisters, with their Indian dresses on, were hustling and bustling hither and thither to wait on their educated brother. They meant to treat me like a real white man.

My little sister pulled out the chair for me to sit down, and there was a knife, fork, and spoon, with all the necessary dishes, but no napkin or finger bowl. After I had been helped, then my father, his two wives, and all the children sat down on the floor to eat their own meal. My sister Victoria was still at Carlisle School, so I had to eat alone at the table.

As I was teaching school I tried to keep myself neat and clean. Indian children are about like their white brothers and sisters — they watch their teacher as an example for them to follow. My stepmother washed my clothes, but she did not know anything about ironing. In those days we did not have the soft collars and shirts such as are now worn. Whenever I desired to 'dress up,' I had to buy a new stiff-front shirt and collar, with stiff cuffs. By wearing the shirt only on Sunday I was able to keep it fairly clean for a whole month. When the shirt looked soiled, my stepmother would wash it; but the collars always had to be thrown away.

When my people began to observe me making friends among the girls, they began to feel anxious about my future welfare. They wanted me to marry in the right way, but, as I had been educated, they could not just figure out what was the right way in my case.

While I was at Carlisle I often had heard the white boys tell about going to call on the girls at their homes. But this was something which the Indian boy was not ac-

customed to do. It was not the Indian way to go and call
on a girl at her home. When an Indian girl was considered
old enough to have callers, none would enter the house or
tipi. All young men who desired to talk to her would come
to her tipi in the evening and wait patiently for her to
come outside. The girls were not at all bold at that time,
and often would not come out at all. The young men who
came to call would all have their heads covered with a
blanket, and would wait in line for an opportunity to talk
to her.

If a girl's mother did not care to have her daughter
marry while very young, she would be very careful of her,
accompanying her on her evening walks so the girl would
not be alone. One woman on our reservation raised several
mean dogs by which she kept all the suitors for her daughter's hand at a distance. Very few of us tried to call on
this girl. But if a head of a family knew that a young man's
character was good, and that he was capable of caring for
a wife, he would encourage the match and do all he could
to win over the young man for a son-in-law.

Some of my 'love-making experiences' in my people's
way may prove amusing to the reader. One evening while
our family was at supper, my father began telling his
wives about meeting an Indian named Yellow Hair, and
the conversation they had carried on. Yellow Hair was a
distant relative of ours. While at the general store one day
he overheard an Indian make a remark about me as I
passed. The man had exclaimed, 'There goes Ota Kte,
the son of Standing Bear; he is going to buy my daughter.'

Let me explain that this remark would be construed
differently by the white people. According to the Indian
custom it merely meant that I was going to give several
presents to the young woman's people to curry their favor,
so I might be able to ask the girl to marry me.

I was sitting at the table eating my supper during this
conversation. My father asked me if it were true, and if I

knew the girl. I replied that I did not know her, and had never even seen her that I could recall. However, this talk aroused my curiosity to such a pitch that I determined to go and see what the girl looked like. So one evening I got into a pair of moccasins, pulled a blanket over my head, and started out to call on the girl.

When I reached her tipi there were several young men already ahead of me. She would not even answer some of them, and these would simply move on and make room for the next. When it came my chance, I spoke to the girl in the Sioux tongue, and she tried to pull off my blanket to see who it was, not being able to recognize me by my walk or my moccasins.

She tried several times to pull the blanket away, saying, 'Who are you?' But I held on to the blanket. All at once I let loose and the blanket fell to my shoulders, revealing my short hair and civilian clothes. The girl was greatly astonished by her discovery, imagining me to be one of the young men with long hair, and not an educated Indian.

Then I told her about the reports which were being circulated about us, and asked her if it were true, and if her father had said that I was to buy her. She replied that both her parents had wished me for a son-in-law, and that if I would give some horses to her brother, we would be married. But I replied that I was a poor boy, and that although my father owned many horses, they were not mine, and that I was not in a position to buy horses, and would not borrow from my people.

This girl was a beautiful Indian maiden, and when I told her all these things she looked sad. I was very sorry to have hurt her feelings, but I could do nothing else under the circumstances but tell her the truth. I was in no position to get married. This was the first time I had ever seen the girl, and I was doing only what my education had taught me as the proper thing to do.

There was another girl who lived near our home, who also interested me very much, and I determined to talk to her alone. I knew, of course, that it was not the Indian custom to visit at the house. So one day, when I observed her going out a certain road, I took a short cut and came into the path some distance ahead of her. She did not see me. This girl had been among the whites, although she had received no school education.

There was a beautiful stream of water close at hand, and she went down to the bank and began to disrobe. She removed her outer skirt, and about that time I concluded it was 'no place for me,' and left. But to this day that girl does not know that I saw her in her underskirt. However, I suddenly lost all interest in her, for I had seen enough to convince me that she wore an underskirt that was far from clean. It was one of the requirements of my life that my associates and family must be neat and clean. Perfumes and fancy powders do not make up for lack of cleanliness.

Being the son of a chief made me quite popular. I worked steadily and had a good reputation — which counted just as much in those days as it does to-day. My own people had known me from a little boy. The whites knew me as a young man who had returned from school and had worked hard ever since. So all the young women of our tribe were very nice to me.

Many of the Indian people wanted me for a son-in-law, but knowing I had received a white man's education, they were shy about asking me.

About this time one of my boy friends from the school, Julian Whistler, came to visit me. He liked my home, so he decided to stay. We were very happy together. We would go out and meet the girls, just as the white boys did, and then return home. I had determined not to marry for a long time to come. But my plans were not kept.

There was a half-breed girl in the camp of whom I began to be very fond. We took many long walks together.

She was very gentle and quiet. Her name was Nellie De Cory. Her mother was a full-blood Indian woman, who could neither read nor write. Her father was a full-blood white man who had come to South Dakota in the early days and married this Indian woman. He was one of the men who gathered up all the things the Indians threw away, not realizing their value. But De Cory did, and he sold them, and in that way made considerable money. He was called one of the wealthiest men on the reservation — also one of the stingiest. He had quite a family of children.

The mother had brought up her children as 'white' as she knew how. She felt that she was a white woman, inasmuch as her husband was a white man. She held herself above us very much. Her children were not trained in the Indian way, for she had tried to follow her husband's teachings and bring them up on the white man's road.

One day when I was out in the field watching some cattle, I saw a man coming toward me in a carriage. It proved to be my father. He had come out to have a talk alone with me about this half-breed girl. He said he had observed that I appeared to be very much in love with her, and he thought it was time we were getting married. He said that he and his two wives would move out of the house, and that it should be my home. It had been purchased with my money from the missionaries, along with some horses and cattle of Father's but he told me that he was going to give me his share in the house as a wedding present.

I got into the carriage with my father and went home to dress for the occasion. We then went to Nellie's house together, where I asked her to come with me to the minister's and be married. Her mother was not at all pleased, but her father was, although he did not exhibit any particular demonstration of joy. In fact, he did not even give us a wedding present.

Nellie and I then packed up all the things she had and brought them to our home. Among these was a doll trunk and a great many toys, instead of the things an Indian girl would have naturally brought. My people had moved out, so we were alone for the afternoon and evening. We managed somehow to get our meals that day, and later, my wife retired for the night. While I was sitting and musing on how my plans had been so suddenly changed, I heard footsteps outside. Suddenly the door opened, and in came the two wives of Chief Spotted Tail, with their daughter Grace.

These two women were sisters. The one who was the girl's mother told me she had brought her daughter Grace to me for a wife! She said she had known me from the time I was a little boy, and knew I would take good care of her daughter. She thought I was deserving of another wife who was a full-blood Indian. She said she was afraid that the girl I had married, and who had been brought up as a white girl, would not know how to cook my meals in the proper manner.

Well, here was an embarrassing situation. After they had both talked, I told them it was impossible for me to take more than one wife at a time, as it was against the laws of the Government, and, further, was against my teachings. But they were so determined that I should be well taken care of that they got up and went out, leaving the girl behind.

My wife, from her room, had overheard all the conversation, but she kept quiet. I had removed one of my shoes just before the trio came in, so I had to put it on again. I then determined to walk over to the agent's house and acquaint him with my difficulties. After some little talk with him, he advised me to go see the chief of police among the Indians. So I walked about a mile to the home of the chief of the Indian police. He had already retired, but got up and listened to my 'tale of woe.' He decided to go back home with me. When we arrived, there sat Grace just as I had left her, and my wife was still in her own room. The chief of police took Grace away to her parents, and we were then left alone.

The following day my father brought me a few horses as a present. Then my father-in-law came. He lived on Antelope Creek, east of the agency about eleven miles. All he brought with him was a mail-order catalogue. He gave this to my wife and told her to pick out just what she wanted. So she selected some household goods. He paid for them and they all arrived in due time.

Then the agent gave me just what I wanted. This was a cast-iron stove for heating and cooking purposes, as well as a new bed, dresser, chairs, table, and other things for the house. He even gave me a spring wagon and a set of harness, and on top of all, he paid me a month's salary in advance!

As soon as the traders discovered that I had been married, they all came to me and said I could purchase anything I wanted from them on credit. But I did not have to take advantage of buying anything 'on time,' so when Nellie and I started housekeeping we were clear of debt. Of course I did appreciate the kindness of the traders.

When Grace Spotted Tail's brother heard that I had refused to take his sister for a second wife, he was quite indignant about it. He felt that I had insulted his sister, and he was out for revenge. But I was not afraid of him. He knew that my work at the agency kept me in touch with the police, so he did not molest me to my face. But he talked about it behind my back in such a way that it reached my father, even saying that he was going to take some horses away from my father because I had refused to marry his sister!

Father was then about forty-eight years of age, and he did not want to fight his own people. He was beginning to study the Christian religion, and he wanted to live a good life. He had some very fine horses, and everybody knew them. He came down to visit me, and told me what Spotted Tail's son had said. He said to me, 'Don't worry, Luther; I will give him a few horses and his temper will cool off.' But I protested against such a move. I told my father not to give him any horses; that I would take care of myself if he tried to make me any trouble. My father then went home, seemingly well pleased, and we never had any more trouble with Spotted Tail's son. But in after years I learned that my father had really given him a few head of horses to save me from any trouble.

Old Peter De Cory, my father-in-law, was very good to me. He came to the house one day with his wagon loaded with all kinds of food and greases, such as we used in making Indian fried bread. One whole hog was killed and dressed for us, and we were very busy getting it in shape so it would not spoil.

A few weeks later he invited my wife and me to his place, and we visited her people for the first time. Before we started back to our own home, her father rounded up all his cattle, and gave us five head of cows to start with. Then he picked out a very fine team of matched horses and two mares, which he also presented us with. We must have resembled a traveling show on our way back home, driving our own buggy and trying to keep the team of horses, two mares, and five cows all together!

For a young couple, we had all we wanted. In addition to these presents, we were drawing rations from the Government at that time. These included one whole beef every two weeks for each household. It made no difference whether there was one person in a household or a dozen — the order held good just the same.

All this taught me that it paid to be kind and gentle to all people at all times, and in all my life, wherever I have been, I have always made friends, and have always got along with any race of people who knew me.

During 1887, my first child was born. I was then only nineteen years of age. What preparations were made in advance for this baby! My two stepmothers and my mother-in-law all were there. We had no doctors or physicians at that time. The old ladies had a beautiful 'postan,' or Indian cradle, all ready for the baby, and when the momentous time arrived, they sent me out of the house.

My father was with me, and after a time we walked back to my house together. Several of the old men of the tribe, who knew what was to happen, met us on the road and walked home with Father and me, so we had quite a houseful of people to welcome the little stranger into the world.

When we entered the house, my stepmother handed me my first-born child, a beautiful baby girl. She was all dressed and lying in a 'hoksicala postan,' or Indian baby cradle, which made it very easy to handle; but I never felt so awkward in my life, and felt quite out of place with so many people around. Noting my embarrassment, my father took the baby from me and crooned over the child as if it were his very own. How I loved this little girl, and how proud I was of her!

She was very pretty, and took after the white side of the family. Her skin was very fair; her hair was a light brown, and her eyes were very dark brown — almost black. We were so happy with this little addition to our family, and she was so fair, that we decided to name her 'Lily.'

I was still teaching school, and when my duties there were finished I would hurry home to my wife and little girl. I was then studying under the Episcopal missionary. When the weather conditions were such that he could not get to the church, I took the pulpit and preached in his place.

When my second child was born, it proved to be a boy and took after my side of the family, being of dark complexion, but was a very fine baby, nevertheless. While both my stepmothers were pleased, my mother-in-law was not at all pleased. She did not like me because I was an Indian, and the thought that her daughter had given birth to a child which was very dark seemed to hurt her feelings very much.

Trying to play the part of a Christian and at the same time being nice to her was very hard to do under the circumstances. You must know that among my people a mother-in-law is never permitted to say a word to her son-in-law, nor even to look at him. However, as I had been to school and had some education, I permitted her to come to the house while I was at home, and tried in every possible way to be good to her. She never said anything to me direct, but talked to her daughter about me.

CHAPTER XX

TROUBLE AT THE AGENCY

Our agent, Mr. Wright, and his daughter Nellie were still at the agency. He was really a very good man, and tried to do all he could for the Indians. The whole tribe seemed to be getting along very nicely; but trouble is bound to creep into one's life at times.

One whole band of Indians moved out on White River, about seven miles west of the agency. There they formed a camp of their own, and had a large tipi painted black at the top, which they used for a dance-hall. This band came to be known as the 'black-top tipi camp.' They made no trouble, but simply indulged in dancing, and enjoying themselves as they did in the old days.

These Indians in the black-top tipi camp learned that we were receiving household goods from the Government, but that they were not. So they held a council about it and decided to come in and see the agent about the matter. Their leader, named Wooden Knife, came into the agency one day with a few of his people. When there was no school, I worked in the agent's office, and happened to be there at the time these Indians came in.

Wooden Knife told the agent that he and his people had come to see about the goods which were being distributed by the Government, but of which they had received nothing. He told Mr. Wright that he knew the other Indians were receiving goods, and he and his people wanted what was rightfully theirs.

After listening to Wooden Knife's speech, Mr. Wright, through the interpreter, replied: 'I know that all you are saying is right, but I cannot issue any goods to you or your people while you are living out there in a camp. Move away from there and build up some little houses for yourselves, and I will be glad to give you all that is coming to you.' He also added: 'I will hold each one of your shares, and will not issue them to any one else. But at present you are doing nothing but dancing the Indian dances, and that is not right. So move away from the camp, and you will have all that is due you.'

Now the interpreter was a man named Louis Lubeteaux. He was a quarter-blood Indian, and had had no education, so was not a very good interpreter; but he was all the agent had.

Mr. Wright had spoken very nicely to the Indians all through his talk, but the interpreter got things mixed up, and translated his talk in such a way that it made Wooden Knife and his people very angry. The interpreter had made an especially bad 'botch' of the talk where he mentioned the Indian dances. Poor interpreters were the cause of a great many rows between the Indians and agents.

Wooden Knife and his band left for their camp in a very angry mood. In fact, they nearly precipitated a battle right there and then. I understood fully about the poor interpretation, but, as I was merely an employee, and not an official interpreter, it was not my business to interfere.

After the Indians got back to their camp, they held a big council. All the chiefs were called together, and it was decided that the agent had no right to withhold anything from them. They said: 'These things he is holding back are ours, and we are going to get them, even if we have to force our agent. Our Grandfather (the President) knows that we have no houses, but he has sent these things here for us, and the agent is holding them back. What right has he to do this? We must get what belongs to us. We will go to the agent again and ask him, and if he refuses, we will throw him out. We know there are plenty of white men who would like to take his place as agent, and some one else might treat us better.'

The agent soon heard about the council which the

black-top tipi Indians had held. It was now very near the time for the distribution of supplies from the Government, and he sent for all the members of the Indian police to be at the agency in case trouble developed. These Indian police had taken oath to stand by the Government, even against their own people. They were paid ten dollars a month for their services, and were ready to shoot down any Indian who would dare harm the agent.

When the distribution of annuities started, the black-top tipi Indians were close at hand, but they did not receive a thing. They could not understand it. Here were goods sent to them by the Government, which the agent was withholding from them.

One morning, bright and early, there was a great commotion. Over the hill came all the black-top tipi Indians. Some were on horseback, others on foot. All were singing brave songs as they drew near the agency. They came directly to the council room, which connected with Mr. Wright's office. All wore blankets. Some covered their heads and had weapons hidden underneath their blankets. They were led by Wooden Knife, a very tall man.

When the council room was filled, some of the Indian police came in and scattered about through the crowd. I managed to work my way inside, close to the office door. I felt that trouble was coming, and I wanted to help my people. As I turned around to face them, they were all seated on the floor. The expression on their faces reminded me very much of the stories my father had told me about how the warriors looked when ready to attack an enemy.

When every one was seated and quiet reigned, the interpreter opened the door leading from the office and a policeman brought in a couple of chairs. He was followed by the agent and the interpreter. Both seated themselves. The agent spoke first:

'You tell these men that if they will talk to me as a friend, I will talk to them.'

Then Wooden Knife, the leader and spokesman, arose. He was a tall, powerfully built Indian, and as he parted his blanket he revealed a large club, wth three knives stuck in the end. He placed this club on the floor in front of the agent and stood on it while speaking. He said:

'Our Grandfather, the President, says if the agent does not treat you right to throw him out. There are plenty more to take his place, and glad of the chance.'

The agent answered, 'Show me the paper.'

'We are not white people,' replied Wooden Knife. 'We do not carry any papers; we only carry what we hear.'

'You have told me what is not true,' answered the agent. 'If you people are going to talk to me like this, I will not listen to you.'

Then he turned toward the office door as though he had concluded the council. That is where he made a mistake. These Indians had come a long distance to be given a full hearing, and they were determined to have it. As the agent turned away, I observed, from the expression on the faces of the Indians, that it meant instant trouble. Weapons of all kinds were suddenly raised, and shouts of 'Kill him! Kill him!' echoed through the council room. One of the Indians grabbed the agent's hand as he was about to enter his office. A policeman inside the office had him by the other hand, and both were pulling with might and main. More of the police came, and the agent was finally pulled inside his office.

But some of the Indians managed to follow the agent inside his office. There were so many of them that the police could do nothing. They did not dare shoot for fear of killing some of their own friends. The agent ran through the office and out into the yard, followed by many of the Indians. As the crowd in the council room thinned out, the police started to show their authority, whereupon both sides started in to fight among themselves.

I ran here and there, trying to make them listen to

reason and stop fighting. I told them I would talk to the agent for them if they would behave themselves, and after a while the trouble quieted down. The black-top tipi Indians went back to their camp, and then I went to the agent, as I had promised, and asked him what he proposed to do about the matter. He said he would issue all their goods to them.

I then went down to the camp and told the chiefs what the agent had said. This pleased them immensely to know that I had kept my word. A few days later each family received a full set of household goods. There were sewing machines, beds, tables, chairs, dishes, dressers, stoves — in fact, everything they needed to furnish a house. But they had them all in their tipis. Some days later I went to visit one of these people who was distantly related to me. I found his wife trying to run the sewing machine while he lay on the bed singing at the top of his voice!

The Indians did not know the uses their new articles were to be put to. All their clothing was in the Indian trunks or parfleches, and nothing in the new dresser drawers. However, they were all happy at receiving the goods, even though they did not yet understand their use.

Shortly after this trouble, Mr. Wright, the agent, left. He felt that one fight with the Sioux was as much as he wanted, and perhaps it might have been his last if I had not interfered at the proper time.

A new agent came named Spencer. He brought a daughter with him, who took Nellie Wright's place. She was not capable of filling the position, but as she was the agent's daughter, she secured the place. This agent was very unscrupulous, although he was very smooth in all his operations.

The Government began issuing large work horses to the Indians for farming purposes, as the little ponies were not big nor strong enough for that sort of work. Instead of giving the large draft animals to the Indians, this agent would look around and if he saw any one with a nice lot of Indian relics he would 'make swap' for them and give horses in exchange. An Indian, of course, would give up almost anything for a nice team of horses. In this manner the agent collected together a great many Indian relics.

My father ferreted out what sort of work the agent was doing, so he went up to visit a man named Red Feather, and between them they concocted a scheme to get rid of the agent by tying him up, placing him in a wagon, and carrying him to the Nebraska border-line and dumping him out there, so as to get him completely off the reservation.

But the agent in some way got wind of what was intended, and he lost no time in packing up and leaving before my father and Red Feather could carry out their plans. The agent could not remain and protect himself, and neither did he dare ask the Indian police to help him out. He knew he was doing wrong, and he knew my father meant all he threatened to do. So he left, and no investigation ever was made to determine what was the reason.

We were therefore left without an agent for several days until George Wright, son of the former agent, came to us. George Wright was a very fine man, and he and I got along together splendidly.

Soon after this, the Government sent some commissioners out to our reservation. The object was to investigate allotments. All the chiefs were against the allotment proposition. They figured that they were to be given a piece of land, fenced in like a white man, but they were to have no openings to and from the land, and would starve.

The agent sent out word for all the Indians to come to the agency. Soon they came trooping in from all directions and made their camps, waiting for the council to open. Of course all the chiefs who imagined they knew something about this allotment proposition had spoken to the other

Indians about it, and they all agreed that there was to be
no more signing of any more papers for the white man.

But my father was in favor of the allotment. He had
listened while I explained it to him. So he paid no attention to either the commissioners or the agent, but went
alone to the council held by the Indians while they were
waiting. Here several of the old chiefs arose to talk. My
father also arose, and as he faced the others, they waited
to hear first what he had to say. He spoke as follows:

'My friends, there are some white men here from the
Great Father at Washington. They have come to see us
about an agreement concerning an allotment of land. Now,
my son has explained the proposition to me, and I consider
that it is a very good one. We are to receive a piece of land,
three hundred and twenty acres, which will be surveyed.
This is for farming. We are also to get a team of horses,
a farm wagon, a milk cow, farming implements, and fifty
dollars in cash toward building a house. This land we live
on is not good for farming, because the seasons are not
right for it. So I am going to ask the commissioners for a
full section of land, six hundred and forty acres. If they
will give us this, in addition to the other things mentioned,
we should sign the paper. Our tribe is to receive three mil-
lion dollars for this land, half of which is to be used to
educate our children, and the balance is to be paid to us
within twenty-five years. If we take a piece of land it will
be ours forever. If any of you old men die, under present
conditions, you have nothing you can leave your children.
But if you have a piece of land, it will be theirs when you
are gone. No one can take it from them. So I am in favor
of accepting this land.'

Then Chief Hollow Horn Bear arose. He was against the
allotment. He was the husband of my oldest sister Was-
tewin, the daughter of my mother by her first husband.
He liked my father, but he was the head of his own band,
and had a right to his opinion. He spoke as follows:

'My friends, you have all heard what my father-in-law says, but I do not think he is right. He believes what the white people tell him; but this is only another trick of the whites to take our land away from us, and they have played these tricks before. We do not want to trust the white people. They come to us with sweet talk, but they do not mean it. We will not sign any more papers for these white men.'

All the Indians grunted 'Hau!' ('How!'), which meant that they agreed with what Hollow Horn Bear said. Then other chiefs arose and spoke. So many of them were against the allotment that it seemed we were not to get it. But these councils which the Indians held among themselves were not recorded, as there were no white persons present.

Finally the Indians became so determined not to favor the allotment that they agreed that the first Indian who signed any more papers for the white men would be shot down. While many of the Indians really agreed with my father, they were afraid to say so for fear of the consequences.

At last the day arrived for the meeting at the agency. All the chiefs and headmen, as well as all the Indians, were gathered together to listen to what the white men had to say. General George Crook, the famous army officer, was the first man to talk. He explained all about what the Indians were to receive, how the children were to be educated, etc. He mentioned the Carlisle School, and the good being accomplished there by Captain Pratt. He was followed by other white men, who asked the Indians if they did not think this was a good thing for them.

Then one of the Indians arose and said they did not fully understand things yet, but if the agent would furnish them with food, they would hold another council, and then they might consider what to do, to which the agent agreed. As soon as the Indians reached their tipis, they held another council.

The following day everybody was at the agency again. The commissioners again spoke, and were followed by several of the other Indians. Chief Hollow Horn Bear, who was against the allotment, spoke as follows:

'You white men have come to us again to offer something to us which we do not fully understand. You talk to us very sweet, but you do not mean it. You have not fulfilled any of the old treaties. Why do you now bring another one to us? Why don't you pay us the money you owe us first, and then bring us another treaty?'

Other chiefs followed and expressed their opinions of the treaties that had not been fulfilled. They argued that if they signed this treaty, then the old treaties would be forgotten. The commissioners tried to explain that the new treaty would be on the same footing with the others — that they were to receive their annuity goods just the same, as well as what was now being promised. However, the Indians did not believe this, so they said they would go home and think it over. They left, and then held another council between themselves alone. My father attended all these councils among the Indians, as well as those held with the commissioners. But he had already told the Indians what his own opinion was about the matter, and what his decision was, and he never spoke of it again; the Indians knew his decision was final.

There was one man in our tribe who never attended any of the councils. His name was Crow Dog — the Indian who shot and killed Chief Spotted Tail. He was permitted by the Government to carry a six-shooter at all times to protect himself. But at all gatherings of Indians — no matter if whites were present — he did not come. He was afraid to do so. However, he heard about my father's talk, and really believed he was right, although he did not dare to say so openly.

The day arrived for the third council with the Indians and commissioners. General Crook made a very strong speech. He told the Indians that they could consider him as their friend. 'Some of you have known me for a long time,' he stated, 'and you can trust me. When the President at Washington asked me to come to you with this proposition, I was glad to do so, because I know it is for your good and the good of your children. We know there are some men in the tribe who are in favor of this proposition, so to-morrow we will hold a meeting in order that you may have a chance to sign this paper. Those who do not believe it will not sign it.'

Everybody wondered just what he meant when he said he knew some men in the tribe were in favor of this treaty. It was well known that my father favored it, but it was also known that he never hung around the commissioners. But news travels just the same.

The following day my father, with several of his friends, went to the agency. All the Indians gathered together as before, but this time they came carrying weapons. The commissioner again spoke, and then he asked if any one present had anything to say. My father thereupon arose and spoke about like this:

'My friends, you all know I have spoken to you about this treaty, because the way my son explained it to me it seemed good for our children and their children in turn. Some day they will have to mix with the white race; therefore, they will need an education. These men have told these things in the way my son told me, and I believe it. So I am going to sign this treaty.'

Then shouts of 'Kill him! Kill him!' went up all over the hall; but my father never even turned his head. He walked straight to the table and touched the pen. That was his signature, as he had no education and could not write. My father's friends became very excited, and kept looking hither and thither. One man had his gun raised, ready to shoot, but some of the men picked him up bodily and threw him out of the hall. My father was the first man to sign the treaty in public, risking his life that we, his children, might receive an allotment of land from the Government.

The other Indians saw that my father signed the paper without getting shot, so they began to have more courage. One after another started for the table and touched the pen. Soon the white men had to get other tables, as the Indians came so fast there was not room at one table. How happy my father was in knowing that the whole tribe believed he was doing the right thing for his people.

Several of the Indians who were not in favor of the treaty walked out of the council hall, among them being my brother-in-law, Chief Hollow Horn Bear. The commissioners remained a few days longer on the reservation, and other Indians, from time to time, came up to sign the treaty. As soon as most of the big men of the tribe had signed the paper, the commissioners went back to Washington. Nobody had been injured, but it took considerable courage to make the first move and be first in line.

Some time after this, my brother-in-law, Hollow Horn Bear, and I were discussing the treaty, and he told me that he really believed in it all the time, but that his band did not. They had asked him to be their spokesman, as he was their leader, and so he had to tell what his people wanted. That was why he had argued against my father.

During the year 1926 I happened to be visiting a friend who had a Government publication on the various treaties. I was examining this book, and found the one which referred to the land allotment. Knowing that my father had been the first man to sign this paper, I was anxious to see just how the Washington authorities had it on record. Imagine my surprise when I saw that the name of Crow Dog headed the list of signers, when, as a matter of fact, he had not attended any of the councils at all, but had gone in the middle of the night secretly to the commissioners and had there signed the treaty. As I was present and saw my father sign that treaty as the first Indian, I know what I am talking about.

But even though Crow Dog's name is recorded as being the first to sign the treaty, I know that is not so. I witnessed the entire transaction, and Crow Dog is getting credit for something he had no hand in at all.

CHAPTER XXI

THE GHOST–DANCE TROUBLES

IT was agreed by the Government that the man of the house was to receive six hundred and forty acres of land for farming. Here my father again spoke. He said the Indians knew nothing about farming, but that they could take the land for grazing. This was satisfactory.

From the day my father signed the treaty, we all began to realize that we were to have something given us which was to be our own — and the thought of ownership gives any one a higher appreciation of life, regardless of how little that ownership may be; so we all began looking around at various sections of the reservation to see where we would care to live.

My father knew all of our country, but when he realized that he was going to have some land for himself, he commenced looking around to see where the best land was. He went over to visit at Pine Ridge Agency, and when he saw the land over there, he liked it so much better than that at Rosebud that he decided to move his family over to Pine Ridge.

But I remained at Rosebud. I had my position as school teacher there. George Wright was still our agent, and he was a very nice young man. My house was close to my work, and my little family was a happy one. My cordwood was all ready for winter; the cattle, pigs, and horses were all well fed, and with the approach of the holiday season, every one seemed to be feeling happy.

And then suddenly great excitement came into our midst. It broke so suddenly over us that a great many of the Indians did not know which way to turn. It was the craze of a new religion called the 'Ghost Dance.' This was in 1890. At that time very few of the Indians had any education, but they were very superstitious and their feelings were easily aroused and played upon.

One day I was called into the agent's office. There I saw an Indian called Short Bull and a young man known as Ce-re-aka-ruga-pi, or Breaks-the-Pot-on-Him. The agent started to question them in front of me, and I shall never forget what Short Bull said. The agent asked him to tell about the new religion which they were all getting so excited about, and why he believed in it. Said Short Bull:

'We heard there was a wonderful man in the Far West. He was a Messiah, so several tribes gathered together to go and see him. We went to the place where the sun sets, and there we saw this man. He told us we were to have a new earth; that the old earth would be covered up, and while it was being covered we were to keep dancing so that we could remain on top of the dirt.

'This man told us that all the white people would be covered up, because they did not believe; even the Indians who did not believe would also be covered. He showed us visions of the olden times when the buffalo were plenty; when the big camps were on the plains. All our people were dancing and having a big feast.

'This man hit the ground and he made fire. He spoke to all of us at once, and all the different tribes understood him. He said that all the white people would be destroyed. He taught us a song to sing during this dance. He showed us where the sun dropped down into the ocean, and it boiled up and became hot.'

At this point I spoke up and said to Short Bull, 'That is not so; the ocean does not boil up with the setting of the sun.'

Short Bull looked straight at me, but he had nothing further to say about the sun.

The agent spoke to both these men politely, and asked them not to stir up the Indians at Rosebud Agency. They both promised, and then left for home.

The first thing we knew, the majority of the Rosebud Indians had joined the ghost dancers. We could see the dust flying skyward from the dancing, and hear the beat of the tom-toms. They would keep up the dancing until they fell from exhaustion.

The ghost dance was being held about eight miles west of the agency on a flat, on the west side of Little White River. We could plainly locate the dancers from the dust they raised. The Indians were really serious about it, and had full faith in what they were doing. They felt that this new religion was going to rid them of the hated pale-faces who had antagonized them so long.

My father's band had not joined the dancers yet. Two of his brothers-in-law were in charge of them. High Pipe (whose name you will recall having been mentioned as driving my father's oxen with a blacksnake whip) was one of the men, and Black Horn was the other. Father had already moved over to Pine Ridge with his family, but had left his two brothers-in-law in charge of the balance of the Indians.

The dust was flying high in the sky every day from the dancing. As the enthusiasm grew, more dancers joined. Then George Wright, the agent, sent for me to see if I would go to my father's band with a message from him. This band was located about five miles west of the agency on the east side of Little White River, so they were only about three miles from the dancers across the river. They could both hear and see the dancers easier than ourselves.

I agreed to go, and Mr. Wright furnished me with a team and driver. He was a white man, and when we reached the camp I instructed him to drive into the center of it before he stopped. The tipis were all in a circle. It was quite a camp — about a quarter of a mile across it. When the wagon stopped, the Indians came out and stood around to listen to what I had to say. There was no excitement, but every one was curious as to the cause of my visit.

I told my people that I wanted to help them, and that was the reason I had come. I said it would not be right for them to join the ghost dancers, as the Government was going to stop it, and it would not be best for them to be found there. I told them the Government would use soldiers to enforce the order if it became necessary.

The thought that the soldiers were coming disturbed them, but I told them if they felt afraid they could move their tipis in and put them up around my house and camp there. My house was only about a half-mile from the agency. They all agreed to come there the following morning. This pleased me immensely to think that my visit and talk had been a success. When I returned and told the agent, he, too, was very happy.

Just after I left the camp my plans were all 'knocked into a cocked hat,' as you might say. One of my uncles, Hard Heart, entered the camp from Pine Ridge. When he saw that the Indians were all getting ready to break camp and go somewhere, he inquired the reason of the sudden move. When they told him they were getting ready to come in and camp by my house, he told them not to go. He said that a new world was coming to roll on top of the present one, and that they must either join the ghost dancers or perish with those who did not believe. Still, that would not have deterred them from coming to me had not some one come into the camp that night and told them the soldiers were coming. That frightened them to such an extent that they were all packed up and gone long before daylight.

When I awoke the next morning and looked out of my window in expectation of seeing their tipis pitched about my house, I was greatly disappointed. There was no sign of their camp. I looked up the road in the direction they would have come, but there was no one in sight. Then I knew something had frightened them from keeping their promise.

The Indians who had decided to remain at the agency held a council so they could discuss the dance. Like all religious beliefs there were those who believed and there were the skeptics as well.

The first thing I knew, all the Indians began to gather at the house of Spotted Tail. He had quite a large residence which the Government had built for him after he traded all the northern part of the present State of Nebraska — our hunting grounds — without our knowledge. Although that chief had been dead since 1881, his home was known as the 'Spotted Tail house.' I still lived in the same house which my father had bought from the Catholic missionary. It stood down a little slope from that of Spotted Tail, so I could plainly see the Indians gathering for the council. After I had observed several of the leading chiefs going in, I decided to go down and find out what they intended doing.

When I arrived, my brother-in-law, Chief Hollow Horn Bear, was speaking, and I stood at the door to listen. He was not a believer in the ghost dance, and was talking very strongly against it. All who were in favor of it exclaimed 'Hauh!' every once in a while. Suddenly we who were standing near the door saw an Indian riding a white horse coming toward the house as fast as he could urge his pony. He had come from the agency and was headed straight for the council. As he dashed up he leaped from his pony and rushed into the council hall. Hollow Horn Bear was still speaking, but this man, Brave Eagle, interrupted him, exclaiming, 'Hey, hey! What are all you men doing here? Don't you know that the soldiers have taken all our women and children away from Cut Meat Creek? Why do you all sit here doing nothing?'

This caused considerable excitement, as many of these men had relatives at Cut Meat Creek. The council broke up, and several of the Indians rushed to the agency. My brother-in-law and I started, but first we stopped at my house. My Winchester rifle, with fifty rounds of cartridges in the belt, was standing in one corner of the room, and it was the first thing he spied. He wanted this gun. 'Let me have it, and I will go over and see what all this means,' he said to me.

When we arrived at the agency, the agent was greatly excited. He was walking the floor, rubbing his. head. 'I can't understand what has happened,' he said to me. 'If there is anything wrong, I should have been sent a telegram.' He had sent for his Indian Police, who were now arriving. The Indians who had gathered were all ready to start for Cut Meat Creek, and the police were likewise impatient to be off. Everybody was on horseback, and I stood and watched them start on their journey of twenty-five miles, none of them knowing what they would find after they got there. I was to remain at the agency until Mr. Wright returned.

Bad news travels fast. None of the Government employees at the reservation cared to work that day. Everybody was just standing around, wondering what was to happen next. Toward evening we saw the men all returning. Their horses were all fagged out from hard riding, and the men were tired, but the news they brought was good for us to hear.

The agent told us that when they reached the camp nothing had been disturbed; that the man who had brought the news had not told the truth. We wondered what his object was in bringing us such a story, and whether he had made it up himself or had been bribed to spread the report. However, the truth never came to light.

My brother-in law did not come back with the others, but went right on to his band, taking my Winchester along with him. That was the last I ever saw of that rifle. However, he had always wanted a good gun, and that was a very nice (?) way of getting it!

Nothing exciting occurred during the night, but the following day one of my distant cousins, Isaac Bettelgeau, a half-breed, came to see me. He was a scout for the Government, and was located on the Niobrara River. He told me that all the agencies on the Sioux reserve were to be surrounded in one night by the soldiers. He stated that he could not tell me when it was to happen, but that it was to be very soon. We were doing nothing which demanded the presence of troops, but they were coming just the same, and we wondered why.

However, this piece of news did not worry me very much and I went to bed as usual. One of my friends, Julian Whistler, was staying with me, accompanied by Frank Janis. We all three slept in one bed, my place being next to the window.

On the second morning, quite early, we heard men marching past. It woke us up, and I raised the shade and looked out. There were soldiers' tents everywhere, and the troops were already up and going through a morning drill. I jumped out of bed and went to the back door. Just as I opened it, I heard the command 'Halt!' I thought it was meant for me until I saw the entire body of troops come to a halt. They were fully dressed, but I was still in my night clothes.

I watched them a minute or two and then went back and woke my friends. They dressed and we started getting breakfast. Soon we saw the soldiers coming over to my woodpile. They began to help themselves, and soon my few cords of wood began to disappear rapidly. I did not say anything to them, not caring to start any trouble. Later, when I was out in the yard doing some work, an officer came to me and told me not to worry about the wood, as the Government would pay me for all they used.

The following morning the news arrived of the terrible slaughter of Big Foot's whole band. Men, women, and children — even babies were killed in their mothers' arms!

This was done by the soldiers. According to the white man's history this was known as the 'battle' of Wounded Knee, but it was not a battle — it was a slaughter, a massacre. Those soldiers had been sent to protect these men, women, and children who had not joined the ghost dancers, but they had shot them down without even a chance to defend themselves.

When I heard of this, it made my blood boil. I was ready myself to go and fight then. There I was, doing my best to teach my people to follow in the white men's road — even trying to get them to believe in their religion — and this was my reward for it all! The very people I was following — and getting my people to follow — had no respect for motherhood, old age, or babyhood. Where was all their civilized training?

More of the Indians joined the dancers after the Wounded Knee affair. They felt that they could not meet with any worse fate than that which had been meted out to their friends and relatives.

Always after a trouble of this sort, rumors were apt to be flying thick and fast. As we had no telephones in those days, we had no way to determine the truth about the fate of our friends and relatives. All we received were rumors—and they were not of the best. One of the Indians came running into the agency with the report that he had overheard a soldier remark that 'they were going to kill all the Indians, regardless of education, because the only good Indians were the dead ones.' That sounded pretty bad, but soon came another rumor: 'All the Indians who stay with the white people and work with them, will be regarded as white people and are not going to be killed.'

It was about two days after the Wounded Knee affair that these rumors began to sift in at the agency. Orders were given that no Indian was to leave his or her house. Everybody's nerves were on edge. My own house was completely surrounded by the soldiers. I did not know whether my own family were alive or dead. My wife and children had gone to her father's before the trouble started.

I talked the situation over with my two friends, Julian Whistler and Frank Janis. We decided to fight if we had to, but agreed that we would not start trouble ourselves. As my brother-in-law had taken my rifle, I was left without any arms. My two friends had no guns. So we went out and each bought a gun and plenty of ammunition, and were ready to fight if it came to a ' show-down.' While we three were Carlisle graduates, we determined to stick by our race.

After getting these guns we felt much easier about going to bed nights. We kept the weapons fully loaded, waiting and fully expecting an attack.

One night during a full moon, when it was almost as light as day, we got a scare. We had been in bed for some time, when suddenly we heard the command 'Mount!' We jumped from bed, grabbed our guns and went outside. It developed that an officer had seen a lone Indian scout coming over the hill and had given the alarm. The order was given 'Forward, march,' and off they started. I turned to my friends, and told them when the shooting commenced that we would open the ball ourselves, and keep on shooting as long as we had any ammunition. However, our plans were not carried into effect. The officer had made a mistake. Instead of an Indian scout it turned out to be only a loose horse. The animal was hobbled, and as he jumped along down the hill it made such a queer sound that the officer thought something serious was happening.

We had a few scares of this sort, but nothing serious happened at our agency. Few of the Government employees did any work, however, as all were too excited, waiting for all the late news to come in. It kept the agent on the jump, though.

Three or four days later I started over to find out how

bad the reports were which we had heard about the fight. My father and mother and their family were at Pine Ridge at this time and I had heard nothing from them. It had snowed in the meantime, and the weather was very cold. It meant a ride of thirty miles on horseback, but I had a good horse, plenty of warm clothing, and I did not mind the jaunt.

When I arrived at the place where the fight had occurred between the Indians and the soldiers, all the bodies had been removed. Here and there lay the body of a horse. The tipi poles were broken and lay scattered about in heaps. Cooking utensils were strewed around in confusion; old wagons were overturned, with the tongues broken off. Everything was confusion. It was early in the morning when I reached this place, and the silence was oppressive and terrible.

There were many little pools of water here and there, some with clear water and others red with the blood of my people. I was enraged enough at this sight to shoot any one, but nobody was to be seen. The place of death was forsaken and forbidding. I stood there in silence for several minutes, in reverence for the dead, and then turned and rode toward the agency.

On the way I met some Indians. My first question was for my father, his wives and my sisters and brothers. They told me that Father and his wives were all right, and that my two brothers, Ellis and Willard, were safe. So I returned to Rosebud Agency without seeing them.

All the Indians who believed in the ghost dance had now rushed into what was known as the 'Bad Lands.' It was located in the northern part of our reservation, and was a hard place to enter. The entrance was only large enough for one wagon at a time to pass in. It was an excellent place to stand off an enemy.

Those who had not at first believed in the ghost dance ran away with these Indians who were bound for the Bad

Lands. After they had seen what the soldiers did to their friends and relatives, they were not taking any more chances. The few who had escaped the terrible slaughter at Wounded Knee also fled into the fastnesses of the Bad Lands, although they had no guns nor anything with which to put up a fight. The soldiers had taken everything away from them before shooting them down. But the other Indians had all brought firearms and plenty of ammunition.

These they divided. They felt sure that now they would have to fight to protect themselves against the white man. *Who could blame them?*

In the Bad Lands they had plenty of wood and water, but they needed meat. Some of the braves sneaked out in the night and rounded up all the cattle they could find and drove them into their place of retreat. There was no high chief left at the agency now, because Red Cloud, who had always called Pine Ridge his agency, was one of the Indians to run with his whole family into the Bad Lands.

Everybody in the camp now felt safe, as they had plenty of everything to supply their needs. They could dance when they pleased, and they had no agent from whom to ask permission. They were not under obligations to the Government for supplies, as they now had all they wanted. They kept two scouts posted at the entrance to the Bad Lands day and night, so there was no chance of interference without being seen. The soldiers did not even try to come near them. They knew better!

The troops realize that the Indians who had guns knew how to use them. Those who had bows and arrows were experts in their use. The Indians were really better armed than at the time they wiped out Custer, fourteen years previously. Had the soldiers tried at the time to enter the Bad Lands, there would have been many deaths on both sides.

General Miles realized all this, so he thought up a plan

toward a reconciliation. He called on a few of the chiefs who had remained at the agency, and asked them if they would not go to their people and try to make peace for them. This was a most dangerous mission to attempt to perform, as the Indians had declared they would kill any one who came to them, regardless of color. The white man had started the fight, and now he wanted the Indian to act as mediator!

My father, who was now the head chief, said he would carry the peace pipe to these Indians if any one else would accompany him. Nine others volunteered to accompany him. These ten chiefs started off on horseback, not knowing whether they would ever return alive. My father carried the pipe, which all the Indians respected at that time.

When they arrived at the entrance to the Bad Lands, they were recognized by the scouts on duty, who allowed them to enter unmolested. They all rode their horses in through the gateway in plain sight of all the Indians. Here they dismounted, my father still holding the peace pipe in both hands, straight out before him. Not a word was spoken. The Indians arranged themselves in a circle and sat down. They were making an appeal to their friends to come and accept the pipe of peace. Everything was as quiet as the grave. Among the Indians at that time, there was a strong superstition that if the pipe of peace was brought and not accepted, great harm would come to them or to their relatives.

The sight of this peace pipe made the fighting Indians wild! They were on horseback, and they rode right toward my father and the other chiefs. Not one of the latter moved, but sat perfectly still. One of these Indians had a loaded gun. His name was Ten Fingers. As he came near my father he said, 'The white people have killed our people without mercy, and we want to fight them. Why have you brought us this pipe of peace?'

As he finished speaking, bang! went his rifle, the bullet

striking the ground between my father's knees and spattering dirt in his face. Father never flinched or said a word of rebuke. He had faith in what he was doing in bringing the peace pipe to these enraged Indians.

You who are Christians — have you ever been in a high temper at a time when some one may have asked you to kiss the Bible? Then you will understand just how these Indians felt toward accepting the peace pipe offered them. However, after a time these wild Indians calmed down, and strange as it may seem, those ten chiefs brought all those hostiles into the agency without a shot being fired! There a peace was effected.

After the affair was over, somebody mentioned to my brother Ellis the incident in which Ten Fingers had fired his rifle between my father's knees while he was holding the peace pipe. This so enraged my brother that after dark he covered his head with a sheet, carried his rifle underneath it, and started out to locate Ten Fingers. He went from tipi to tipi, but could not find him — and it was probably lucky for Ten Fingers that he was not located.

Now that peace was finally restored, who was given the credit for it? Did the Indian who had brought the peace pipe receive any honor for the part he played? No, indeed! All the credit went to General Miles, who was proclaimed the 'great peacemaker.' Perhaps his salary was raised, or possibly he received a few more stripes to his sleeves. The Indians came to my father about it, and my father, who was the head chief throughout those ceremonies, went to General Miles for an explanation.

He told the General that the Indians thought they (who had remained loyal and at the agency) should have something from the Government to indicate that they belonged to the Progressives — something to show that they had not run away; some sort of emblem for them to wear to commemorate this great peace and the part they had in it.

The General said he would accede to this request of

my father's. He secured the names of all the chiefs who had accompanied my father. He must have submitted their names to the officials at Washington, because in a short time some buttons arrived — one for each man. They were about an inch and a half in diameter, and were worn fastened to the coat lapel, much the same as a lodge emblem. On the face of these buttons was emblazoned a rising sun, and in the clear sky above were the words 'Peace, Good Will.' Below were two clasped hands, on each side of which was a shock of corn; at the extreme bottom was a plough. They were made of some cheap metal, silver-plated.

When these buttons arrived, General Miles sent for my father and gave him the buttons to distribute. The chiefs were greatly pleased to wear them, showing that they belonged to the Progressives. It was a mark of distinction and honor. But I often look back to this incident and wonder if the general public knows that the men who really settled the greatest trouble between the whites and Indians at Pine Ridge each received a dinky button worth about fifty cents!

CHAPTER XXII

AT PINE RIDGE: SCHOOL, STORE, AND POST OFFICE

I was still residing at Rosebud Agency, teaching school. Now that peace was restored, we had no further excitement the balance of that winter. During the following vacation season I went over to Pine Ridge to visit my father. It seemed good to be with the family again. Many things had happened since we had seen each other and there was much to talk about and discuss. One thing I was very desirous of learning was how many were dead since we had last met? How had my brothers got along while they were acting as scouts? How were the Indians paid for making peace? Then my father and brothers told me the whole story just as I will here relate it:

My father and his wives were living at the agency. They had not gone to camp with those at Wounded Knee. My brother Ellis was employed as a scout for the soldiers. Willard, my other brother, was to be a scout at the agency. When each agency was surrounded by soldiers, Ellis was with those at Pine Ridge. He was present at the killing of all of Big Foot's band, and was a witness to everything that happened. Here is what he related to me:

The whole band of Big Foot had their tipis in a circle. They were quiet, but the soldiers surrounded their camp, on horseback, with their guns pointed right into the faces of the Indians. An officer gave the command to disarm all the Indians. Their guns and knives were to be taken away from them, leaving them without any weapons.

A few of the soldiers went forward to collect the weapons of the Indians as they stood and sat around. Among this band was one boy who was not as bright as he might have been, being somewhat half-witted, and hardly any one ever paid any attention to whatever he did or said. In times of a crisis such people are the sort to be watched.

He stood around with the rest of the Indians while the soldiers held them with covered guns. This fellow saw that the weapons of his people were being taken away without resistance. He kept saying in the Sioux tongue, 'Don't give up your guns and knives; I am going to shoot.' However, his talk made no impression on any one, as he had always been considered harmless and not accountable for his speech or actions.

As a soldier approached him for his gun, he did not hand it over, but suddenly raised it and emptied the full contents right into the soldier's face. The man dropped dead.

Most of the weapons of the Indians had already been collected, and this half-witted youth was the only one who shot at that time. The next instant the command came from the officer in command of the troops, 'Fire!' The soldiers were in a circle, surrounding the Indians, and when they began shooting, many of their bullets went across the circle and killed their own men.

When the shooting began, my brother Ellis knew there was no chance for the life of any one who remained within that circle, so he ran his horse at top speed to the highest point of a hill about a quarter of a mile away. There he was a witness to all that happened. The soldiers kept shooting until nothing stirred within the entire camp. Little babies were shot to death right in the carriers strapped to their mothers' backs. All the trouble was due to the foolish, uncalled-for act of one half-witted Indian!

In the white men's accounts of this slaughter, it states that many soldiers were shot. So they were, but they were killed by their own comrades, as there was not a gun among the Indians at the time the shooting began.

My brother Willard, who was a scout at the agency, then told me what happened after the slaughter was over. Some of the scouts ran their horses to the agency to let the people know what was happening. To many this meant great sorrow, as they had relatives among Big Foot's band. The Episcopal Church was immediately turned into an emergency hospital. Here the wounded were taken to be cared for.

The Indians out in the Bad Lands wanted to rid the earth of the brand of whites who came when they felt like it and killed as many of the Indians as they pleased. There seemed to be no justice for the Indians, so the leaders of the hostiles in the Bad Lands wanted all the Indians there to stick together for one final battle. Some of them went to the church to see those who were wounded. They talked to them, but when they saw that they intended staying there until they had recovered, it made them very angry. In this way some of the wounded were killed by their own people because they would not leave the whites.

When I was ready to start home, I thought I would go and see the agent and find out what sort of man they had in charge. When I entered the office, there sat Captain Brown. He had been assistant superintendent for a while at the Carlisle School, and we were greatly surprised to see each other. He remembered me very well, indeed, and asked me a great many questions regarding myself and what I was doing. I told him I was the assistant teacher in the day school at the Rosebud Agency.

'But, Luther,' said he, 'why don't you move over here? If you will, I will put you in charge of one of the day schools.'

That sounded very good to me, so when I arrived home I went to Mr. Wright and told him what Captain Brown had mentioned to me, and that the change would mean an increased salary for me.

However, Mr. Wright said: 'Standing Bear, I do not want you to do such a thing. We are going to raise your salary here this coming year, so you had better remain here with us.'

But as my whole family were at Pine Ridge, I told him I thought I would be better off with them. Accordingly I traded my house for thirty head of cattle, and moved over to Pine Ridge Agency without a transfer from the agent. The house I exchanged was the one my father had bought from the Catholic missionary.

For about three months it was see-saw back and forth between these two agents. The Rosebud Agent would not give me a transfer, and the Pine Ridge Agent could not put my name on the books there as long as I officially belonged at Rosebud. The school there I was supposed to take charge of was not quite finished.

While I was waiting for a position to open for me, I thought it a good time to visit some of my relatives. One of my uncles, Charles Turning Hawk, had married Chief Little Wound's daughter, and had moved down to Medicine Creek. So I went down to see how they were getting along. Charles had started a little general store there.

After having worked in John Wanamaker's great Philadelphia establishment, my uncle's tiny store seemed very small, but, as I had had some experience in selling goods, Charles made good use of me during my visit. One day we were talking about the mail facilities in that section, as some of our letters had been delayed in transit. I told my uncle that John Wanamaker, the man for whom I had worked in Philadelphia, was Postmaster-General, and that I would write and see if we could not have a post office established at his camp. I suggested that we call it Kyle. It was a short name, and easy to spell.

When Mr. Wanamaker received my letter, he replied immediately. He was pleased with my suggestion, but said that he could not appoint me postmaster, as I was an Indian. It would have to be some white man. There was a Joseph Taylor who was one of our missionaries, and we sent his name. He received the appointment, but I took care of the office.

The post office was started in a corner of my uncle's store. Our mail carrier was a white man. He delivered the mail on horseback. Shortly thereafter he had a buggy for his use. This office was started in 1891, thirty-five years ago. I think now they use an automobile to deliver the mail during the summer months and a team in the winter. With the establishment of the post office of Kyle, South Dakota, we felt that we were at least on the map.

During the fall of that year I went back to the agency to take charge of the school. It was at Allen, South Dakota. The Government furnished nearly everything, and I was getting along splendidly — far better than I had at Rosebud Agency. The children were anxious to learn, and we gave little entertainments for them, which pleased both the children and the parents as well.

One evening I recall that we gave a little play called 'The Landing of Columbus.' My brother Henry played the part of Columbus. Of course the acting was not very good, but we did the best we knew how at that time, and it brought out one point in American history of which the people knew but little. Then we had some 'shadow-graphs.' This was something new to the Indians, and it took very well with them. This was helping the younger generation, but I knew that something should be done to assist those who had not had the chance or opportunity of any schooling. The idea kept working in my head until I finally decided to call all the adult Indians together and talk the matter over.

So I prepared a feast and called together all the Indians in the Allen district. After every one had eaten, and was feeling good and comfortable, I broached the subject of the meeting. I told them we ought to organize a club, like the white people, where we could discuss matters of importance to the tribe, and suggest ways and means to better our conditions.

Everybody agreed with my proposition, and we started

these meetings. I would furnish the food for all who came. After we had eaten, then some question was brought up on which to debate. One of these questions was: 'Which is the more useful — salt or tobacco? Which could we do without best?'

These debates brought up all sorts of topics. As the whites say nowadays, 'we got a great kick out of it.' I was really surprised to hear some of the long-haired, uneducated Indian boys talk. They would roll their blankets around their waists and make really sensible remarks. They did not have the learning from books, but from their own personal experience.

I kept this up for about a year, then I told them that I thought it would be a fine idea to tell the other Indians about our meetings, and possibly we might be able to do more for our people. We could study up on the old treaties and know more about them. So a committee was appointed to go among the other Indians and let them know what we proposed doing.

Shortly, the committee returned with the information that the Indians all agreed to attend a meeting in a few days. Everybody seemed pleased The first big meeting was held on the Big White River. Nearly all the Indians from Pine Ridge Agency were there, and we had a great time.

Officers were elected at this meeting as follows: For president, Louis Shangreau. He was a half-breed, uneducated but very smart nevertheless. My brother, Henry Standing Bear, was elected secretary. We did not elect any treasurer, because we had no money to collect. The name adopted for our 'club' was the 'Oglala Council.'

My brother, Henry Standing Bear, was a graduate of the Carlisle School, so he could explain things which were incorporated into the different treaties which many did not thoroughly understand. There were no 'big words' in our language, but Henry could interpret everything so that all understood. I started this organization in 1892. None of the Indians, up to that time, had had any experience in public speaking. They were naturally a quiet people; but at these councils they were given a chance to talk.

I was still teaching school, but I started a small general merchandise store of my own. I engaged my brother Ellis to take care of the store for me. He had started for Carlisle, but only remained there three months. He never went back. However, he made a splendid storekeeper, and we got along together without any trouble.

One evening a man, Henry Twist, rode his pony to the school. He was greatly excited, and stated that an Indian named Two Sticks and his sons had killed some cowboys and were headed our way. He reported that the murderers had said they were going to kill all the teachers as they went along, as well as all the white people that they could. He warned us not to light any lamps that night.

Henry Twist said that Two Sticks might mistake me for a white man and kill me. That was not very comforting news, but the following morning worse tidings came.

The Indians came to me and said that the whites had warned them that, if any more trouble started, they (the whites) would kill all the Indians. I said to them, 'If any further news comes of this nature, come to me, and move all your belongings to my place. Then if the soldiers come, I will face them, and try to explain to them; but if they refuse to listen, then we will fight them to a finish; there will be no more peace with them.' They all agreed with me on this.

But we had good reason to congratulate ourselves that no further trouble developed. Shortly after, we heard that the two sons of old Two Sticks had been killed by the Indian Police. Two Sticks himself was arrested and taken to Deadwood, South Dakota, and there the old man was hanged.

A long time after this occurrence we heard the true story of the Two Sticks affair. It seems that he and his family went out north on a hunt. They were unsuccessful in securing any game, and started back for home. They were very hungry, and while riding along they saw a ranch in the distance. It occurred to them that perhaps they could trade one of their ponies for a cow, or something to eat.

They rode up to the ranch house and entered. A bunch of cowboys were there playing a game of cards. Ordinarily the cowboys and Indians got along very well together, but I think these must have been drinking or else were new to that section of the country. They did not give Two Sticks and his sons any chance to explain their presence, but began cursing them. They abused them in this way for some little time, and finally kicked them outdoors.

Of course this angered the Indians. Soon they again entered the house, but this time it was to kill. They shot the four cowboys who had abused them, leaving their bodies in the house, just where they fell. Then they went out and killed a steer or two and had a grand feast, which lasted for several days. After this, the whole party started back for the agency, sending one of their number on ahead to the agent, with the information that they had killed some cowboys, but were not going to surrender, but would fight to the finish.

This made the agent greatly excited, and he called his Indian Police together. Then he issued an order for them to go out and bring in Two Sticks and his band. He was really afraid to face them himself, but sent the Indian Police to carry out his orders; so the police started out to bring Two Sticks and his followers in, dead or alive.

There was a fight, in which the sons of Two Sticks were killed and the old man captured. They took him over to Deadwood, where he was convicted, after a sort of trial, and sentenced to hang. When he was on the scaffold they asked him if he had anything to say. The old man raised his face skyward and sang a brave song. He was not afraid to meet his Maker. He was then dropped to his death. This whole thing was simply the result of a few drunken cowpunchers trying to be tough, and it resulted in the death of seven persons.

During the early part of 1894 word came that the Government were going to hold civil service examinations for all teachers. It really was not necessary for the primary education of the smaller Indian children. I had proved this by holding competitions between my own scholars and those taught by the white teachers, who got their knowledge from books, but outside of that, they knew nothing.

The Indian children should have been taught how to translate the Sioux tongue into English properly; but the English teachers only taught them the English language, like a bunch of parrots. While they could read all the words placed before them, they did not know the proper use of them; their meaning was a puzzle.

CHAPTER XXIII

RANCHER, CLERK, AND ASSISTANT MINISTER

CAPTAIN BROWN, our agent, was a very fine man. He had been assistant superintendent to Captain Pratt at Carlisle, and he knew something about Indians; and not from what he had read about them in books, but from personal relations with them. He knew that if they were given half a chance they would make good. So he determined that the Indians should have the chance. He did not go about as many of the agents had been in the habit of going — in a buggy, with some man to drive him around. He had a horse, and many times he took long horseback trips alone to look the country over. In that manner he could best determine what could be done to help the Indians.

One day, when out on one of these trips, he observed a long strip of land. Above it there seemed to be plenty of water which appeared to be going to waste, while down below, on the prairie, the land was not getting sufficient water to grow the crops. He determined that if a dam could be built to catch and hold all this waste water, it could be brought to the fields and properly utilized.

So he wrote to the Interior Department about the matter, and suggested building the dam, asking for an appropriation of several thousand dollars, and advising that the work be started at once. The news soon spread among the Indians, and they were greatly pleased that at last they had a man who was working for their interest and welfare.

But great was our disappointment when word was received from Washington that Captain Brown was about to be transferred to another reservation. This was one way of getting rid of a man who was working for the good of the Indian and not for the good of the political parasites at Washington.   And so the irrigation proposition, upon which we had built such fond hopes, 'went glimmering.'

Some time after this, I went to the head of Pass Creek and bought a ranch from Frank Janis, a half-breed.   We moved out to the ranch and started raising cattle and horses.   We shortly had a very fine place, and I was doing nicely.

Soon afterward, many white people were sent out from the East to teach our schools.   The instructors were men, and they brought their wives along to be given places as assistants.   While they knew quite a bit about book-learning, and could pass the civil service examinations, that was about the extent of their knowledge.   The assistant teachers were supposed to instruct our girls properly in household duties, such as cooking, washing, ironing, etc., and how to make their own clothes and take care of a house according to the white man's viewpoint.   We now had thirty-two day schools on our reservation.   A supervisor was appointed to visit all the schools and report on the progress they made.

I was busy at my ranch.   We had a comfortable home and were very happy.   My home was on the head of Pass Creek, about halfway between two agencies, and it soon became quite a stopping-place for both white men and Indians, going and coming from the reservations.   We were still drawing rations from the Government, and the Indians, as a whole, were quite happy, as they appeared to be getting about everything they wanted.

Then like a thunderbolt from a clear sky came an order from the Interior Department that all rations and annuity goods which had been issued to all able-bodied Indians were to be cut off unless the Indians were willing to work for them.

A man who owned a team, and who was willing to use it, was to receive $2.50 a day, while those who simply worked 'on foot' were to be paid $1.50.   Various jobs had been mapped out, one of which was the construction of a dam, another to build a road for our honorable agent to ride over. Other men were to build bridges. While all this work took us away from our homes, it meant money and something to eat.

Being an able-bodied man, I now had to get out and hustle. When the agent called for more men, I went to him, and was assigned to help build a fence around the entire Indian reservation. This seemed like a funny proposition to us — fencing us in like a lot of wild animals — and the Interior Department had approved such an order! However, we all got busy fencing ourselves in, at $2.50 per day for a man and his team. It seemed like a positive disgrace to construct this fence around a race of people who had always been free to roam where they chose.

All summer while we worked, we had no ready cash to buy groceries — and we also had to have feed for our horses. So the agent arranged matters for us to get our supplies on time from the storekeepers. That fall, when we were about ready to quit, our horses were all tired out. They had not been used to doing such heavy work. The Indians were all heavily in debt to the storekeeper. Our houses needed repairs before winter came on. We had no chance to put up hay for our stock, as only the women and children were at home, with the aged and infirm. We had no wood cut for the cold weather which was close at hand. Our stables were in need of repairs.

When we received our money, the first thing we had to do was to pay the storekeeper. After that, we had very little left; not sufficient to purchase supplies for the winter. So we had to go in debt again, which meant that we would have to work hard all the following summer in order to get caught up.

This working out one year put me back two years. There was no encouragement in such an arrangement for any of us. We were in the clutches of the white man — and the Interior Department was behind him!

So I knew I would have to get into some other line of work, for I had a family to support, and I was determined not to be forever in debt. My wife suggested that we move in to the agency, as I was well known there. So we drove there to look the situation over. I had really intended asking the agent for a position of some sort. When we got near the place I saw hotels, stores, livery stables, and a church, all of which had been erected since I last came into the agency. It looked as if there ought to be work there for me.

I noticed the general store of George Caloff and Dick Stern. I went in and asked for work, and was given a job immediately as clerk in the store. We rented a little log house belonging to the missionary. It was handy to my work and we liked it.

One day, the missionary, the Reverend Mr. Snevelly, asked me if I would like to assist him in his work. He wanted an interpreter when he was preaching; so I accepted his offer. Now I had two jobs.

Not long after, Captain Clapp asked if I would take a position as assistant clerk in his office. I said 'yes.' So I arranged matters in order to hold down all three positions, as follows: I worked in the agent's office from 8 A.M. until 4.30 P.M. Then I went home to supper. After supper, I went to the store and put in the balance of the evening there. The church work occupied my time two nights a week and Sundays. I had to be there as interpreter; but after a time I conducted the services myself.

All the Indians were proud to have one of their own race in positions where he could compete with the white people. When they came to the agent's office for their money, I gave them the book in which they were to sign their names. In the evening I was at the store to wait on them, talking to them in the Sioux tongue. When they went to church,

I stood before them and preached to them in their own language. It kept me very busy to hold three positions.

While we were living at the agency, my father came to see me and my family very often. He would go to the store and sit around with the old chiefs and warriors as they talked of the days gone by. Their experiences were very interesting indeed, and attracted a considerable crowd of people, both whites and Indians, who would stand around and listen to these tales of the old-timers.

About the first of the year 1898, my father came to visit us as usual. He remained until about the middle of March. This was during the time I was living at Pine Ridge Agency. When he was ready to leave, he told me he was going to hire one or two young men to go out to my ranch and round up my horses and colts, so they could be branded. He got his men, and everything was in shape for them to start on March 20th. Father was then to go to my ranch house at the head of Pass Creek and remain there until after the round-up.

On the morning of the 20th, my father had breakfast with his family, after which he arose, got a rope and started to go for his horse. He stepped out of the door, but almost immediately came back, saying that he felt very dizzy and would lie down awhile. He made no particular complaint, and the family gave it little thought, expecting that he would get up in a short time. A few minutes later when they tried to awaken him, they discovered that he had died in his sleep. He had passed away, just as he had lived — without complaining. In his last years he had been a good Christian — just as he had been a great fighter in his early life. He always did what he thought was best for the good of his people, never receiving anything for himself alone unless his people received an equal amount. Thus ended the career of my father, a man who had done much good for his own race.

His death was a great shock to us all, as we had never

expected him to pass out in this manner. I was working at the agency when the news was brought to me. There had been a terrible snowstorm. The drifts were very high in places. And worst of all, I was called upon to hold a funeral service over an Indian who had just died at our agency. I could not help thinking of my own father, lying in death, thirty miles away. The snow was so deep that the missionary could not reach the church, so he sent word for me to preach the funeral sermon.

The services were to have been held in the afternoon, but the storm became so violent that the people were delayed in getting to the church, and it grew dark. Coal-oil lamps were lighted, and I came out to preach the last service over this man. How terribly solemn it all seemed to me that evening! When I came to the last few lines of my sermon, the tears were running down my face, and I was glad when I could sit down and let the choir sing a hymn.

My father's remains were taken to the church he had been attending, and buried about two days after the funeral of the Indian I had preached the service over. The Reverend Amos Ross, a Santee Sioux of mixed blood, held the services. The year following his death, I erected the highest tombstone in the cemetery over his grave. During all my father's life I had always shown him respect, and now in death I had finished my work.

At Allen, South Dakota, a man who was running a store wanted to go away for a time, and wrote me asking if I would come and take charge during his absence. Things had not been going exactly to my liking where I was, for some months, and I accepted his offer.

One day a relative of mine named Black Horn came into the store. He said, 'I have come after you to tell you that Buffalo Bill's show is going across the big water, and all the interpreters he had hired have backed out. Why don't you apply for the job?'

I had never been in the show business, and such a life never had appealed to me. An Indian in the store named Bad Hair laughed when Black Horn spoke to me about the job of interpreter. He also made jeering remarks about my going across the big water. 'Why,' he sarcastically remarked, 'you couldn't go across there with a show.'

'Well,' I replied, 'I have never been in the show business, as you all know, but as long as you think I can't go, I will show you that I can.' It made me exceedingly mad to think that I was considered incapable for such a job.

The next day Black Horn came around to the store with his horse and buggy and we started for Rushville, Nebraska, just across the State line, to see William McCune and Jim Esay. McCune hired the Indians for the Buffalo Bill show, and also acted as a sort of bodyguard for Colonel Cody. Esay had a store and provided costumes for those of the Indians who had none themselves.

We drove in the buggy as far as Gordon, Nebraska, and there took the train for Rushville. Neither Black Horn nor I had ever met McCune or Esay, but we found them in the store together. Black Horn was to do the talking, but, as he used no English, I had to interpret for him. This is about what he said: 'My friends, I have brought my younger brother, Standing Bear, to you to say that he can go across the big water as interpreter. We all know that he is a good man.'

Then Esay spoke up and said he had heard of me before, and knew that I was considered one of the reliable men of the reservation. McCune then remarked that he was sorry, but he had already promised the position to another man, Frank Goings, who had been the chief of police at our agency for some time, as well as their interpreter.

'My brother here told me that all the interpreters you had engaged had backed out,' I said. 'That is what brought me over here to inquire about the job.'

McCune and Esay put their heads together and spoke

in low tones for a while. Then McCune turned to me and said, 'If you will go home and return about next Wednesday, we will be better able to determine just who is really to be given the position.'

But I said it would be too much of a trip to go back home and return the following Wednesday, just for that purpose, and that I preferred to stay right there until the matter was settled. So Black Horn and I went to a hotel near by and ordered breakfast.

While we were eating, McCune and Esay walked into the hotel looking for us. McCune said they were going to telephone the agent, and if he said he could not spare Frank Goings, I could have the place. They went over to the depot and called up the agent. Before we had finished eating, they were back again and McCune said, 'We are going to take Standing Bear.' Black Horn was delighted that they were going to take me. So that is how I came to join the Buffalo Bill show.

CHAPTER XXIV
WITH BUFFALO BILL IN ENGLAND

MY wife was greatly pleased when I told her the news that we were going to have the chance to go abroad. We had only three days to get ready, so there was considerable hustling to be done. My horses I turned over to my brother-in-law, Frank Conroy. The wife of White Bull Number Two was to look after our house until we returned.

We were to meet the entire Indian delegation at Rushville. When we reached the top of the hill looking into Rushville, there lay a full Indian camp spread out before us, with all the tipis arranged in a circle. Many of these people already had registered to go with the show, and their relatives had come along with them to see them off. We selected a place to pitch our tent and my wife started to cook over a square tin stove.

After finishing our meal, Black Horn and I hunted up Mr. McCune. We both wanted to take our wives along, but had forgotten to find out if they were to be allowed to accompany us. McCune said it would be a good idea to have them along. This meant that we had to hire some one to take our teams back home, but that was quickly arranged.

As this was my first experience in the show business, I did not know just how much responsibility was really on my shoulders. There were seventy-five Sioux for me to look after, many of them a great deal older than myself. Among the Indians was a young man named Samuel Lone Bear who had been out with the show several seasons, and who spoke fairly good English.

Without going into the details of the trip, we arrived at Jersey City, New Jersey, a few days later. Here we took a ferryboat for New York City, and there boarded an elevated train for the hotel we were to stay in until we left for Europe. Black Horn and his wife and little girl, and my wife, my boy, and myself, all stayed together.

My luggage consisted of two suitcases, but Black Horn had a long sack made of striped bed-ticking, somewhat like the bags carried by sailors, but much larger. In this he had rawhide, tanned skins, awls, sinew, clothing, and all their other belongings. The sack was so full that Black Horn had to carry it in front of him, like a tree trunk.

We had got along splendidly in the cars en route from the West; also on the ferryboat and in the elevated train, but just as we stepped off the elevated train to the sidewalk, the string to Black Horn's bag broke, and clothing, skins, sinew, awls, and all the other contents were scattered in all directions. While we were recovering the things, a great crowd gathered to watch us and to learn the cause of the excitement. When we piled into a trolley car and arrived at our hotel, we each breathed a sigh of relief.

After supper that night, a meeting of all the Indians was called, at which several of the men talked. Finally a man named Rock called on me for a few words. Then I arose and said:

'My relations, you all know that I am to take care of you while going across the big water to another country, and all the time we are to stay there. I have heard that when any one joins this show, about the first thing he thinks of is getting drunk. I understand that the regulations of the Buffalo Bill show require that no Indian shall be given any liquor. You all know that I do not drink, and I am going to keep you all from it. Don't think that because you may be closely related to me I will shield you, for I will not. I will report to Colonel Cody immediately any one I find drinking.'

That was all I said, but it meant a good deal to my

people, and they knew it was said with malice toward none of them.

We remained at this hotel three days, then several large busses called for us and our belongings, and we were carried down to the dock, where a big ship was waiting to receive us. As soon as I stepped on board, there was something about the smell of that ship that made me sick. As I knew nothing about steamships, I am under the impression that we traveled in the steerage, for we were all in one big room. Our bunks were not wide nor long.

The ship was soon under way, and as we got out on the ocean, the water became very rough. All the luggage was scattered about this big room, and the motion of the ship sent it rolling from one side to the other. The women and children became greatly frightened, and even some of the men began to wish for Pine Ridge Reservation. I include myself among the latter. I soon became so sick that I even hated to hear the dishes rattle, and for nine days I suffered the tortures of the damned. There were plenty of the others who could keep nothing on their stomachs at all. It was only Indian corn and dried meat that kept me up. Some of the Indians did not get sick at all, but ate their meals regularly and laughed at the rest of us who could not. As a whole, however, there were very few who were able to walk around.

When the ninth day arrived and our ship docked, we were very happy to feel again the land under our feet, although for some hours we all walked with a peculiar motion after being so long on the water. We landed at Liverpool on a very drizzly morning. Here we were put in some very funny-looking cars with doors on each side. There were two seats to a compartment, and one could not see who was in the compartment behind. No conductor came through the train to tell us where we were, and no fares were collected from any of us. Every time the train stopped, the Indians stuck their heads out the windows to see where we were. As many of the boys had their faces painted and wore feathers in their hair, this sight must have appeared funny to onlookers.

Finally we reached a large city called London. Here we were taken to a big house and quartered upstairs. We found ourselves in a large round room, which had partitions in it somewhat like horse stalls. On the floor of each stall was a nice mattress, and to those who had their families along, this was a very nice arrangement, as curtains could be hung up in front, which gave privacy to those inside. After we had our belongings all arranged, we were called downstairs to a big dining-room.

The smell of that meat cooking was mighty comforting to me, after nine days of 'total abstinence.' It was mutton. We sat down to the tables and waiters came to serve us. The meat was cut into small pieces and served with potatoes and other vegetables and some greens. We cared nothing for the greens. All we wanted was meat, and plenty of it. So we would take the meat off the platter and hand the platter back to the waiter with the potatoes and other things still on it. We certainly kept those waiters busy bringing in meat and carrying out the vegetables.

After the meal was over and everybody was ready to go upstairs, I sent for the head waiter. I told him that Indians did not care for a lot of mixed-up foods such as had just been served to us, but that they wanted meat — lots of it. He was very nice to me, and promised that their wants should be supplied.

None of us wanted to stay up late that night. We were anxious for a good night's sleep on dry land again, so everybody was soon in bed.

The next morning, while we were all waiting to go to the dining-room again, in came a very finely dressed man, wearing a high silk hat, Prince Albert coat, kid gloves, silk handkerchief in his pocket, and carrying a cane. He was so dignified-looking that all the Indians wondered who he might be. He went all around looking in each compartment. He spoke to no one and none of us spoke to him. After I had watched him awhile, I concluded he must be either a fire inspector or the proprietor of the place. I so remarked to the Indians and then we all went down to breakfast.

After finishing the meal and returning to our room, what was our amazement to find our late dignified caller, minus all his finery of silk hat, gloves, Prince Albert coat and cane, making up our beds.

We had to await the arrival of our horses from the United States, and, as there was nothing to do until they came, we put in the time walking around and taking in the sights. But when it came near to meal time we were back at our hotel very promptly.

After we had been in London about a week, Lone Bear came to us with the information that the horses had arrived, but that they were so weak from seasickness it would be several days before they were in shape for active work.

The place where we were quartered I had supposed to be a large hotel. In reality, it was the Olympia Theater, the largest at that time in England. It was somewhat on the order of Madison Square Garden in New York City, but much larger, with rooms upstairs for the actors and actresses. There was a large arena in connection with the theater, in which the Buffalo Bill show gave their performances.

So we went down to look over the arena. Here we found our horses — black, white, bay, and buckskin-colored animals. While all the Indians belonged to the Sioux tribe, we were supposed to represent four different tribes, each tribe to ride animals of one color. So we began to pick out the horses we wanted to ride. Then the fun commenced. The animals began bucking, throwing the Indians hither and yonder; but none of them seemed to mind it. They just got up and climbed on again. Sam Lone Bear was here very much in evidence. He told me I was to have a very gentle horse which had been used by Johnny Baker, a young protégé of Buffalo Bill, and an expert rifle shot. This horse had only one eye, but was a good show horse, and had been used in the arena so much that he was well broken in all that was required of him, and needed no 'gentling.'

This horse really knew more about the show business at that time than I did myself. Of course a lot of practice was required before the show was ready to open to the public. Sam Lone Bear saw my confusion at the start, as I did not know what was required of me, and he came to me and said that all I was to do was to sit at the gate on my horse all through the show; so I did as he told me, but I got mighty tired sitting on that horse in one spot while all the others were going through stunts of various kinds. However, I received no orders from any one else, so I supposed it was all right.

But Johnny Baker observed me sitting on that horse in the same place every day, and he finally came over to me and said, 'Standing Bear, what are you sitting here for? Do you want something, or what is the matter with you?'

'No,' I answered. 'Sam Lone Bear told me that I was to sit right here in this spot all the time, in case you wanted me for anything.'

Then Johnny laughed. 'Why,' said he, 'you are not to stay here at all. After the Indians go out of the arena, you are to go with them. Go home after you have turned your horse loose. Don't mind what Sam Lone Bear says to you. You are in charge of these Indians, not he. Just because he has been out with the show a few times he imagines he has some authority around here. If I ever want you I will send for you.'

That awakened me to the responsibility of my job. I

found out then and there that I was to take orders from nobody but Buffalo Bill or Johnny Baker.

Every day we had a rehearsal, and at last came the day for the opening performance. Everything was in readiness. Each tribe was on horseback, as were the various nations represented. The announcer would call out, 'The Sioux Nation,' and out would dash the Sioux, riding beautiful white horses. Then would come the chief of the Sioux. This part was taken by Black Horn, my cousin. Next came the Cheyennes, Arapahoes, etc. Then the announcer called out, 'The Chief Interpreter of the Sioux Nation,' which was my time to come racing into the ring and around the arena. The performers went through their various parts admirably.

Buffalo Bill was well pleased to note how well the Indians minded me in all our work. I was wearing a very fine outfit, and the damp weather of London was not doing it any good. So after we had given a few shows, Johnny Baker came to me one day and said it would be a good plan if I did not wear my best clothes on the days when the attendance was not large, but that on such days I might take the part of a cowboy if I chose. This was a change for me and I enjoyed it very much.

One day Colonel Cody sent for me to come to his private office. Wondering what he could want of me, I knocked at his door. He invited me in, remarking, 'Sit down, Standing Bear. I have sent for you because I want to tell you something of importance. The Big Chief of this country — the King of England — has promised to attend a performance of our show. Now I want you to go back to your people, call them all together, and tell them all about it. Tell them to be very careful about their clothes; to see that they are perfectly clean and neat for that particular performance. If anything needs repairs, tell them to attend to it at once. We must please the King at this performance. Rehearse your Indians well so they will do their best for me. If the King likes our show, it will please the people of this country. I have observed your own costume. It is very fine, and when the King attends the show, I want you to do an Indian dance in front of his box. Will you do this for me?'

I answered, 'Yes, sir, I will. You can depend on all of the Indians to do their very best.'

'That will be fine,' gleefully replied Colonel Cody, as I walked out of his office.

I went back to my people and we got together in council. I told them everything that Colonel Cody had requested me to. All the Indians promised to do their very best. While we still occupied our little compartments upstairs, now that the show was on we had a little Indian village built up inside of this big theater. When our part in the show was over, we went to our village, where the visitors had a chance to see how we lived.

At length the day arrived for the special performance for the King. The best seats were reserved for his party, in the center of which was the seat for the King. All of these had been decorated in gold, and made a beautiful appearance. The theater began to fill up very early that day. Buffalo Bill was very nervous, lest something should go wrong. Finally there was a great stir out in front, and we noticed that the King and his party had arrived. Everybody in the theater arose as they entered and remained standing until his entire party were seated. They were all very elegantly dressed, the gentlemen in full dress, with silk hats, and the ladies in very low-necked dresses with long trains.

Buffalo Bill came to me several times and said, 'Don't forget, now, Standing Bear, to have your boys do their very best. And dance your very best before the King.'

I promised to carry out all his wishes faithfully, and the show started. Everything worked splendidly. When it came time for the Indians to come in with their village in the center of the arena, we started the dance in which I was to appear before the King of England. I had a beautiful lance, and as the dance proceeded I worked over toward the King's box. There I shook the lance in his face and danced my very prettiest, you may be sure. The King had been very dignified thus far and had not even smiled. But when I got down to doing my fancy steps and gave a few Sioux yells, he had to smile in spite of himself. I saw that I had made a hit with him, and was very happy.

After the show, Buffalo Bill brought the King and his party around inside the arena. In front of him walked a big man who seemed to keep his eyes roving about all the while. I think he must have been the King's personal bodyguard. Buffalo Bill brought the King over to me and we were introduced. We shook hands, although neither of us said a word. But I had the honor of being introduced to King Edward the Seventh, the monarch of Great Britain.

Not very long after this, we began to have trouble with the Indians. They were commencing to get liquor somewhere, but I was unable for some time to locate the place. As soon as the show was over, they would skip out and nobody knew where they went. Finally I went to see Mr. McCune about it. I told him that something had got to be done to keep the Indian boys straight as long as I was with the show. I suggested that we have some cards printed with each man's name and a number on them. Whenever a man left the building he was to take his card and hang it on a board by the gate-keeper's stand. Then we would know just who was out and who was in.

McCune thought it a good plan. This scheme worked all right for a few days, but the Indians did not take very well to the new arrangement. Without letting me know anything about it, they sent for McCune. But he told me they had sent for him, and requested that I go with him to find out what their grievance was.

So I went in with him. The Indians were greatly surprised to see me, as this was something they had not expected. McCune said, 'You people have sent for me to see you in council, so here I am. I have brought your interpreter with me so I will be able to understand all you say to me. Now, then, what is the trouble, and what do you want?'

Then Chief Rock stood up and said, 'Mr. McCune, we have sent for you to ask why it is we all have to have tickets which we must hang up on that board every time we go out? Now, our interpreter is one of us, but he has no ticket. We think he should have one, just the same as ourselves, so if he is out we will know it.'

Poor old Chief Rock! He simply wanted to know if I was out so he would be more careful about buying liquor!

McCune smiled. Then he winked at me and said, 'Well, Standing Bear, I guess you will have to make out a ticket for yourself, too.'

That was perfectly satisfactory to me, and everybody seemed pleased. When we got outside, I explained to McCune what the ticket scheme meant, so he said, 'We'll fix them. You just hang your ticket up by the gate-keeper's stand, and I will fix things with him to leave it on the board all the time. Then they will never know whether you are out or in.'

It was amusing to note the effect that card had on the Indians who wanted their liquor. They would go to the gate, and as soon as they saw my card hanging up they were afraid to go out, lest they run into me somewhere on the street. And very often I was right in the building at the time!

But in spite of our best efforts, the Indians managed to get their whiskey. The craving for the vile stuff made them go to extremes and they would come in rather 'loose in their feet.' One day after the performance three of the Indians were missing. Nobody knew where they had gone;

so I started out to see if I could round them up. I was in civilian clothes, and not conspicuous. Once outside the theater building I walked rapidly to the corner, and away up the street I saw a red blanket. I walked fast and observed the wearer go down a few steps where there was a barroom. Finally the door opened again and out came one of the old men of the Sioux. He was staggering a bit. He did not recognize me immediately, but saw that I was watching him closely. So he started talking what few words of English he knew. 'Me whiskey — not much,' he grunted.

I never answered him, but brushed him aside and went down into the bar-room. There sat Chief Rock and Red Star, two of the men who were playing the parts of chiefs. They were seated at a little table with a bottle between them. I walked up to them before they recognized me, and it was too late to hide the bottle. They were so surprised that they were just speechless. I ordered them to come with me. Although there was quite a bit of liquor left in the bottle, they obeyed my orders. We walked back to the theater together. I did not scold them.

The next day I went to see Colonel Cody about the matter. I told him about the men who had gone against my orders. He said, 'This is the first time they have been caught, so we will let it go this time; but if they are caught again, we will punish them in some way.' If I remember correctly, we did not have any further trouble with the Indians about liquor while in London.

The English people were very good to us. They would invite the Indians to their homes and give them plenty of good things to eat. One lady in particular stands out in my memory. She was of middle age, and she always came twice a week to see the Indians. She always carried a pocketbook made of wire — one of the kind the white people call a 'mesh-bag.' You could look right through and see what was in it. In this pocketbook she always carried gold pieces. She would take out men or women — sometimes an entire family — and treat them until her pocketbook was empty. The Indians soon 'got wise' to this particular woman, and thought it a great treat to go out with her, because, if they happened to see a pin or a ring that sparkled and took their fancy, she would always buy it for them.

We remained at the Olympia three months and had a royal good time. Finally we were told that the show was going to move to another city. Then everybody had to pack all his belongings. I was sorry to leave this city, because I had been given a chance to see many wonderful sights and visit many interesting places. I recall that one day I visited the house where all the toys were kept with which Queen Victoria had played as a child, and I was shown where all her jewelry was on display. I also visited Westminster Abbey, one of the most beautiful churches in the world, and a very historic spot. The King's palace was also a place of great interest. So I, for one, was sorry when the show came to an end in London, and we had to leave the beautiful Olympia Theater.

The weather in England does not compare with that of the United States: there is so much fog, especially in London, and the roads were always muddy.

Everything was arranged to move like clockwork. When we would arrive in a new town, early in the morning, the Indians would all get their horses and ride out to the grounds where the show was to be held, which was usually on the outskirts of the place. Sometimes we would have to wait until the 'big top' had been erected. The 'big top' was the dining-tent, and you may be sure we kept our eyes open for that. The Indian village would always be located not far from the dining-tent.

When the wagon carrying our tipis arrived, some of the boys would roll their blankets around their waists and help unload the wagon. Each man knew his own tipi, and as

fast as they were unloaded we would set them up. It was
hard work, especially in wet and muddy weather. Bales of
straw would be distributed about to put on the ground inside the tipis to keep us out of the mud. In the center of the
tipi would be a space for the fire, and after this was started
it would not be long before the inside of the tipi would be
nice and dry.

Breakfast would shortly be ready. Our appetites were
sharpened by the work we had been doing. In the dining-
tent was one long table for the Indians, with other tables
for the various other nationalities represented in the show.
We always had plenty to eat, so there was no complaint
in that direction.

One morning as I came into the dining-tent I noticed
that everybody but the Indians had been served with hot
cakes. This did not bother me very much, as Indians do
not eat such food. At dinner-time that same day, when I
sat down to our table, I saw to my surprise that there were
pancakes before us. These were the 'left-overs' from the
morning, and now the cook wanted to feed them to us. Although I was very angry, I made no remark, but quietly
left the table and went over where Buffalo Bill and the
head officials of the show were eating dinner.

Colonel Cody asked, 'What is it, Standing Bear?'

'Colonel Cody,' I replied, 'this morning all the other
races represented in the show were served with pancakes,
but the Indians were not given any. We do not object to
that, as we do not care for them; but now the cook has put
his old cold pancakes on our table and expects us to eat
what was left over from breakfast, and it isn't right.'

Buffalo Bill's eyes snapped, as he arose from the table.
'Come with me, Standing Bear,' he exclaimed. We went
direct to the manager of the dining-room, and Colonel
Cody said to him, 'Look here, sir, you are trying to feed my
Indians the left-over pancakes from the morning meal. I
want you to understand, sir, that I will not stand for such

treatment. My Indians are the principal feature of this show, and they are the one people I will not allow to be misused or neglected. Hereafter see to it that they get just exactly what they want at meal-time. Do you understand me, sir?'

'Yes, sir, oh, yes, sir,' exclaimed the embarrassed manager. After that we had no more trouble about our meals.

In all my experience in the show business I have met many Indians of various tribes, as well as many interpreters, and to me it did not seem right for Indians who cannot understand a word of the English language to leave the reservation to engage in the show business. They are certain to meet with some abuse or mistreatment unless they have an interpreter who is 'right on the job' and who will watch out for their interests and see that they get just treatment; otherwise they are not going to get the best work out of the Indians.

Right after breakfast, in a new town, we would get dressed for the big parade which was always held. This usually occupied the time until dinner. After that, we had about an hour before the afternoon performance began. When that was over we had a few hours before supper and the evening performance.

At this time, many of the Indians would want to go out and buy trinkets and things to carry back home, such as nice blankets and shawls. But during the rainy weather some of them thought they had an excuse to drink. They said they thought it kept them warm. I saw at once that this must not go on, as a little whiskey always calls for more. So I called all the Indians together in council, and explained to them that I had noticed they were beginning to look for liquor again and that it was not good for them. Then I said:

'I am going to make a new rule with you. Every man and woman hereafter will receive only half their pay. The balance will be kept in my care until near the end of the season. Then those of you who think you must be spending your money all the time will have something to take home with you when your work is done.'

Some, of course, did not like this plan. While they knew it was for their best interest, still they did not want to do without their liquor. But the majority fell right in with my proposition. They knew I would be honest with them, and that their money was safe with me. So it was agreed that on each pay-day half of the money should be put away until the show closed. Further, each man was warned that he must be more careful about drinking.

After the evening performance everything had to be packed ready to move again. This was when we were making only one-day stands, and it was very hard on us. We had to ride our horses over to the train and see that all our property also went. If the depot was not far away, the women would walk, but if it was some distance I would hire a big bus to carry them there.

After our horses were properly loaded, we would hunt up the small lunch counter which followed the show, just for the purpose of giving us a chance to get coffee, frankfurters, and chopped meat sandwiches, somewhat like what the white people now call 'hot dogs.' A cup of hot coffee and a good sandwich, on a cold night, tasted mighty good.

And so it went, day after day and week after week, as long as the season lasted. In some places in England I have seen those fogs so thick that one could not see across the arena in which we were giving our performance, and we had to ride very close to our audiences so they could see what we were doing. We suffered very much from wet feet, as we wore moccasins, which are not made for wet weather.

My cousin, Black Horn, his wife and daughter and myself and my family were always together. We did not like the arrangements on the show train, and we decided to ask

Colonel Cody if we could not have a special car to ride in, where we could be by ourselves. The cars for the show people were too 'stuffy' and we wanted more fresh air; so we told him we were willing to pay for the special car. Colonel Cody laughed and informed us that we could not hire a car, but would have to buy one, and that it would cost ten thousand dollars. We were somewhat surprised and likewise shocked, as we had no idea about such things, so we concluded we would have to 'grin and bear it.'

On rainy days we always sat inside the big tent. There we could talk about home, home cooking, and the good things we wished we could have to eat that were cooked Indian fashion. Some of the old men would wish for wild peppermint tea and fried bread. Others wished they could have dried meat and bacon, while some wanted roast ribs or choke-cherry soup. We really had plenty to eat, but it was not cooked 'Indian style.'

There were a great many cowboys with the show. There was a chief of the cowboys who had general supervision over both horses and men. When an unbroken horse would be brought in, this cowboy chief would give it to an Indian to ride bareback. After the animal was well broken, it would be taken away from the Indian and given to a cowboy to ride. Then the Indian would be given another unbroken horse. For quite awhile we said nothing about it, but finally it began to be just a little too much to stand. One day one of the Indians came to me just before it was time to enter the arena. His horse was saddled and bridled, but he was leading the animal by the bridle. I asked him what was the matter, and he said it was a wild horse and he was not going to ride it into the arena.

I went to the chief cowboy and said, 'I do not think you are doing right. You know our Indian boys have to ride bareback, but you always give them the wild horses to ride. Then, when they have the horse nicely broken, you give it to a cowboy. Why don't you give the wild horses to the cowboys to break in? They ride on saddles, and it would not be so hard for them.'

But the chief cowboy only said, 'Well, I can't be bothered by a little thing like that. You will have to see Buffalo Bill about the horses.'

But I retorted, 'You know very well that Buffalo Bill does not know what you do with the horses. He does not know that you give the wild ones to the Indian boys to ride until they are broken in. Give that horse back to that Indian boy or he will not go into the arena to-day.'

That was all — but the boy got his horse in time to enter the arena with the others. Just as I was ready to go back to the Indians, I looked at Buffalo Bill, and he had a twinkle in his eye. After that, we had no more trouble with the horses. Although Buffalo Bill never said anything to me, I knew he had fixed things to our satisfaction.

While we were traveling about England, one of the Indian boys came to me one evening and said he would like some kidney fat, raw, with his fried steak, for breakfast, so I went to the chief of the dining-tent and told him what the boy wanted. 'Why, yes, of course he can have it,' was the reply. 'Now, is there anything else any of the others would like?'

'Yes,' I answered, 'they would like some of those big sweet onions.'

The next morning when we went in for breakfast, there was plenty of fried steak, kidney fat, and sweet onions. That was surely a treat for all of us!

Buffalo Bill saw that I never drank nor smoked, and that all the Indians listened to me, and that I treated them all alike and showed no partiality. He became so interested in me that one day he sent for me to come to his tent. There we discussed Indian affairs. He queried me about my tribe; asked how we got along and what was really needed to help us. We had quite a pow-wow, and

when I went away he said that he would send for me again
very soon.

We had several of these talks together later. One day
he told me that he and President Roosevelt were very good
friends, and as Roosevelt was then in the presidential chair
he felt that he could use his influence to help my people,
providing he could get the authority from Washington.
He asked if I would write home and ask all the old chiefs
to appoint him as their helper. He said he would then
engage some good attorneys to bring the grievances of the
Sioux tribe before the President.

So I wrote home about the matter. At first the old chiefs
were puzzled a bit. They could not quite understand why
a white man wanted to help them when he was not even
married to an Indian woman. The letters were read in
council at which Charles Allen and some other squaw-men
were present. A 'squaw-man' is a white man who has an
Indian wife. Some of these squaw-men said that as President Roosevelt was a Westerner, he could do wonders for
the tribe. The old chiefs listened to what the squaw-men
said because they were married to our women.

Then they wrote back to me, telling me what they
thought should be done, and who should go ahead with
the matter. At that time I was not a chief, and my father,
who had been their chief, had passed on to his eternal rest,
so I could do nothing more at that time. So through these
squaw-men talking too much, Buffalo Bill gave up the idea,
and once again we failed in securing some one who would
take an interest in our welfare. And the squaw-men, of
course, never did anything for us. 'Talk is cheap.'

After a time the show reached Birmingham. This was a
beautiful city, but we had an arena there. While we were
showing in Birmingham, a little daughter was born to us.
The morning papers discussed the event in big headlines
that the first full-blooded Indian baby had been born at
the Buffalo Bill show grounds. Colonel Cody was to be its

godfather, and the baby was to be named after the reign-ing Queen of England. The child's full name was to be Alexandra Birmingham Cody Standing Bear.

The next morning Colonel Cody came to me and asked if my wife and baby could be placed in the side-show. He said the English people would like to see the face of a newly born Indian baby lying in an Indian cradle or 'hoksicala postan.' I gave my consent, and the afternoon papers stated that the baby and mother could be seen the following afternoon.

Long before it was time for the show to begin, people were lining up in the road. My wife sat on a raised platform, with the little one in the cradle before her. The people filed past, many of them dropping money in a box for her. Nearly every one had some sort of little gift for her also. It was a great drawing card for the show; the work was very light for my wife, and as for the baby, before she was twenty-four hours old she was making more money than my wife and I together.

With the coming of the new baby came added cares, of course. Our little boy, who was named after me (Luther), had to be rigged up for the part he took in the show. He had a full costume of buckskin, very much like the one I wore, and every day his face must be painted and his hair combed and braided for the two performances. The Indian boys seemed to think it was a pleasure to get the little chap ready for exhibition. After he was 'all fixed up,' he would stand outside the tipi, and the English-speaking people would crowd around to shake his hand and give him money. This he would put in a little pocket in his buck-skin jacket, and when it was full he would refuse to accept any more, although the crowd would try to force it on him. Then he would leave, in apparent disgust, and come inside the tipi. He kept us all laughing.

It was now getting near the end of our stay in England. One day Buffalo Bill brought a tailor into the Indian encampment. All the men were called together and told that they were to have new suits of clothes as a present for the good work they had done while with the show. The tailor had samples of cloth, and each man was measured for a tailor-made suit. How pleased all the men were over this!

Each woman was to receive a gingham dress and a blanket.

CHAPTER XXV

I AM MADE CHIEF

WE had now been in England eleven months, and during all that time I had kept back half of the pay of every Indian, so it amounted to quite a sum of money. Those who had not spent their money foolishly had purchased blankets, shawls, dresses, and other pretty and useful articles. Just before the show closed, the new suits and dresses were delivered, and each Indian received the back pay due him. They were a happy and well-dressed looking crowd then.

Before we sailed for the United States, I told the Indians that if any of them became intoxicated during the voyage they would lose their last month's pay. All agreed to abide by my decision. With the others I had received a new suit, and in addition, Buffalo Bill made me a present of fifty dollars in cash. He said that was in appreciation of the good work I had done in keeping the Indians sober and in good order.

The Indians had made so many purchases that they wanted some trunks to pack their things in, but I advised them to wait until they reached the United States. So they tore up the old tipis, which were practically worn out, and wrapped their belongings in them.

When we reached Chicago I took all the Indian men up to Marshall Field & Company's store. They all wanted to buy fur overcoats. Twenty-seven of these were sold. I selected one for myself, upon which they gave me a discount for bringing in so many good customers. Then at another place we all bought new trunks. Some of the boys even indulged in some 'make-up,' such as they had seen white girls using, and it was not long before they could decorate their lips, cheeks, eyebrows, etc., as expertly as any white girl.

Then we started for Dakota and home. When we reached Nebraska and the train neared Rushville, every one became excited. All the Indians from our reservation had come down to meet us, and had erected their tipis in a circle, just like the old days, and everybody was cooking and getting a good meal ready for us.

When we left the train the Indians all went to McCune and Esay's store, and there I paid them off. I had not realized until then what a strain I had been under for nearly a year, and I began to feel very tired and went to our tipi and lay down for a nap. When I awoke, I observed several of my wife's relatives in the tipi, all crying. They said a relative had died while we were away, and now they were all having a good cry together.

To this day I am proud of the success I had while abroad with the Buffalo Bill show, in keeping the Indians under good subjection. It seems to me that when any one joins a show of any sort, about the first thing he thinks of is drinking. That is wrong. It makes your employer angry and disgusted and does the person himself no good. It also takes courage to say 'no' when thrown in with people who drink; but it pays. I respected my people and talked kindly to them.

All during the fall and winter after reaching home, I was quite ill. I had a contract to put up cordwood for two day-schools. Three men were working for me, and during that time a great many Indians came to me to sign up for the Buffalo Bill show the next season. But I told them I had not heard a word from Buffalo Bill, and did not know whether I was going out with the show the coming season or not. It became noised around that Frank Goings was to have charge of the Indians the following season. He did not deny the report, so I just said nothing.

Along toward spring I received a letter from Colonel

Cody saying he wished me to get ready to go out with the show again. Neither my wife nor myself said a word to any one about this, as I did not want to be bothered. My wife was not going to accompany me on this trip, as she had the new baby to care for.

Rushville was to be the meeting-place again, and when I arrived there I was surprised to see all the Indians from my reservation there, waiting. They had a big camp. It seems they had found out in some manner that I was again to be in charge and when I entered the camp I was besieged on all sides from those who wanted to go out with the show.

McCune and I gave a feast, to which all the Indians who wanted to go out with the show were invited to come in full costume, so we could 'size them up' and select those who had good outfits. We watched their dancing very closely, and some of the young people did look very pretty indeed. We selected those having the finest outfits and who were the best dancers, and who, in our opinion, would not drink.

Two days before we started, our little baby girl, born in England, became sick and died. Mr. McCune and Mr. Esay took full charge of the funeral, and as an honor to my family they had all the Indians who were to accompany me with the show dress in full Indian costume and march to the cemetery through the town of Rushville. It was a solemn and impressive sight.

We were to leave for New York the following day. Early in the morning, two of the Indians came to me and said they had changed their minds about going. When I asked the reason, they said they had had bad dreams the previous night, which made them feel that something would happen to them if they went away. They were very superstitious and afraid. It was no trouble to get two others to take their places.

Everything went along nicely, once we were on the road, until we reached Maywood, Illinois. On the morning of April 7, 1903, I was sitting in the last car of the train. It was very early, but we were all up and dressed. I was riding in such a position that I could look out the rear door and see the railroad track winding in and out. Several of the men were singing and I joined in. One man who was sitting next to me did not sing, but seemed very quiet as if worried about something.

We were rounding a curve, when suddenly I saw a train behind us coming at lightning speed. Then came a terrific crash. There was not even time to cry out. When I opened my eyes again, the seats were piled up on top of us and the steam and smoke from the engine were pouring in on us in great clouds. My legs were pinned down, and I was perfectly helpless. The moaning of the injured and the screams of many of the white people in the car were terrible. Blood was everywhere. Overhead I could see the blue sky shining. I started to sing a brave song. One of my cousins, who had not been injured, came over to me and offered me a drink of whiskey; but I remarked that I had lived all these years without it and did not intend to commence right there.

In this railroad wreck three young men were killed outright and twenty-seven of us badly injured. Some had mangled arms which had to be amputated; others lost their legs. My own injuries consisted of a dislocation of both hips, left leg broken below the knee, left arm broken, two ribs broken on the left side, and a broken collar bone. Three ribs on the right side were badly sprained, my nose was broken and both eyes seriously cut, and I sustained a deep gash across the back of my head.

A box car was brought up, and the dead and injured loaded on it. When they dragged me out of the wreckage, they laid me out with the dead. When we reached the hospital and they carried me in on a stretcher, one of the doctors said I was just as good as dead. In the first newspaper accounts my name was included among those killed.

The news reached the reservation that I had been killed;

so my sister, the wife of Chief Hollow Horn Bear, cut her hair very short. All my sisters and brothers were in mourning. They even gave away horses and other valuables, according to the Indian custom.

At the hospital, one of the doctors came in and saw that I was conscious, but unable to talk. He held out no hope whatever for me. I was not worrying about either living or dying. I knew I had terrible pains in the region of my stomach. Suddenly something inside seemed to burst, and I threw up great quantities of blood. After that, I felt greatly relieved, and told Mr. McCune to send a telegram to my relatives that I was not going to die.

Of course that 'settled me' and a great many others, so far as going out with the show was concerned, for that season, at least. McCune went to Rushville and secured other Indians to take the places of the killed and injured; and so the Buffalo Bill show went to England that season without us.

Shortly after my return home, my little son Luther, who had been with us in England, passed away. He was beloved by all, particularly the old people. Whenever the little fellow saw an old man or old woman coming down the road, he would run out, take them by the hand, and lead them in to his mother, asking her to feed them. So his untimely death was an occasion for great mourning throughout the tribe.

The year prior to his death he had been honored by being selected to act as the council drum-keeper. This position meant that he collected whatever was offered as sacrifices at any dance given. The significance of it is that, if a dance is in order and a song is sung for some particular individual, that individual must arise and dance and say, 'I give this (or that) for my song.' Sometimes these gifts might be money, bead-work, or cattle or horses — whatever they felt able to give. So my little son had the honor of caring for the gifts. But now he was taken away and I was to take his place in collecting the offerings given.

This was early in 1905, and I had quite a collection of various kinds of presents. Even the Omaha Indians who met my boy brought blankets, bead-work, horses, and money.

Soon the time arrived for the 'big time.' In the olden days it was known as the Sun Dance, and it was to be held on the 4th of July.

You will remember that I explained about the bower which was made for those who were to watch the dancers, with the pole in the center. All the tribe brought their tipis and they were set up in a great circle, as in the olden days, making a village about a mile in circumference.

We had a big tent erected, and everything inside looked very nice. Some Omahas and Pawnees came to visit us, and, as it was just about noon, we were sitting on the ground eating our lunch when two old chiefs of my tribe walked in. Without saying a word or making a sign, they took me by the arms, lifted me from the ground and led me outside. There stood two horses. They motioned for me to mount one of them behind one of the chiefs. I did so and off we rode.

They took me to the center of the big camp where this great bower was erected. At the extreme end sat all the old chiefs in a half-circle. I was led up in front of all of these old men and told to sit down. It then suddenly dawned upon me that they wanted me to be made chief in my father's place, as our band had now been without a chief for seven years.

At the time of my father's passing, there were six brothers of us. No mention was ever made as to which one would take his place. I now began to realize that I was the chosen one, and a great responsibility suddenly seemed to fall upon me.

Then one of the old chiefs arose with the pipe of peace

in his hand. Wrapping his blanket around his waist, he came over in front of me. There was strict silence while this old man handled the pipe. Lighting it, he pointed it toward the blue sky, or heaven, thence to the east, north, south, and west respectively; then lastly to Mother Earth. Stepping up to me, I was commanded to stand. Then the old man held the pipe before me crossways. I held my two hands over the pipe, palms down, not touching it, but just over it. My body bent slightly as I made the motion with the hands of going over the pipe. This I did three times; then the old chief turned the mouthpiece toward me. As I never smoked, I simply put both hands over the stem about halfway up, and drew them toward me, which signified, 'I accept the pipe.'

As I finished this part of the ceremony, the old chiefs exclaimed, 'Ha ye,' meaning, 'Thank you.' Such is a description of the manner in which I went through the ceremony and accepted the title of chief, which my father had previously held. One of the old men then arose and recounted many interesting incidents about my father; what a brave man he had been, and not afraid to stand up for his people, but had fought for their rights.

Another of the old chiefs then spoke to me. He said, 'We have made you a chief because we feel that you will be able to take the place of your father.' He then told me all that the people would expect of me, and for me to do all I could for the sake of my people.

I told them I did not expect ever to be as great a man as my father had been, but that I would do all in my power to help my people at all times, regardless of where I might be. That was the oath I took when I became chief of the Oglala Sioux, the greatest Indian tribe in the United States.

The chiefs then began to sing a brave song, and all got up to dance. Now that I was one of them, I had to dance with them. That was the first time in my life that I had the honor of dancing with the old chiefs. As I was expected to give something away on this occasion, I said that I would give away ten dollars to-day and to-morrow would be there again.

Early on the morning of July 4, 1905, I hitched up my two teams. I had a lumber wagon and a top buggy, with two beautiful teams of horses for them. Both were new vehicles, and the harness was spick and span as well. The lumber wagon I loaded with groceries, meats, bead-work, blankets, dry goods, and many other articles of value. The buggy was filled with beautiful bead-work. On one side of it we hung the full costume of my little boy who had died — buckskin suit, beaded vest, moccasins, and little blankets. These were to be given away in remembrance of him. Before taking these things over to give them away, I had two different bands of Indians from Rosebud Agency act as escorts. One of the chiefs was Hollow Horn Bear and the other High Pipe.

My wife drove the buggy and I drove the wagon, while we were escorted around the camp by these two bands of Indians. Everybody was on horseback, even the women. The various bands of Indians were camped together, with each chief's tipi in front, and, as we came in front of a chief's tipi, our escort would stop, dismount, and have a short dance. Then all would mount again and move on.

In this way we made the rounds of the camp. Many of the people, upon seeing the clothing of the little boy hanging from the side of the buggy, would cry. It was a sorrowful gathering as well as one of rejoicing, for I was now a chief. After going the rounds of the camp, we came back to my tipi and then started for the big hall, or bower, to give the presents away. How excited all the people were to see us!

In different places they started to sing songs of praise for me. Frank Goings, the chief of the Indian Police and interpreter at the agency, had brought over the Boys' Band from the boarding-school, with all their instruments. In between the Indian songs, the band would play. I then started giving away the things I had brought along.

I kept this up until I had given away everything I owned, and my wife and I walked away with practically nothing. We figured that we gave away that day about a thousand dollars' worth of goods ourselves, not counting all the presents that had been donated to be distributed. We were certainly good and tired when the day's festivities were over.

There were many tribes present that day — Omahas, Pawnees, Winnebagoes, Crows, Cheyennes, Arapahoes, as well as the Sioux. So I was made a chief in the Indian custom in front of all these different tribes; therefore the title of 'Chief' is now right and proper for me to use, whether in California or in any other part of the United States; and my people know that as long as I live I will do what is right and proper for them.

A chief receives no salary, and at gatherings it is up to him to see that everything is done properly. We have no more war councils, but if a Commissioner is sent from Washington to make any sort of contract with the tribe, it is up to the chief to be present and investigate the matter. That is the law among the Indians. It is a great honor to receive the title of 'Chief,' but there is much hard work about it also.

Whenever an Indian leaves his reservation and comes among the white people to-day, either to go on the stage or in the moving pictures or with a Wild West show, he is always greeted with 'Hello, Chief.' This is most decidedly wrong. Suppose when you visited an Indian reservation, the Indians should say to you, 'Hello, President,' or 'Hello, King.' You would think it not only silly, but it would be most embarrassing. Then sometimes the white people call a woman of mixed blood 'princess.' How can that be right and proper when Indians have no kings or queens, and therefore there can be no 'princesses'? The highest title an Indian woman can receive is wife or mother. And where is there greater honor than that?

The expression 'chief' and 'princess' has become so common nowadays that various impostors have seized upon it as a means of collecting money, supposedly to go to help their tribe. There are many such in Los Angeles, my home city. These are the facts as I have found them. When I go to such impostors, they just say, 'Oh, well, Chief, we are only doing this for the sake of publicity.' Don't you white people see how and in what manner you are being swindled and tricked? It would be well for the white race to learn who is the true American. It is high time they knew the difference.

With all my title of chieftain, and with all my education and travels, I discovered that as long as I was on the reservation I was only a helpless Indian, and was not considered any better than any of the uneducated Indians — that is, according to the views of the white agent in charge of the reservation. He had been given the authority at Washington to look after us. If I tried to better the condition of my people, while on the reservation, I found it was an utter impossibility. So I had to do one of two things — keep my mouth shut or fight the agent all the time.

CHAPTER XXVI

AMERICAN CITIZENSHIP

About that time a party of Indians were going to New York City in charge of my brother, Henry Standing Bear, to appear at the Hippodrome in an act which brought in all the nations of the world. I decided to join them and see how life off the reservation would be. 'Perhaps,' thought I, 'things have changed quite a bit since I got out of Carlisle School.'

We stayed at one of the big hotels in New York, and had two acts a day in which to appear. We had a six months' contract, so when that ran out, all the Indians went home except myself. I concluded to stay and see if I could make my living among the white people. I appeared in theaters and side-shows. I lectured, and did any sort of work I could find. While lecturing I met many people who were really interested in learning the truth in regard to the Indians. I determined that, if I could only get the right sort of people interested, I might be able to do more for my own race off the reservation than to remain there under the iron rule of the white agent.

After several months I made a trip back to the reservation to visit my folks and tell them what I intended to do. My brothers and sisters wanted me to remain, but I told them if we were free it might be different, but as for myself, I had come to the conclusion that the reservation was no place for me.

About that time (1907) I was given my allotment of land, six hundred and forty acres. That was in Bennett County, South Dakota. You will remember that in an earlier part of this book I told how my father had risked his life to sign the paper that gave us our allotment of land. We had waited all that time to learn where we were to live.

Now that I had received mine, I did not want to stay on the reservation. But how could I get away — that was the question!

Several educated Indians and some half-breeds had tried to get fee patents for their lands, and were refused. Even a highly educated Omaha Indian named Tom Sloane, who was a practicing attorney, was turned down by the Government. This fee patent was a paper giving us the right to sell our land if we chose, and go elsewhere to make our living. It would make citizens of us. That was the reason the agent did not want us to get such privileges. If all the Indians left the reservation, the agent would lose his job — and the job of Indian agent in those days was a money-making one.

So it appeared to be up to me to get my citizenship papers. According to the Constitution of the United States, we did not have to become citizens, because we were born here.

One day I went to Omaha to see Tom Sloane, the Omaha Indian lawyer. I asked him if he would help me make out an application so that I could get a fee patent to my land. He did this, and then we went to the agent's office to see if he would endorse the papers. He signed them, and I gave them to Sloane to take to Washington, where he was shortly going on business.

I concluded that, as an Indian attorney had charge of my case, all would go well, and I would soon be a free man — free to come and free to go. In a few days a long official-looking envelope arrived from Washington for me. I opened it, and great was my disappointment when I found inside a letter which said, 'Some one left these papers in this office. We noted your name and address on them, so we are returning them to you.'

Mr. Sloane's name was never mentioned. I stood there dumbfounded for a time. Everything seemed to be working against me. Finally I concluded to go to Washington

and investigate for myself. I determined that if they
turned me down in the Interior Department and closed
the door of freedom in my face, there was nothing left in
this life for me. I telegraphed the Commissioner of Indian
Affairs, asking if it would be necessary for me to come to
Washington. He wired back that he would be pleased to
see me, but that I had better make out my application for
a quarter-section of land, or one hundred and forty acres.

I made up my mind to be free entirely, so this was how
I figured the way out: I made out two applications, one for
a quarter-section and the other for three quarters. Then
I sent both applications to Washington and as soon as
possible I packed my suit-case and set out for the United
States Capital.

When I arrived in Washington, the first thing I did was
to go and see Representative Curtis and ask if he would
introduce me to the Commissioner of Indian Affairs. He
said he would gladly do so. When we reached the office we
found the Secretary of the Interior, the Commissioner and
Assistant Commissioner of Indian Affairs there. I was
there introduced and talked to both the Commissioner and
his assistant. I found them both real gentlemen, totally
unlike our agent on the reservation. I told them I wanted
a fee patent for my whole section of land. That would
make me a citizen of the United States.

'You have been taking care of my property all these
years,' I said, 'and I have received no benefits from it. I
want to take care of my own property, like any other man.
I am old enough to do so, and perfectly able to. You put
me in school and educated me to be a man. I never drink
whiskey or smoke. Now, I want you gentlemen to give
me my freedom. If you refuse, I will go to Congress and
ask them for my citizenship.'

They both listened to me very attentively. Finally the
Commissioner turned to his assistant and said, 'Mr. Belt,
will you take care of this case?'

To make a long story short, I stuck around there for five weeks, going there daily to see how things were progressing. The principal question was, 'Do you drink whiskey?' I said 'No, I do not.' Right away, they wired to Mr. Brennan, the agent of my reservation, to find out what he knew about me. He wired back, 'Luther Standing Bear never drinks, but he is always away from the reservation.' Evidently he thought that by saying I was away, it would go against me; but it helped me along. The Washington authorities concluded that, if I stayed away from the reservation most of the time, I must be able to make my living. That was in my favor.

While in Washington I met General Nelson A. Miles, who had been such a friend of my father. He was glad to see me and asked if there was anything he could do for me. He wanted to know what I was doing there in Washington, and I told him. As I had things coming my way, I did not bother General Miles.

One day the Commissioner said to me, 'Standing Bear, we will have everything fixed up for you and send it on. There is no use of your staying here under expense any longer; it is costing too much money.'

'Mr. Commissioner,' I replied, 'I am spending my own money, and I want to stay right here until I am a full citizen of this country. I came here for that purpose and I am going to stay here until the matter is decided one way or the other.'

'Oh, well, as long as you are using your own money no one can say anything to you,' he replied.

Finally a happy day arrived for me. I got my papers signed by the Commissioner, the Assistant Commissioner, the Secretary of the Interior Department, and President William H. Taft. All my money which was in trust with the Government I drew out, and when I had those papers and my money in my pocket, nobody can imagine how I felt!

When I was made a chief, before sixteen thousand of my own people, besides other visiting tribes, I thought it was a great moment; but when I got my freedom from the iron hand of Brennan, the Indian agent at my reservation, I began to feel that I had been raised higher than a chieftainship.

I now felt that I could come and go as I chose, and I went to Sioux City, Iowa, and bought a nice home for myself. I then secured a position in Fuller Pierson's wholesale drygoods house, as shipping clerk, and soon was doing nicely; had my own telephone in my house and would call up my friends on the reservation occasionally. I also invited them to come down and visit me, and a delegation of them did so. How pleased they were to see the fine home in which I lived, and to learn about the good position I held!

When these visitors went back to the reservation and reported the success I was having since securing my citizenship, many of the Indians decided that they, too, would like to become citizens. My visitors had told me they were going to have a talk with those at home and see if they would have me go to Washington for them. As I had got my own rights, it was pretty evident that I should be able to do something for the others.

Shortly, I received a letter from Pine Ridge, asking me to come up and talk the matter over, as the old men of the tribe wished to consult with me. I went, and we called a large meeting. I told them I would be pleased to go to Washington to represent their interests.

But the agent got wind of the proposition and began to worry. Here was I, just an Indian, who had gone right over his head in securing my rights. He knew if I went to Washington again for the good of my tribe, it would go against his own plans, and he did not want to lose an easy job nor get in bad with the Washington authorities.

So he began to do some talking among the Indians. He

said, 'Why, Standing Bear is no better than you are. He has no more right to go to Washington and fight for your rights than you have. He is only a plain Indian, but he wants to get a pull with the Government. If you people vote to let him go and intercede for you, he will make lots of trouble for you. You better vote against him if you do not want to lose everything.'

Some of these men were already under the influence of liquor, and I suppose they could 'see red.' So they started around the reservation, reporting what the agent had said. Soon the time came to decide the matter. Some of the older people began to wonder if my contact with the white race had changed me toward them. They apparently seemed to think that, now that my father was gone, I was about to grab everything I could lay my hands on. They were afraid to go against the agent's wishes, and, when the test came, I was voted out, and there was no one to go to Washington for them, and once again they lost out.

I returned to my work at Sioux City. The work in the store was hard and the worries about my people began to tell on me. At last the combination broke down my health. I had no appetite and grew steadily worse. So I went to see a doctor, and he advised me to get into a different climate where I would have a complete change.

I wrote to Miller Brothers, who run the 101 Ranch in Oklahoma, and was given a chance to go to work for them. There I met several tribes of Indians and we had several dances together. The fall and spring weather there was all right, but in summer the heat was terrific, and I saw that I was not going to be able to stand it.

I had heard a great deal about the wonderful climate of Southern California, and concluded to go there. I wrote to Thomas Ince, then one of the big moving-picture magnates. He had some Sioux Indians with him, and I thought I would like to be with them. He wrote me a nice reply and sent me transportation for Los Angeles.

When I reached Southern California I began to improve and feel better right away. Mr. Ince's moving-picture studio was located at Inceville, five miles above Santa Monica, the beach city, and when I reached the Indian camp it certainly looked good to me.

That was in 1912. Up to that time I had never worked in the 'movies,' but this was to be my start in an entirely different line of work from any I had ever before engaged in.

As I look back to my early-day experiences in the making of pictures, I cannot help noting how we real Indians were held back, while white 'imitators' were pushed to the front. One of these was Ann Little, who afterward became a star. There was also a white girl named Elenore Ulrick, who played the part of an Indian girl represented as my daughter. There was also the wife of a famous Japanese star, Sessue Hayakowa, who also played as my daughter. All these people have risen in the ranks, but we Indians have been held back.

In those early days I worked with Douglas Fairbanks, William S. Hart, Charles Ray, and several others who are now top-notchers in the moving-picture game.

One day Tom Ince was talking with me about the making of Indian pictures. He told me it was through making that sort of pictures that he got his start. Then I told him that none of the Indian pictures were made right. He seemed quite surprised at this and began asking me questions. I explained to him in what way his Indian pictures were wrong. We talked for a long time, and when I arose to leave, he said, 'Standing Bear, some day you and I are going to make some real Indian pictures.'

Ince had a man in his employ who conceived the idea that, if he could get some more Indians from the reservation who could tell the stories I told, they could direct them. The Sioux who had been with the camp wanted to return home, as their six months' contract had expired. So Ince got sixty more Sioux to take their places.

The new bunch of Sioux had had no experience in moving pictures, and they knew nothing of stage work or about writing a story. They were simply 'up against it' and at a loss to know what to do. The moving-picture managers tried to get these people to relate some stories, but the Indians refused to do so. So Mr. Ince asked me to tackle the job at sixty dollars a week.

I wrote Mr. Ince that I was willing to work for my people and to help him, if he would accept my ideas and my stories. I waited for a reply, but none came. Then, as they could get nothing out of the new bunch of Sioux, and they had nobody who could talk their language and direct them, they had to return them to the reservation.

I have seen probably all of the pictures which are supposed to depict Indian life, and not one of them is correctly made. There is not an Indian play on the stage that is put on as it should be. I have gone personally to directors and stage managers and playwrights and explained this to them, telling them that their actors do not play the part as it should be played, and do not even know how to put on an Indian costume and get it right; but the answer is always the same, 'The public don't know the difference, and we should worry!'

Bert La Monte, a manager in New York, wired me to come on to take a part in a play he was producing, called 'The Race of Man.' This was during the World War, and it caught the public fancy and took well. But it was hard work keeping a company together. Just when we would be getting along splendidly, one of the actors would be drafted to go to war. The play finally had to close down for lack of men.

During my travels on the stage my people at home kept in touch with me. When they started to draft the Indian boys, who were not even American citizens, I wrote a strong letter to the old chiefs, advising that the boys demand their citizenship if they were to be expected to go abroad and fight for Uncle Sam. Even my own brother, Ellis Standing Bear, wrote me that he had to go in the next draft. He was greatly worried as to who would care for the children he had adopted, as he and his wife were childless.

One of my own sons was rejected in the draft because he was tubercular. He has since passed away. Our tribe, the Sioux, is the largest in the United States to-day, and during the World War more than *eight thousand* of our boys went across. We certainly feel that we have done our duty to the land that really belonged to our fathers, and is the land of our birth. It is ours, and we are always ready to protect it against any enemy.

I went to Florida with my company to make a picture, and then came back to California, the State that I love so well. I went down to Venice-by-the-Sea, an hour's ride from Los Angeles, and started in business for myself. While there I was elected president of the American Indian Progressive Association, holding the office two years. I tried to help my own race whenever I could, either in getting work for them or introducing them where they could receive aid. I lectured in high schools, churches, and grammar schools to show the white race what the Indian was capable of doing.

A few months after opening my concession at Venice, a man called on me to say that the Mission Indians of California were holding a council, and as I was a chief who had been to Washington they wanted to meet me in council. I accepted the invitation, and the pow-wow was held in Riverside, lasting three days.

There are about six different tribes of these California Indians, each one of which required an interpreter. None of these Indians understand the sign language, like the plains tribes, so all the talk had to be spoken. If it had been a council of the plains Indians, one of them would have got up and talked in the sign language, which is a universal language among all plains tribes, and, if there had been eight or ten different tribes there in council, all would have understood it perfectly.

I spoke to these California Indians regarding affairs at Washington, and they seemed pleased to hear from me. One day of the council had been set apart for white people to be present. I gave a talk on that day, and after I had finished, a lady sitting at the back of the room arose and said, 'I wonder if Standing Bear remembers me?' I arose and looked at the lady, but could not recall her. I asked one of my nieces who was with me if she knew who the lady was, but she said no. There seemed to be something familiar about her, and finally it dawned upon me that it was my first school teacher at Carlisle, Miss M. Burgess; and such it proved to be.

How glad we were to see each other again! We had not met since 1883, but she had recognized me from my resemblance to my father. To the Indians who were present, it was a great surprise, but no more so than to myself, as I had never expected to see her again.

During 1924 I was chosen to go to Oklahoma as a representative of the city of Los Angeles to invite the Indians of that State to have their next council in California. I went to Tulsa, and the day of the parade I hired an automobile, dressed myself carefully in full Indian regalia and represented the city of Los Angeles.

I was now getting along in years, and my family advised me to give up hard work, and some of my friends suggested I write a book detailing my experiences 'from the cradle up.' Two of my personal friends in Los Angeles, Mr. Clyde Champion, to whom I am indebted for the photographic work in this volume, and Mr. E. A. Brininstool, a writer of true Western history, and both greatly interested in the Indian question, were especially urgent; so in July, 1925, I gave up my place of business and began the writing of this book. And what you have been reading between these covers is the true history of my own people as I have lived my life among them.

It has taken many weary months to prepare this book, but I trust as you read these pages you will voice my plea to help my people, the Sioux, by giving them full citizenship. They are willing to fight for you and to die for you, if necessary.

The old saying that 'the only good Indian is a dead Indian' is no longer a popular expression. The Indian has just as many ounces of brains as his white brother, and with education and learning he will make a real American citizen of whom the white race will be justly proud.

As I am writing these last lines, on July 25, 1927, I am starting an Indian Employment Agency, which I trust will be for the betterment of the whole race. The Indian is bright, and he is capable of holding good, responsible positions if he is only given a chance.

And why not give the Indian that chance?

THE END

*Other titles by Luther Standing Bear
available in Bison Books editions*

LAND OF THE SPOTTED EAGLE, New Edition

MY INDIAN BOYHOOD, New Edition

STORIES OF THE SIOUX, New Edition